About the Author

Dr Kojo Sebastian Amanor is a Ghanaian anthropologist who was educated at the School of Oriental and African Studies and University College, London University. He has conducted field research for a number of institutions including the Overseas Development Institute (ODI), London, where he was a Research Associate (1988–90) and the United Nations Research Institute for Social Development (UNRISD), Geneva, where he was a consultant (1991–2). He is currently a Research Fellow at the Institute of African Studies, University of Ghana.

Dr Amanor is co-editor, with W. de Boef, K. Wellard and A. Bebbington of *Cultivating Knowledge: Genetic Diversity, Farmer Experimentation and Crop Research* (Intermediate Technology, 1993) and has compiled *Analytical Abstracts in Farmer Participatory Research* (ODI, 1992).

About UNRISD

The United Nations Research Institute for Social Development (UNRISD) is an autonomous agency that engages in multi-disciplinary research on the social dimensions of contemporary problems affecting development. Its work is guided by the conviction that, for effective development policies to be formulated, an understanding of the social and political context is crucial. The Institute attempts to provide governments, development agencies, grassroots organisations and scholars with a better understanding of how development policies and processes of economic, social and environmental change affect different social groups. Working through an extensive network of national research centres, UNRISD aims to promote original research and strengthen research capacity in developing countries.

Current research themes include Crisis, Adjustment and Social Change; Socio-Economic and Political Consequences of the International Trade in Illicit Drugs; Environment, Sustainable Development and Social Change; Ethnic Conflict and Development; Integrating Gender into Development Policy; Participation and Changes in Property Relations in Communist and Post-Communist Societies; Refugees, Returnees and Local Society; and Political Violence and Social Movements. UNRISD research projects focused on the 1995 World Summit for Social Development include Rethinking Social Development in the 1990s; Economic Restructuring and New Social Policies; Ethnic Diversity and Public Policies; and The Challenge of Rebuilding Wartorn Societies.

A list of the Institute's free and priced publications can be obtained by writing to: UNRISD, Reference Centre, Palais des Nations, CH-1211, Geneva 10, Switzerland.

About CTA

The ACP-EU Technical Centre for Agricultural and Rural Cooperation (CTA) operates under the Lomé Convention between Member States of the European Union and the African, Caribbean and Pacific States.

CTA collects, disseminates and facilitates the exchange of information on research, training and innovations in the spheres of agricultural and rural development and extension for the benefit of the ACP States.

To achieve this, CTA commissions and publishes studies; organises and supports conferences, workshops and seminars; publishes and co-publishes a wide range of books, proceedings, bibliographies and directories; strengthens documentation services in ACP countries; and offers an extensive information service.

Headquarters: Galvanistraat 9, Ede (The Netherlands)
Postal address:
Postbus 380, 6700 A J Wageningen, The Netherlands
Telephone: +31 8380 - 60400
Fax: +31 8380 - 31052
Telex: +44 30169 CTA NL

The New Frontier

Farmer Responses to Land Degradation: A West African Study

Kojo Sebastian Amanor

UNRISD
Geneva

Zed Books Ltd
London & New Jersey

The New Frontier was first published by Zed Books Ltd, 7 Cynthia Street, London N1 9JF, UK, and 165 First Avenue, Atlantic Highlands, New Jersey 07716, USA, in association with the United Nations Research Institute for Social Development (UNRISD), Palais des Nations, 1211 Geneva 10, Switzerland, and the ACP-EU Technical Centre for Agricultural and Rural Co-operation (CTA), Galvanistraat 9, Ede, The Netherlands, in 1994.

Cover designed by Andrew Corbett.
Laserset by Opus 43, Cumbria, UK.
Printed and bound in the United Kingdom
by Biddles Ltd, Guildford and King's Lynn.

A catalogue record for this book
is available from the British Library.

US CIP data is available from the Library of Congress.

ISBN 1 85649 241 9 Cased
ISBN 1 85649 242 7 Limp

Contents

List of Tables

LIST OF FIGURES AND MAPS

Special Acknowledgement to Michael Kwabla Odjidja

I am deeply grateful to Michael Kwabla Odjidja for his great input into this work. Odjidja is a small farmer at Odometa, who formerly worked as a nurseryman before retiring to his plot at Odometa Piengwa. He has considerable knowledge of the Krobo area and has assimilated a vast store of Krobo folk knowledge on plants and agriculture. He has the ability to identify a vast range of trees and shrubs. During my apprenticeship carrying out research as a graduate student he patiently devoted many hours explaining weed ecology to me. When I returned to carry out this research he was one of the first people I consulted with my questionnaires. From this it became obvious that it would be sensible to engage him in this venture. At first he was hesitant and felt he would be unable to do the work. Once started he responded to the work as an intellectual challenge. I look back with fondness at our many adventures on our old constantly breaking down motorbike, the numerous times we fell down in the mud 'slightly' inebriated on local gin, the farmers who believed we were coming to cart all their topsoil away to search it for gold when we told them we were carrying out a soil survey, the terrible mosquito nights on the Volta Lake, being miserably drenched by rain, and his fatherly advice. Last time I saw Odjidja he had started a *nyabatso* nursery, experimenting with implementing some of the results of the survey.

ACKNOWLEDGEMENTS

I would like to thank Daniel Abbiw, curator of the herbarium at the University of Ghana, Legon for his help in the identification of plants collected in Krobo and the knowledge he has shared with me about plants. Drs E.A. Gyasi, S.T. Addo and J.K. Ametekpor of the University of Ghana, Legon also gave useful advice on some aspects of the logistics of field research. Jessica Vivian made many useful comments on the first draft of the manuscript. Research was made possible by support from the United Nations Research Institute for Social Development (UNRISD). I would also like to thank Moses Nomo of Awoweso Adome for help in collecting soil samples at Adome, and all the farmers who patiently participated in the survey, offering great insights and interesting perspectives. The study also draws on research I carried out as a graduate student at the Department of Anthropology, University College London.

I also remember my uncle, Sam Asare Mate Kole, who cultivated an agriculture which blended scientific knowledge with folk knowledge and who inspired in me a great interest in agriculture. He died the week before I went out to the field.

Note on Orthography

The symbol ɔ represents the phonetic 'open o' roughly corresponding to the vowel in dog. The symbol ɛ represents the phonetic 'open e' sound roughly equivalent to the vowel in beg.

Many of the burnt tree-trunks were now putting forth fresh green shoots, and the clearings were bright with colour. New roads were already in existence, and with the winter rains flowers sprang up around the crosses that had been planted in the ground the winter before. This year alone the forest of Sequeiro Grande was diminished by almost half. It was now surrounded by clearings and burnt tracts and was, in brief, living its last winter. On rainy mornings workers would go by, scythes on their shoulders, singing their sad songs, which died away in the mysterious depths of the giant wood:

Cocoa is a good crop,
And there's a new crop coming …

Jorge Amado, *The Violent Land* (Collins Harvill, London, 1989)

1

INTRODUCTION

The expansion of the world capitalist market has involved the opening up of new geographical, socio-economic, cultural and technological frontiers. The emergence of the European world economy is entwined with the rise of large maritime commercial centres. These centres have been able to organize trade, capital, communications and warfare to bring the economies of the periphery into the ambit of world commercial centres. Areas on the fringes of commodity production have eventually contributed to the vast store of wealth of world commercial centres, as producers of commodities and as consumers of the wide array of articles gathered in the great metropolitan warehouses. From 1500 the burgeoning world economy grew from a centre in the Mediterranean and Western Europe to embrace all the maritime regions of the world by the beginning of the nineteenth century. During the nineteenth century the expansion of the world economy proceeded inland from the maritime trading centres established in earlier epochs on the seaboards of the five continents. Various cities in turn have been at the throbbing centre of this world economy, from Venice in the fifteenth century to Antwerp, Amsterdam, London and, in the present era, New York.

The expansion of the world economy has transformed the populations and cultures of the world. Faced with the burdens of poverty and frustration in old world centres, people have migrated to these new frontiers of untold opportunity. In some areas, such as the Americas and Australia, the old populations of these frontiers have been decimated to pave the way for the conquest of the wilderness by commodity production, while in other instances new heterogeneous populations and cultures have often emerged from the miscegenation of frontier life.

The expansion of the frontier has often been carried out by indigenous producers and traders. The people involved in the opening up of frontiers are socially differentiated and involved in commodity production in different ways. The dominant social classes within the expansionary movement bring to the frontier a knowledge of the metropolis, a taste for metropolitan commodities and a cosmopolitan culture rooted in commodity fetishism. They bring the promise of new opportunity, of the untold wealth of the metropolis; they bring dreams which often shatter into the bleak reality of economic stagnation, marginalization and impoverishment.

The frontier is a creation of the metropolis and its economy arises as an extension of the metropolis – an extractive economy provisioning the metropolis with a 'windfall', a 'free gift' (Webb, 1952). As the world economy expands, the new frontier increasingly becomes a caricature of an economy, an area in which one easily exploitable resource is writ large and determines the fortunes of the inhabitants. This is a reflection of the constraints of administering the natural resources of the world from the metropolitan centre, and the rapidity with which new frontiers have been assimilated into the world economy in the last two hundred years. Given the impulse of frontier conquest, the incorporation of new areas into the world market could not be based on a balanced exploitation of resources. It was founded on the extraction of easily exploited resources. Considerations of quantity rather than quality informed the administration of the world's resources. History was impelled by the desire to increase the metropolitan storehouse of commodities rather than to develop stable and balanced economies in specific localities, districts and regions.

In the metropolitan mind, colonies were often synonymous with commodities:

Gold Coast: cocoa	Ceylon: tea	Brazil: coffee
Malaya: rubber	Zanzibar: cloves	Madagascar: vanilla
Jamaica: sugar	Cuba: sugar, cigars	Dominica: banana.

This was glorified in classical economic theory by Ricardo's conception of *comparative advantage* in which foreign trade

> binds together, by one common tie of interest and intercourse, the universal society of nations through the civilized world. It is this principle which determines that wine should be made in France and Portugal, that corn shall be grown in America and Poland, and that hardware and other goods shall be manufactured in England (Ricardo, 1955: 81).

However, such a division of labour results in inequality in the intercourse of nations, and those who continue to be providers of single commodities for the dining table of the metropolis remain its servants. Only those who decide to enter into the production of 'hardware and other goods' are guaranteed any security, a place at the world dining table.

For the colonies this mode of exploitation of resources, in response to the insatiable but shifting desires of metropolitan commodity markets, has often resulted in serious land degradation. Previously diverse but backward economies are replaced by monocrop economies. Natural environments are felled and destroyed to make way for cultivation and extraction of these resources. In this fashion, the forests of the world have been felled to make way for sugar estates, coffee plantations, cocoa, cattle ranches, etc. Timber has become a synonym of forests. Colonial foresters sought to poison non-economic timber species in forest reserves to promote maximum growth of prime timber species. While the history of resource exploitation in tropical colonies preceding their integration into the world economy has often involved utilization of a wide range of forest products:

> somewhere down the course of history, timber and timber products assumed such major importance in human affairs that they appeared to be the only significant output of the forests. They dominated in national and international statistics, were promoted rigorously in all sorts of media, adapted rapidly to the changing tastes of urban consumption, and generally basked in an exaggerated measure of self-importance (Francois, 1992).

Resources have also moved around the world as centres of world commerce opened up new areas to develop the most favourable terms of trade for the metropolitan markets. Tea was moved from China to India, rubber (*Hevea brasiliensis*) from Brazil to South East Asia, the oil palm from West Africa to South East Asia, and cocoa from Latin America and the Caribbean to West Africa. At each juncture old markets were displaced, leaving behind decaying settlements with only memories of their former glory.

The frontier is completely expendable. It is mercilessly exploited for today, and tomorrow the great waste of lost environmental and economic potential is left behind for posterity. Meanwhile, the frontier moves further into the interior or into completely new geographical regions. In a study of the history of the frontier in the São Paulo area of Brazil, Dean (1983) concludes:

> The fate of the São Paulo frontier was to be despoiled of its easily exploitable resources and to suffer extreme degradation of its ecosystems. The process was nevertheless regarded by those who accomplished it as a brilliant achievement. It was accompanied by genocide. It did not result in a broadening of human potentialities of the victors, since it replicated, and even caricatured, the inequality of the metropolis. It is true that the export of coffee made possible the importation of an array of human and capital resources that soon produced a higher level of material standards, but this form of development thereafter suffered the consequences of a weakened agricultural base. In the wake of severe environmental degradation, the successors of the original settlers have undertaken to manage their remaining resources rationally. Nevertheless, extractive practices

> and attitudes have persisted into the present because the frontier itself continued its march into Paraná, Mato Grosso, Goiás and beyond, to the borders of Peru and Colombia (pp. 97–8).

Today the last frontiers are being opened up. The expansion of the commodity markets has filled every nook and cranny in the world. The frontier is no longer so expendable. The waste in the vast old frontier areas is now becoming evident. The remaining frontiers, as in Amazonia, have become a rallying ground for the new global environmentalism, which is emerging as the champion of indigenous peoples – those who still lie beyond the fringe of commodity fetishism. A grand ode is now being sung to the cultural systems of these native peoples, to their vast knowledge of forest plants and medicines. This knowledge is being fetishized, however, fashioned into a commodity, a new commodity for the age of biotechnology. Popular knowledge has become exotic, transformed into a catalogue of exotic commodities and natural resources with rich promises for the future, like the spice trade of old. Knowledge is being deprived of its dynamism, its history, its experiential base, its relation to social, economic and political processes.

Meanwhile, what about the forgotten peoples of the old frontiers – those tainted and immersed in commodity production, those who have seen the environment and their livelihoods crumble under the insatiable desire of frontier colonization, those who can reflect on the futility of past developments, and have observed processes of degradation and decline, those who have undertaken 'to manage their remaining resources rationally', those who have been consumed and are now marginalized? These are the people who inform this investigation, which examines their experiences of land degradation and their responses to their plight.

This study critically explores contemporary policy frameworks for the environment and for development. It places land degradation and economic decline within a political economy framework. Since it focuses on agriculturalists, it also examines agricultural development frameworks in the context of paradigms of development and institutional frameworks for technology generation. It is concerned with the interface between science as a system of understanding and changing the world and the production systems and aspirations of the people as an expression of humanity and its relationship to nature. Finally, the study is concerned with commoditization as it affects both the frontiers of science and popular production.

Environmental Policy

There are two conflicting paradigms of the environment. The first is concerned with the limits which nature poses to human growth, and is characteristic of environmental determinism, Malthusianism, and much of recent debates on population control and carrying capacity. The second stresses the potential of human labour to transform nature and the capacity of peoples to create new systems of material production which transcend contemporary economic constraints and the environmental problems which are symptomatic of economic malaise. In the latter approach the major economic and environmental constraints are seen as emanating from the world capitalist system and the economic structures of the world commodity markets (Redclift, 1989).

These conflicting paradigms underlay many of the debates at the 1992 Earth Summit. A Northern industrial perspective of environmental problems, broadly shared by the centres of world capitalism, confronted a Southern developing perspective, broadly shared by dependent former colonies. The Northern perspective was based essentially on constraints and the Southern perspective on the notion that a more stable utilization of the environment could only be attained once basic levels of economic development are achieved. Conservation could be undertaken by Southern governments, however, in return for Northern aid to facilitate development.

The environment as constraints paradigm, as developed in the North, also revealed political and economic self-interests. From the US perspective, the interests of the US market and free consumer choice were considered sacrosanct: the environment could not violate the narrow economic interests of powerful multinational firms. As George Bush commented, 'we cannot permit the extremes in the environmental movement to shut down the United States'. William Reilly, administrator of the US Environmental Protection Agency, commented that the biodiversity treaty would have 'blown away' intellectual property rights and patents of US companies in the business of marketing genetic materials. Yet these same intellectual property and patenting rights are freely drawing on and appropriating the genetic materials developed by farmers in the South without acknowledgement (Kloppenburg, 1988; Berg *et al.*, 1991; Mooney, 1983, 1993). Furthermore, patenting rights and commoditization of science are seriously eroding the freedom of exchange of research information between scientists in the North.

Northern environmental frameworks reflected the globalization of capitalism and the impact that degradation in the South may have on the world economy. Thus concerns with protecting tropical forests as international property resources reflect interests of preserving them as carbon sinks for Northern industry and as hunting grounds of biodiversity for biotechnology and pharmaceutical firms. Ecotourism reflects the expansion of the Northern tourist industry and its penetration into the South, and not the interests of local peoples who are unlikely to manage or gain access to the major profits of this industry.

A critical point arises from the environment as constraints argument: who is going to be constrained, and who will do the constraining? At this juncture, the definition of causes and parameters of environmental degradation becomes political and ideological. Attempts to use notions of carrying capacity as a basis for policies of sustainable development in dependent countries are blatantly ideological in conception (Martinez-Alier, 1990). Their ideological nature is reflected in the highly simplistic solutions offered in much recent discourse on population and degradation, which, should they be implemented, may have alarming implications for the freedom of peoples to determine their own destinies:

> projects focusing only on soil and water conservation or prevention of salinization may turn out to be ineffective in the long run because they deal with symptoms and not underlying causes. Similarly, projects that encourage commercial cropping to raise rural incomes may intensify pressures on the land. In the long run, birth control programmes may be the most effective policy to halt land degradation (Dixon *et al.*, 1990: 45).

Attempts to define degradation as the result of poverty are also ideological, shifting the onus of environmental degradation onto the developing world and absolving the rich lifestyles, industrial waste and parasitism of the North from the environmental debate. This critique was a major element in the Southern Earth Summit perspective. It was argued that the contrast in the total and *per capita* consumption of energy and non-renewable resources of peoples in the North and South was more relevant than total population figures.

Emphasis on environmental constraints and the rural poor also carry disquieting political implications. They converge with policy trends of the 1980s at international and national levels to shift the burden of the world economic crisis onto the backs of the people. The growth of recent political liberalism and concern with social inequity in international policy frameworks is paradoxical, since increasing poverty, immiseration and affliction have arisen from the economic policies of the 1980s which are still in place. Within many developing countries, regimes with reputations for afflicting the people are enthusiastically developing environmental policies which point to the poor as the main perpetrators of environmental degradation. The new global environmental thinking opens up possibilities for further political intervention into the ways of life of the people, appropriating their resources and patterns of resource utilization in the name of protecting the environment. In this respect, global environmental managerialism opens up avenues for the development of what has been termed 'ecofascism' (Pepper, 1984; Guha, 1985): the legitimation of oppressive actions against the poor in the name of protecting the environment.

The main limitation of the Southern perspective at the Earth Summit was its failure to question seriously the whole process of development over the last two hundred years of colonial and neocolonial domination. There was a reluctance to envisage a new course of economic development responding to both popular aspirations and ecological concerns, based on a more diversified utilization of the environment and involving a break with dominant patterns of commodity trade.

Despite the articulation of a Southern perspective on the environment, there is not a great variation, in practical reality, between environmental policy in developing and industrial nations. Most developing nations are implementing institutional frameworks for environmental policy which are based on Western European and US models, and which are supported with funding from these donor nations (Hosier *et al.*, 1982; Conlin, 1985; Perry, 1986). This policy direction is essentially based on a technocentric, managerial model for the environment.

Environmental Technocentrism and the Globalization of Research

The technocentric approach is characterized by a belief that environmental problems can be solved by the introduction of new methodologies, technologies and controls based on a combination of the following elements:

- the incorporation of environmental costing into economic planning and legislation which will require that companies and producers pay for the cost of the degradation they cause;
- the development of 'green' technologies in soil and water conservation, reafforestation and agroforestry;
- the introduction of population control;
- the promotion of equity by developing technologies relevant to the needs of the poor and improved access to and distribution of resources, and through increasing participation of rural peoples in implementing and carrying responsibility for environmental projects;
- the conceptualization of environmental objectives within the strictures of the free market and trade liberalization, and an unwillingness to examine the impact of the ideology of the free market on the environment.

This central framework is usually articulated through an environmental protection agency, which coordinates the environmental programmes of various ministries, government research sectors and projects, and which builds linkages with community-level projects and non-governmental agencies (NGOs). However, within many developing countries, particularly in Africa, the capacity to carry out research into the environment is seriously limited.

RESEARCH, DEVELOPMENT AND THE ENVIRONMENT

The constraints and limitations on research in developing countries are rooted in both national underfunding and an international research structure in which the research institutions of developing nations are expected to focus on adaptive research – the fine tuning and packaging of technologies developed in international centres to suit national conditions. The serious business of basic and applied research is carried out in international centres. International research is considered to be superior since it has 'universal appeal', technologies of wide applicability and generalized data which can be processed easily by international policy and fund-disbursing agencies. As a result, international centres can command the lion's share of resources and the cream of developing country scientists, who are accorded higher prestige, better remuneration, and broader support for research activities. Poverty of research at the local and national level will result, however, in inappropriately conceived problems, methodologies, and structures of research at the international level.

Regional and national environmental problems are frequently defined at the international level and do not arise from ongoing research within national research centres. The national structures of environmental policies are often carbon copies of their Western counterparts, which have been foisted on dependent nations by aid-disbursing agencies. The fact that these institutional frameworks have no track record of solving environmental problems in industrial nations does not seem to be relevant. Developing nation states willingly put these structures in place since they are prerequisites or inducements for the disbursement of aid. As a result of this utilization of credit, sector and ministerial agencies of the state are drawn towards international environmental prescriptions and have much stronger linkages with international science and policy than with the people. Weak research traditions and poor understanding of problems are covered up by a disdain for the people and a lack of willingness to investigate their problems. The espousing of old and worn international prescriptions is given more priority than encouraging new and innovative national research into environment and production systems. Frequently the various sector organs and ministries merely paraphrase international environmental proclamations while bemoaning the ignorance of the people.

Within the technocentric model of environmental managerialism the international centre is the font of all knowledge and the national agency the expert in implementing this knowledge within the confines of the national state. Environmental actions are thus defined by the technologies and policy frameworks generated by international centres. The main research structures at the national level are concerned with implementing policy rather than with evaluating critically its short-term and long-term implications, investigating the way of life, problems and aspirations of people, and seeking for innovatory alternatives generated within the milieu of the nation.

Researchers working in institutes at the developing national level are frequently marginalized when they are interested in pursuing their own research findings; or in forms of research concerned with the life of the people and their cultural, production and technical domains; or in the complexity of interactions between social, historical and environmental factors. Researchers willing to allow their own research agendas to be defined by international centres are gaining new leases of life. In the natural sciences, researchers interested in developing projects concerned with biodiversity for biotechnology, or with aspects of local genetic materials in which international research is interested, are likely to find research funding. Meanwhile, researchers interested in developing taxonomies or creating national floras are marginalized for their interest in basic research. Yet the classification of plants must form a basic requisite for the development of a genuine interest in biodiversity. This, however, constitutes a form of pure and independent research which is given low priority in international research funding for developing or dependent nations. The international structure of science reflects global political and economic relations, and research is constrained by dependency in developing countries. Consequently, there is little scope or support for national research to carry out innovative and critical research, appraising the peculiarities of the natural and social environments within the confines of the nation state and opening up new lines of enquiry which can make fresh contributions to world science.

COMMODITY SECTOR RESEARCH

Environmental policy frameworks are being globalized. But this globalization is taking place through a fracturing of the social and natural world into commodity sectors. Despite attempts to develop an increasing interdisciplinary focus within international agencies, this only takes place within the confines of the policy agenda of the agency. There are rarely overarching structures which enable the development needs and environmental problems of particular localities to be articulated in an integral framework which relates technology development to the socio-economic context. While a large number of international and national agencies are employing social scientists, they are usually confined to the role of brokers between technicians and their 'clients'. They are usually employed to work within existing policy frameworks rather than to develop a critical policy analysis which incorporates political economy perspectives and opens up new frontiers for subsequent development.

Few international centres have a competence to develop true interdisciplinary research, despite recent attempts at reform within the Consultative Group for International Agricultural Research (CGIAR) system to develop multidisciplinary approaches, increasing orientation towards natural resource management and ecological zones. Attempts to develop a new international research centre with a mandate to cover agroforestry and forestry have likewise failed. The International Council for Research in Agroforestry (ICRAF) has been unable to accept changes to its mandate to include forestry. As a result alternative plans have been put into motion to create the Centre for International Forestry Research (CIFOR), as a new forest commodity-based research institution (Ravnborg, 1992). Since justifications for research in agroforestry include the extent of degradation of the forest and the impact of forms of shifting agriculture on forest lands, agroforestry needs to develop a conception of the interaction between forests and social systems before it can claim to transcend narrow commodity-oriented approaches and contribute towards the development of an interdisciplinary environmental science. While ICRAF feels unable to include research into the forest environment in its mandate, the products of its research into fast-growing leguminous trees are being rapidly promoted and disseminated as the solution to the problems of shifting cultivators within the forest. Most of ICRAF's work on farming systems has focused on inventories of economic tree species utilized on-farm and not on interactions between forest tree species, fallow regeneration and cycles of crop production. Despite these shortcomings, ICRAF has been one of the international agencies most concerned with developing an interdisciplinary approach and participatory social science research methods (Nair, 1989).

The environment is being perceived through a series of narrow commodity-sector windows, which see resources as things in themselves, rather than as integral parts of processes. Frequently, the complex interaction between social relations, the production base and natural systems are disregarded. Miracle solutions to the problems of the developing world, extolled with a missionary zeal, often give disappointing results when taken up in popular production systems. Given the international emphasis on applied research in developing countries, knowledge of human ecology and popular production systems is limited. In place of the emergence of an approach to the environment rooted in the history of land use, settlement patterns and environmental change, feasibility studies and environmental impact assessment often approach localities with pre-established parameters rooted in commodity sector development.

Since commodity research is internationalized, it searches for standardized solutions applicable to a wide range of environments. In the Green Revolution approach, this has been achieved by fostering a technology which is intended to minimize the impact of the host environment and to create an artificial environment of high-input technology (including pesticides, fertilizers, herbicides and irrigation) which protects the technology from stresses in the host environment. However, in many areas this technology interface is difficult to achieve as a result of remoteness, poverty, and highly fragile or harsh environments. The Green Revolution has failed to march into many marginal areas where local resilient varieties and techniques still dominate, despite an agricultural extension system promoting modern techniques.

The successful uptake of modern variety technology has resulted in environmental problems. These include pollution from pesticide and fertilizer residues, and salinization from prolonged reliance on irrigation. Another serious problem is genetic erosion. This is the result of a narrow range of high-yielding varieties (HYVs) replacing the wide variety of landraces which characterized the agricultural endeavour when seeds were bred by farmers in specific localities rather than multinational agribusiness (Mooney, 1979; Cooper *et al.*, 1991; de Boef *et al.*, 1993). Genetic erosion of landraces has disturbing implications for the seed industry, since the future development of germplasm is dependent upon access to a wide range of genetic materials with new traits which can strengthen the vulnerability of the narrow genetic base of modern varieties (Frankel, 1970; Harlan, 1975; Wilkes, 1983).

Even when dealing with technologies which are not highly commoditized and which have been developed specifically for poor people and to promote environmental conservation, modern technology still tends to produce highly standardized, uniform packages which can alienate farmers. Much of the technology and many of the species utilized in agroforestry have been drawn from the fallows and experiences of small-scale farmers in the tropics. But these resources have been developed into packages which often alienate farmers by failing to take into account specific environmental characteristics and the production factors available to farmers (Thrupp, 1989). Modern agricultural science tends to regard the agricultural system as divorced from the natural environment and frequently fails to consider synergetic interactions between the agro-ecosystem and nature.

This emphasis on commodities rather than systems, processes and interfaces results in an institutional structure of development which gains its strength from its knowledge of a particular standardized brand of commodity, and its ability to create the conditions through which this commodity can thrive in a wide range of environments. In this system it is not necessary to have specific knowledge of particular environments. It is thus difficult for sector specialists to understand the environmental interactions of technology, or the specific needs, aspirations and long-term strategies of producers. These factors lie beyond the realm of commodities. The focus on commodity packages leads to a top-down structure of research and development based on a *transfer of technology* mode (Biggs and Farrington, 1991). Technical solutions are transmitted without specific problems and interrelationships of problems being understood within their context. Commodity sector agencies can easily alienate producers, through making technical recommendations which do not fit their struggles, aspirations, preoccupations and life experiences.

The *transfer of technology* approach to development is rooted in *dualism*, a bygone model of economic development which arose in the 1950s (Lewis, 1954; Higgins, 1956; Jorgensen, 1961; Myint, 1958). This views underdeveloped economies as consisting of an introduced, progressive, modern industrial sector and a backward and static traditional sector. Development comes through the expansion of the modern sector and its ability to transform the traditional sector. The dualist thesis was a product of the peculiarities of the post-war boom, with the rapid growth of agro-industries and expansion of tertiary consumer and light processing industries. It was linked with the pumping of bilateral aid and loans to developing countries to purchase machinery and technology and invest in import substitution industry. It encouraged the investment of capital in the purchase of agro-industrial and manufacturing equipment as a means to modernization.

Recent global policy frameworks implicitly reject the dualist thesis, and recognize the fact that the enclave of the modern 'progressive' state sector, has been a failure – a drain on resources. This is reflected in policy frameworks concerned with divesting the state sector of its sector agencies and in growing concern with small-scale producers. Concerns with equity, poverty alleviation, the environment, and linkages, are a recognition of the fact that social and institutional factors are as important in development as technology dissemination.

Nevertheless, the institutional frameworks of commodity sector institutions are rooted in technicist conceptions. At present, there are growing tensions between global policy objectives, which often lack a theoretical grounding and consistency, and commodity sector organizations, which are unable to reform to carry out the new objectives required of them. In many cases, sector agencies declare new objectives but continue working in the old familiar modes. Many agricultural sector agencies are now proclaiming the need for sustainable agriculture. Sustainable agriculture is defined in terms of the need to replace the backward traditional farming systems of the peasantry which encourage environmental degradation. This is the very same framework in which it was declared that farmers need to take up modern input farming. But with what sustainable technologies are farmers going to replace their outmoded techniques? The technologies promoted by extension services over the last thirty years can hardly claim to be rooted in sound environmental frameworks. Thus the authoritative proclamation of the age of sustainable technology heralded in by expert commodity sector agencies is misplaced. Nevertheless, these strains and contradictions are opening up debates and searches for new paradigms of development.

Popular Participation in Research

During the 1980s popular participation became an important buzz word in international development circles. There are different senses and objectives with which the term is employed: as a mode of political administration, as a paradigm for processes of technology generation, and as a conception in examining policy and institutional frameworks.

The origins of popular participation in development can be located in disillusionment with the large-scale projects of the 1960s and 1970s which were often poorly designed, failed to take local realities into consideration, and alienated local people from developing initiatives within them (Pearse and Steifel, 1979). During the 1980s, however, community participation developed another relevance in relation to decentralization of the state and its apparatus (Vivian, 1992). This is associated with the crisis of the state and its need to cut public sector investment, and with the uptake of structural adjustment prescriptions which seek to reduce the burden of aid-disbursing nations funding inefficient dependent states. Concepts of community participation often entail shifting the burden of the provision of the basic infrastructural amenities of life from the state to local communities. From this perspective, the participation of local communities is limited to the provision of labour for specific projects (Oakley, 1991). Such projects often bear a striking similarity to colonial conceptions of forced or communal labour. In many African countries local chiefs are experiencing a new resurgence as the agency with power to enforce participation in public works programmes. During the early independence period chiefs in several African countries experienced a waning of power as they were identified as collaborators in colonial domination (Crowder and Ikeme, 1970).

Within many sector agencies community participation has been picked up as a means of both rationalizing public expenditure on infrastructure development programmes and producing more appropriate management and technology design. Agencies are shedding their roles as implementers of projects to NGOs and community organizations, and developing new roles of monitoring, evaluating and providing technical assistance to independent programmes. The emphasis is on developing more appropriate feedback mechanisms from producers or 'clients' to sector agencies, which can be utilized in fine-tuning technology options or result in more appropriate management practices. This conception is perhaps most highly developed in agricultural technology development.

PARTICIPATION IN AGRICULTURAL TECHNOLOGY DEVELOPMENT

Several studies have pointed to the abilities of small-scale farmers in experimentation and adaptation of technology to their needs (Johnson, 1972; Box, 1986; Richards, 1985; McKorkle *et al.*, 1988; Haverkort *et al.*, 1991; de Boef *et al.*, 1993). Several projects have attempted to use the skills of farmers in testing and evaluating in their programmes (for references see Farrington and Martin, 1988; Amanor, 1990). At the International Potato Center (CIP) Rhoades and Booth (1982) developed the 'farmer back to farmer' paradigm of a participatory approach to technology generation. Research is a continuous, interactive process in which farmers participate in an ongoing appraisal of technology problems. After a participatory diagnosis of problems and possible interventions, information is carried back to the research station for incorporation into technology testing and development programmes. This feedback generates a process of continuous technology adaptation and improvement which refers to farmers' experience with the technology for further development. In this conception of participation farmers help researchers to continually improve technology. However, the researcher still has monopoly control over technology and technology generation, and success in fine-tuning will strengthen this monopoly over research.

Richards (1987) argues that the conception of farmer participation may actually marginalize farmers' own experimenting traditions, by coopting them into formal research programmes. Essential elements of this experimenting tradition which do not fit into formal research procedures may be relegated from research programmes and marginalized by researchers, while other elements less alien to formal science may be encouraged. This may distort farmers' independent research traditions and threaten their integrity and autonomy.

Van der Ploeg (1990) has argued that the research traditions of farmers are built on disparate traditions from those of modern commercial agriculture. They are characterized as 'l'art de la localité', a system based on continually adapting and matching technologies to changing environmental conditions. The system is threatened by modern agricultural technology which seeks to transform farmers into consumers of commodity technology, and to replace the dynamic process of adaptive responses to changing micro-environments with the consumption of standardized inputs which transform and mask human interactions with the environment.

More sensitive targeting of small-scale farmers by agricultural science and participation in programmes generated by research institutions and technicians may undermine farmers' own adaptive responses and their independent technologies. The development of farming systems research and farmer participatory research may form part of the onslaught of the commoditization of agricultural technology, a long-term strategy to transform the remaining independent farmers into consumers of agribusiness technology. Thus, issues of participatory technology development need to be viewed in a wider institutional and political economy setting.

STRENGTHENING FARMERS' OWN TRADITIONS OF EXPERIMENTATION

An alternative approach to the interface between farmers, research and technicians is to use research facilities to strengthen the experimenting traditions of farmers. Researchers act as a catalyst to local development, evolving forms of support which enable local communities to transcend existing constraints (Biggs, 1989a).

This requires new institutional arrangements and paradigms of research systems (informing research organization) which incorporate a recognition of the fact that farmers are not only consumers but also generators of technology (Röling, 1990), with their own networks of experimentation (Box, 1986). A paradigm of the international research system needs to recognize that technology is generated from multiple sources, including farmers and interactions between farmers and NGOs (Biggs, 1989b).

In recent years a number of projects have come into being which focus on the knowledge systems of farmers. Many of these projects have been initiated by NGOs and are concerned with natural resources, farmers' genetic materials and the conservation of local crops and landraces from the onslaught of modern varieties. This research is often highly critical of the commercialization of modern agriculture, its reliance on petrochemical inputs, and the negative impact of the promotion of Green Revolution technologies on small-scale farmers (Altieri, 1987; Altieri and Hecht, 1990; Tan, 1986; Cooper *et al.*, 1991; de Boef *et al.*; 1993).

Formal sector plant breeding research institutions are also developing an interest in linking up with such projects. This has grown out of a recognition that the genetic diversity of landraces is based upon human–crop interactions and a system of crop development played out in small farming systems. *Local crop development* (Hardon and de Boef, 1993) refers to a conservation activity based on supporting farmer–crop interactions within specific localities to complement both *in situ* conservation (in wilderness areas) and *ex-situ* conservation (preservation of genetic materials in gene banks). The aim of local crop development is to foster, support and strengthen existing farmer activities of crop conservation and improvement, to maintain processes which have resulted in the development of landraces and to increase the potential of research to develop improved varieties for marginal environments, outside of mainstream commercial breeding based on standardization. This also involves strengthening farmers' ability to organize autonomously or building new development initiatives into older modes of social organization (Berg, 1993). This support may include provision of new germplasm for farmers to experiment with, or the preservation of farmers' existing landraces in gene banks, to enable farmers to experiment adventurously, knowing that if they make mistakes they can go back to their old proven varieties (Worede and Mekbib, 1993).

The concept of local crop development is important in according the knowledge of farmers a dynamic role, and in associating it with development in addition to conservation. It provides a context in which peasant societies can contribute to modern science. This contrasts with much of the literature, which sees indigenous knowledge as a static system rooted in endless tradition disrupted by social change and modernization. Unlike some of the literature on farmer experimentation, the concept of local crop development also provides an environmental context in which innovation takes place, which is independent and autonomous of international agricultural research.

Knowledge, Commodity and Political Economy

Mooney (1983, 1993) raises important issues concerning the ulterior motives for interests of international agricultural research in indigenous knowledge of genetic materials. He points out that for many years the international agricultural research centres have been collecting genetic materials from farmers in tropical regions and making them accessible to commercial firms and agribusiness in the North. This genetic material is used in the development of modern varieties which are then patented. The contribution of the farmers to this is largely unacknowledged and uncompensated. The expansion of patenting laws into developing countries also threatens the basic right of farmers to produce and experiment with their own seeds. Alternative Technologies Project (PTA), a Brazilian NGO working on rescuing and developing farmers' varieties of maize, has found that the development of patenting laws in Brazil will enable seed companies to establish a monopoly over the breeding of local varieties and threaten the right of access of farmers to germplasm (Cordeiro, 1993). In India, on 29 December 1992, angry farmers stormed the offices of Cargill in Bangalore and destroyed seeds. They were protesting against changes in Indian patenting laws which would give agribusiness companies monopoly rights in the production of seeds. They were demanding 'the rights of farmers to produce, modify and sell seeds' (*The Ecologist*, 23, 2, 1993).

Researchers championing indigenous knowledge of genetic materials and farmer participation in genetic resource conservation and development may unwittingly be furthering the process of the expansion of agribusiness, and laying conditions for the further marginalization of farmers. Since control over plant genetic resources includes control over knowledge about seeds, indigenous knowledge of germplasm is important to the biotechnology industry.

These developments are mirrored in other industries. While an emphasis on indigenous knowledge may appear to be new in agricultural and environmental science, biologists collecting taxonomies of plants and the pharmaceutical industries have long collected inventories of the local uses of plants, which are often tested for the development of medicines. Juma (1989) comments:

> The search for knowledge and new plants was already part of the culture during the early period of colonial expansion and imperialism. The role of genetic resources in the rise of the British Empire is an example of this process and the imperatives that led to the redrawing of the global genetic map (p. 48).

In his introduction to *Plants of the Gold Coast* (1930), Irvine is largely concerned with indigenous perceptions of plants and their uses. He concludes:

> The field of investigation on the value of such West African native medicines is one that is full of scope for further enquiry, especially along pharmaceutical lines, and much valuable information remains to be brought to light (p. xxiv).

Thirty years later, in his introduction to *Woody Plants of Ghana* (1961) Irvine writes:

> Special attention has been given to the economic uses of plants, including local medicinal uses. The names of active principles are given, where known, as are details of any scientific experiments made to demonstrate their medicinal uses. It is hoped that there will be further research along these lines, as the knowledge of medicinal uses by African herbal doctors is still enormous (p. xiv).

The local knowledge of colonial peoples has made great contributions to science, including such important medicines as quinine taken from the bark of Chinchona (Juma, 1989), and contributions of crop genetic resources (Mooney, 1983; Kloppenburg, 1988; Juma, 1989). While the North seeks to patent its knowledge of genetic materials, the genetic knowledge from developing countries has often been appropriated for free. In the case of

Chinchona, genetic materials were smuggled out of Bolivia for cultivation in India by British botanists, in contravention of Bolivian national laws which stated that export of the plant was a government monopoly (Juma, 1989).

An emphasis on the knowledge of rural producers is not new in science. What is new is the incipient critique of the commoditization of science which accompanies much recent discourse on indigenous knowledge and promises of empowering local communities.

Empowerment is associated with the end of marginalization, and the development of a science which 'listens' to the people, respects their knowledge, and builds this knowledge into processes of technology generation. This tends to neglect the fact that marginalization is not only associated with the perimeters of scientific interest but also with market forces. There are many agricultural communities which were formally centres of production and now lie marginalized because market forces have left them behind, seeking greener pastures elsewhere. This is not only applicable to agricultural communities in developing countries, but also in Europe and North America. Many former centres of industrial production have experienced similar fates, with generations of the children of workers doomed to unemployment as industry relocates to more profitable areas of the world.

While the discourse on indigenous knowledge is critical of commodity-oriented science, it has not been able to free itself of commodity orientation. It is still largely concerned with knowledge of commodities or potential commodities, of particular crops and genetic resources, rather than the framework of the generation of knowledge about production and its relation to the agricultural environment, the natural environment, and the position of producers in society.

Popular Perceptions of the Environment

Folk knowledge is largely considered to be utilitarian, and its role in development is now defined by the interests of science and capital rather than by the producers themselves. That is to say, indigenous knowledge tends to be robbed of its own autonomous consciousness and a global consciousness is imposed on it.

Some recent research on the environment stresses the ways in which traditional African societies used their knowledge of the environment to create systems of production which ensured the protection of the environment. These systems are now supposed to be breaking down because of modernization and population growth. This approach marginalizes local knowledge, by questioning its relevance in the present period, and by giving it an unconscious conservation objective or ethic, which mirrors modern international environmental and development concerns, but may be at odds with the present 'unsustainable' livelihood strategies and aspirations of the people.

Theoretically, this approach is in danger of teleological functionalism, of reducing technical knowledge and knowledge of the environment to a purposive action solely concerned with preserving the environment. This mirrors earlier developments in social anthropology and sociology which saw social institutions as functioning to preserve the stability of society, and in cultural ecology which saw ritual and social institutions as functioning to preserve an equilibrium with the environment.

Human Ecology, Equilibrium and Consciousness

In the study of human ecology or human interactions with the environment, human interpretation of the environment has often been ignored and social organization and culture assumed to respond mechanistically to the environment (Ellen, 1982). In much of the anthropological tradition, the ritual domain is the focus of human interactions with the environment, where homeostatic pressures on human utilization of the environment, or the regulation of ecological and social systems, are worked out in symbolic systems which lie above cognition of the natural world. In his analysis of Maring ritual cycles in New Guinea, Rappaport (1968) argues that a complex chain of events and signals serves to determine pig festivals, which regulate the pig population and ensure that the environment is not degraded. He sees this as forming a homeostatic mechanism, which lies beyond conscious awareness. Such an analysis is functional in that it reduces human organization and consciousness to a regulative mechanism for preserving an equilibrium. It robs society of its history.

While theories of equilibrium, homeostatic and cybernetic systems have made a major impact on studies of human ecology, equilibrium models of the natural world have been questioned by a number of biologists (May, 1973; Holling, 1973; Levins, 1968; Levins and Lewontin, 1985). They argue that nature is not in a state of self-regulatory balance, but in a continually transient state, being disturbed from time to time, moving in one direction and then another under the influence of climatic and other geographical processes. Throughout history natural species have changed; some have disappeared and others have come into being.

History also furnishes many examples of pre-modern land degradation (Westoby, 1989; Hughes and Thirgood, 1982; Thirgood, 1986). The problem then facing neo-functional models of human society is to analyse and account for the conditions under which nature and human consciousness breaks out of homeostasis, and the effects of changes in nature on human–environmental equilibrium.

Alternatively, an analysis of human–environment interactions must examine human perceptions of the environment and give an account of purposive behaviour which focuses on the transformation of the natural world through the utilization of natural resources to meet specific objectives (Bennet, 1976). As Levins and Lewontin (1985: 69) argue, 'consciousness allows people to analyse and make deliberate alterations, so adaptation of environment to organism has become the dominant mode'. Thus, human conceptions of the environment are concerned with transforming the environment to meet production goals, and reflect the negative and positive results arising from this transformation.

While knowledge of the environment may be manifest in classificatory systems of nature (see Ellen, 1982 for a review of the literature) which arise out of a familiarity with a relatively stable environment, the act of transforming nature gives rise to an understanding of the process involved in harnessing natural forces and the 'capability of becoming aware of the disturbances created by humans in the milieu, and how these might be avoided if there is evidence of danger' (Bennet, 1976: 35). This will give rise to a knowledge which is more process oriented than that rooted in classificatory structures. This type of knowledge may be characterized as an *adaptive system* (Bennett, 1976). Adaptive systems are:

> open systems – they freely exchange energy with the environment, and contain internal innovation. Adaptive systems are dynamic systems, because the innovative solutions to problems tend to create new problems, which must be coped with some time in the future. Adaptation is a behavioural process that seeks satisfaction for present needs, with greater or lesser concern for the future: where there is great concern, the system will change slowly and undesirable consequences may be avoided; where the concern is weak, the system will change relatively rapidly and easily, and the problems will accumulate (Bennett, 1976: 94).

Periods of change will be characterized by much searching for solutions to problems without knowing the precise outcome. The environmental knowledge brought into play will be based on a reflection and knowledge of the responses of nature to the interventions of humans, and on the unintended outcomes of human interventions. This knowledge will be innovatory, experimental, interactive and dialectical, rather than arising from an intimate and timeless relationship rooted in equilibrium with a static nature. While it may not be concerned with wide and broad classificatory systems of natural resources, it will contain knowledge of process, energetics and ecology. It will arise from a tendency of humans to play with and explore the environment (Campbell, 1966). The unforeseen consequences of these interactions will give rise to new perceptions of the environment.

In times of crisis, this knowledge may be concerned with solving environmental problems. In other periods, knowledge of ecology and energy flows may be harnessed for different purposes, and subsumed under different adaptive strategies, which seek to harness energy to accommodate nature to particular objectives. Thus, shifting agriculturalists may harness the energy of fire to minimize labour inputs on the farm. In contrast, high-input agriculturalists may harness the energy of petrochemicals to raise yields to the maximum possible.

In each instance, interactions with the environment are influenced by the nature of social relations and the development and utilization of technology. Human relations with nature are a reflection of social and production relations. The social and production relations change in relation to interactions with the natural world, the responses of the natural world to productive activity, and new knowledge about nature and natural resources. As Bennett (1976: 41) writes, 'we act on Society just as we act on Nature, and our actions toward Nature may be defined for us by actions on Society. Hence Nature becomes Society'.

The study of human ecology has much to contribute towards an understanding of popular perceptions of nature and natural resources, which goes beyond the narrow utilitarian approach of the development commodity disciplines. However, the roots of human ecology in functionalism, and concerns with equilibrium models and adaptation to nature, have limited its scope to examine the impact on the environment of societies drawn into commodity production and incorporated into the world economy. The dominant concerns are with small-scale social formations and tribal people rather than with peasant societies organized around large urban centres and nodes of world trade. In reality, many of these societies will be involved in commodity production and participate in wider political and socio-economic formations, but the integration of these wider social formations has not been the object of study.

Bennett (1976) argues that human ecology needs to develop into a policy science of the adaptive consequences of human activities. However, by focusing on culture, on the behaviourial aspects of human relations with the environment, and in relegating the socio-economic and political economy, Bennett is in danger of producing an overgeneralized methodology concerned with an essential human nature, in which social dimensions are subsumed under the problem of the human need for gratification and its impact on the environment. The impact of political and economic systems on human–environmental interactions is removed from this equation. The central question is one of how policy makers can control human actions which result in land degradation within a democratic system. This is in danger of producing a technocentric approach to the environment, in which the central problem is seen as the introduction of regulation to control environmental utilization and the use of coercion to enforce this. However, the perceptions of what needs to be regulated and who does the regulation are socially constructed.

This raises similar problems to the 'lifeboat ethics' of Hardin (1972). Hardin, one of the early progenitors of global environmental technocentricism, argues that the overpopulated masses of the Third World are a major threat to the survival of earth. They are in danger of capsizing the lifeboat, the 'spaceship Beagle' (global environmentalism) which is destined to save the world. Only those underdeveloped countries which show a willingness to control their population should be helped aboard the lifeboat or should be provided with aid by the developed world. The rest are a dispensable entity threatening the global environment or modern society. Those who obey what the captain says will be helped, but those who persist in their own viewpoints will be allowed to perish. The sensibilities of the lifeboat captain reveals an ethnocentrisism in which the concept of the environment is equated with the world view of Western capitalist life, from which other parts of human diversity and experience can be cut off.

Environmentalism of the Poor

Recent literature has unearthed the phenomenon of environmental movements among the marginalized, poor and dispossessed tribal and peasant peoples in developing countries. This includes social movements which oppose the actions of the state and large companies which result in land degradation and threats to popular livelihoods. These social movements oppose deforestation, large dam projects, enclosure of common lands for agribusiness, and the extension of patenting laws.[1] In contrast with the consumer environmentalism of well-endowed middle-class Europeans and North Americans, these movements are rooted in production and livelihood struggles. They represent the interests of people whose livelihoods are threatened by the increasing commoditization of the environment and the expansion of capitalism into the last frontier areas. They represent a desperate defence of the people against the enclosure of the common lands they have utilized for centuries, and against the appropriation of nature by large-scale

---

1 See Hecht and Cockburn (1990) on Brazilian rubber tappers and Indians; Guha (1989) on the Chipko movement in India, with strong representation from tribal people, which seeks to protect forests from deforestation; Shiva (1988) and Agarwal (1993) on women's environmental movements in India, including movements against dams; Colchester (1992) on a wide range of popular movements in South and South East Asia; *The Ecologist* (1993) for movements concerned with agribusiness control over seeds.

commerce. They represent the right to use land and resources on the basis of established historical and cultural experiences and in ways which are determined by local needs and livelihoods rather than commodity markets. They represent local consciousness of the environment (including the human environment and precapitalist values) defining its space outside of global environmentalism, and challenging capitalist economic development.

While these social movements are being interpreted as something new, they are part of a continuum, with roots in popular rebellion and resistance to the encroachment of the world economy (Colchester, 1992; Jackson, 1993; Guha, 1989). Colchester gives examples of popular resistance to imposed development projects in South East Asia resulting in the use of intimidatory tactics by the state and culminating in popular uprisings. He also notes that not all these social movements are environmentally benign. Tribal people in Bihar who have lost rights to land have mobilized against official forestry programmes, and developed a 'forest cutting programme'. They use forest clearance as a means of asserting rights to land which can be upheld in the context of forestry law. In Karnataka and Thailand people have mobilized successfully against the appropriation of land by forestry programmes, sabotaging eucalyptus plantations and uprooting seedlings, bringing development projects to a standstill, and winning the right to manage land.

If these movements are not new, international recognition and support for their struggles are. In the past, popular resistance to the march of progress has often resulted in decimation and genocide. Increasing familiarization with the state and the politics of development has also enabled popular movements to articulate their struggles in modes through which they have been able to gain public support at the national and international level. At the international level many struggles of tribal or indigenous people have attained the status of icons, while national environmental movements rooted in the middle class or commodity-producing peasantry are marginalized (Viola, 1992; Redclift, 1989), as are the environmental struggles of working people and national minorities in developed countries against their living conditions.

International recognition for environmental movements, and incorporation of them into international development objectives, may form part of a process of cooption (Vivian, 1992). The struggles of tribal peoples may in the end be packaged into new rainforest flavours of ice-cream for the environmentally sensitive consuming classes of the North (May, 1992), a symbolic representation of the new frontier of genetic resources. Support for the struggles of the common people for the common land may reflect a larger conflict between international and national capital for access to land for different resource usages. The interests of international capital may be associated with preserving the resources of tropical forests as international 'common property' resources, since the enclosure of the tropical rainforests by national capital may preempt the future interest of international capital in genetic resources.

Environmental movements are seen as important levers for the creation of sustainable development agendas, bringing local knowledge and experiences of the environment into the development debate, containing the cost of development and enlarging the benefits (Redclift, 1989). They have also been seen as contributing to the emergence of ecological economics by forcing capital to internalize some of the externalities of environmental degradation (Martinez-Alier, 1990).

Environmental movements have not emerged uniformly throughout the world. Their existence is likely to be related to political conditions, traditions of struggle and organization, and the reality of marginalization. The lack of environmental movements in particular areas does not preclude the emergence of an awareness of the political economy of the management of resources. This may take the form of disquiet about certain forms of national and international development policy, or resistance to adopting forms of development behaviour promoted by the state and its allies.

To divorce environmental movements from their historical and socio-economic context and to promote them as a lever for environmental accountability and sustainable development agendas is to reduce them to functionalism. They need to be studied in the context of how economic, social and political factors influence the utilization of resources; the ways in which people associate resources in particular niches of production, the articulation of the expansion of commodity markets and the world economy in patterns of utilizing resources, and the responses of people to change and encroachment on their livelihoods, their neighbourhood and their way of life.

Political Economy and the Frontier

The study of environmental perceptions and consciousness among rural people can be carried out in a political economy framework which examines the relationship between people and the natural environment, the relations of people to production, and the incorporation of the production interface between people and nature into wider political and market relations, into the nation state and the world economy.

This requires a framework which examines the interaction between local production and global markets and between global and local socio-economic stratification. In this three levels of analysis need to be combined: local production and economy within the context of the regional economy, the regional economy in the context of the national economy and state, and the nation state and its economy in the context of the world economy.

Production is a useful activity around which the interaction between people and the environment can be observed, but analysis needs to go beyond examining those commodities produced for markets, to the perceptions of the producer of nature and natural resources and the impact of the market economy and its associated political and social outlooks on the utilization of resources. The interaction between people and the environment must go beyond an understanding of a few principles of ecology and introduction of systems analysis into socio-economic frameworks. It must document patterns and ranges of resource usage and perceptions of resources, and their relations to socio-economic and micro-environmental differentiation. It needs to develop a historical dimension which incorporates changing patterns of resource utilization and perceptions of the environment with the dynamics of socio-economic transformation, economic growth, decline and marginalization.

The concept of the frontier is a useful tool for the building of such an analysis, uniting a wider world economy with the local economy, and society with nature.[2] Frontiers represent first encounters between nature and society, arenas in which society shapes nature in its own image, and where people are eventually shaped by the dominant political and economic structures in society. People migrate to the new frontier with hope of starting a new life. But often they find themselves caught in a web as society reconstructs itself in its old image. In recent years the frontier has received much attention as a result of growing world awareness of tribal peoples, particularly in the Amazon. However, few studies examine old frontier areas, districts which have been despoiled and now lie forgotten.[3] These areas have usually become marginalized because of the culmination of land degradation resulting from the ramifications of frontier ideology and the pressures of frontier markets; and because settlers can move to the new frontier beyond, which will be more profitable to exploit than solving the mounting environmental problems.

---

2 There is now a large literature on the frontier. Some notable examples include W. P. Billington (1966), *The Frontier Thesis: Valid interpretations of American History*, which examines the frontier thesis as originally developed by F. J. Turner, and its subsequent reinterpretation. *The Great Frontier* by Webb (1951) is a particularly stimulating extension of the frontier thesis, which examines the implications of the decline of the frontier for American society, and the impact of the frontier on the development of capitalism in both Europe and America. *Essays on Frontiers in World History* edited by Wolfskill and Palmer (1983) is a useful collection on the application of the concept of the frontier worldwide. Moran (1981), *Developing the Amazon*, and Hecht and Cockburn (1990), *The Fate of the Forests*, examine the ecological and socio-economic implications of the opening up of new frontiers.

3 One notable exception is Dean's study (1983) study of the frontier in São Paolo, Brazil. This traces the whole history of frontier development in this area up to the time when the frontier moves to new districts. Webb (1951) also provides a framework which considers the whole history of the frontier.

The whole process of frontier expansion is important to policy frameworks of the environment and for the analysis of the unevenness of development throughout various regions within a nation. While people remaining in old frontier districts have to contend with environmental degradation, they are frequently marginalized since development resources, infrastructure, and resources for the maintenance of infrastructure have moved to the new frontier areas. In this respect, marginalization does not only apply to peoples beyond existing technology (the sense in which it is frequently used by commodity sector disciplines) but also to people who have been consumed by previous modes of technology utilization, and are left to suffer the consequences and find their own solutions.

The dynamics of frontier development introduce new dimensions into the human-environmental interface, not accounted for by systems analysis with its focus on the matrix of environment, technology and demography. This relates to the movement of peoples, infrastructure and market places, responding to the opening up of new markets, which develop the capacity to despoil an environment rapidly through intensified production. The expansionary nature of capital ensures that the potential of a windfall profit at the frontier is highlighted, but not the consequences – which capital does not have to bear as long as new frontiers exist.

Commoditization and Value

Commoditization is used here in two senses: it refers to the processes by which science becomes increasingly subject to commercial pressures and seeks to promote commercial values; and to the processes through which farmers become captured by commercial agricultural input markets, and increasingly dependent upon the consumption of agribusiness packages for production. Commoditization involves the incorporation of farmers into markets for modern genetic materials and increasing dependency on packages of chemical inputs, labour and technical advice. At its most developed, it involves dependency on marketing outlets through outgrower and contract farmer schemes in which agribusiness chooses the varieties which farmers grow and markets them. Agribusiness firms control the markets in seeds and inputs, and are also monopoly buyers and processers of farm output (Bernstein, 1976; Levins and Lewontin, 1985; van der Ploeg, 1990).

Development programmes often seek to create an interface between farmers and agribusiness. They create infrastructures of credit and technical support to encourage farmers to consume the products of agribusiness. They create a dependency, based on the integration of rural society with dominant market relations (van der Ploeg, 1990). Farmers may respond by attempting to develop a relatively autonomous agriculture, which creates buffers against the market. This may include mechanisms which promote forms of self-sufficiency; which value autonomy, inventiveness and the freedom to pursue independent strategies and styles of farming beyond commercial considerations. This involves forms of economy in which resources are valued and utilized as use values as much as exchange values. This enables producers to resist total incorporation into unfavourable markets and to maintain autonomous forms of production and relations to the environment which are not determined solely by market conditions (van der Ploeg, 1990). This may be interpreted by the forces of development as conservatism or a sentimental attachment to the land.

In recent years the agricultural and development disciplines have become increasingly aware of their limitations, the negative environmental impact of modern technologies, and the implications of reliance on non-renewable petrochemical resources for expansion of yield, and the potential of new unexploited genetic materials. Increasingly they are interested in a range of genetic resources which were previously marginal, including minor crops, new crops, landraces, and medicinal plants. They are also interested in environmental considerations as a result of the failure of standardized technology packages to make inroads into marginal environments, the consequences of environmental degradation, and the widespread erosion of genetic resources as a result of development initiatives.

Approaches to these resources, however, reveal frameworks which if logically developed will lead to the total commoditization of nature. This includes environmental accounting, the attempt to place exchange values on environmental degradation, genetic resources, and the associated local community knowledge. This may lead to a validation of the knowledge of rural communities, in which their contribution is recognized and recompensed to a certain degree. But it may also lead to the introduction of a degree of commoditization in rural life which may threaten its intellectual frameworks and information networks. This may lead to the guarding of knowledge and genetic resources in much the same way in which genetic science in the US and Western Europe is a protected world, highly commoditized, and plagued by patenting laws and commercial considerations which threaten the free exchange of knowledge. This commoditization of genetic resources and associated human knowledge systems may have a negative impact on the cultures of rural communities, and create conditions for further appropriation by agribusiness. These are complicated issues which are not easily resolved. They show that in the study of environment the concept of value (and the nature of value) is of central importance in the nexus of relations between producers, markets, science and the environment.

This Case Study

This study is concerned with how rural people utilize resources and the impact of markets, national policy and environmental degradation on the utilization of resources. It is not concerned with specific prized genetic resources or highly cherished environments, such as centres of genetic diversity or pristine rainforests. It focuses on marginalized environments in areas which were formerly centres of export crop production but now suffer from increasing degradation and are conveniently forgotten. It deals with small farmers who are involved in commodity production; with cultivators on the edge of the forest who have not embraced modern high-input farming and who have reservations about modern technologies and development prescriptions.

This book is based on a case study which focuses on a line of settlement in the forest ecotone of south-east Ghana, in the Manya Krobo district of the Eastern Region. This a highly fragile area on the edge of the forest, with markedly different micro-environments, ranging from areas with relict forest to grassland. It is one of the oldest frontier areas in Ghana and was incorporated into the world economy in the early nineteenth century. Manya Krobo was first known for its oil palm production but decline in the oil palm world market in the late nineteenth century led the area to convert to cocoa production. By the 1940s cocoa had been decimated by disease and the Krobo next focused on food crops, becoming Ghana's largest food-producing area for the home market. However, movement to food in a predominantly export-oriented economy signalled the beginning of marginalization in Krobo. This was compounded by the opening up of new agricultural frontiers in Brong Ahafo in the 1960s and 1970s, which became a central focus of the drive for agricultural modernization. The Manya Krobo area has been forgotten and left to deal with its own problems. Land degradation is pronounced, the result of one hundred years of export-oriented production with a frontier consciousness. With decline, many people have moved on to the new cocoa frontier, the new oil palm frontier and the new food-producing frontier. The once thriving market of Asesewa, the largest food wholesale market in Ghana between 1940 and 1970, has declined pitifully, although it is still recognized as a market of quality palm oil and maize.

Those left behind are forced to struggle with an increasingly harsh environment, in which the former forest has been invaded by aggressive pan-tropical and savanna weeds, in which rainfall has become increasingly unreliable, and yields have fallen dramatically. People still move to newer frontier areas as life becomes increasingly difficult, but this option is less and less attractive as land becomes scarce in these frontiers and stories are carried back of the hardships people have to withstand at the hands of rapacious landowners.

The state agricultural services have a poor presence and are demoralized by the lack of uptake of the technology they promote. Without help, farmers are left to reflect on their experiences of frontier development, on the crisis in the agro-ecosystem, and on the responses of the environment to their interventions. They adapt and experiment in adapting to changing conditions, and some attempt to ameliorate environmental degradation. The study examines the ways in which farmers utilize and interact with the environment. It contrasts the adaptive responses of farmers in the worst degraded micro-environments, which are dominated by grassland, with more forested environments. The more degraded environments are found to be hotbeds of experimentation and innovation, with a high consciousness of environmental issues. However, there is no support for this spirit of innovation within the agricultural and development services, which are busy promoting their own solutions emanating from the international circuit of technology development. These international solutions sometimes have shortcomings already realized by farmers. The different perceptions of farmers, researchers and policy makers are examined, as are the implications for the frameworks of development.

Chapter 2 looks at the wider regional setting, placing the agrarian system within its historical context. It examines the factors which have influenced the emergence and decline of frontier agriculture. It also explores the impact of the frontier on socio-economic relations and integration into the world economy, and on the formulation of agricultural policy. International and national policy frameworks are still rooted in models of export crop production and frontier colonization. They are trying to recreate the golden years of frontier boom, to extract the last windfalls from the frontier (particularly in the form of timber) and to rehabilitate cocoa in areas in which the frontier has gone. Without any conception of the role of the windfalls of frontier colonization, they face a task as herculean as the one that confronted Don Quixote and Sancho Panza. Unlike Don Quixote, they have the power to pull levers and exert pressures to reorganize agrarian production and to aggravate the growing immiseration of the rural folk.

Chapter 3 develops a detailed analysis of the impact of the frontier within the Manya Krobo district. It traces the relationship between the expansion of the frontier and integration into the world economy, and shows how farming strategies and farmer perceptions of the environment have changed with the transformation of the frontier.

Chapter 4 moves into the locality of Upper Manya Krobo in which research was carried out. It investigates the social conditions of production, the relations of production, access to productive factors within communities, and the impact of micro-environmental variations on production. The interaction between commoditization and land degradation results in an economy in which the cost of production is high and returns are declining, resulting in a highly capitalized neo-subsistence economy.

Chapter 5 is concerned with changing patterns of resource utilization within communities in response to degradation and the market. It examines the diversity of natural resources used in communities and problems emerging from the interactions between a diversification of use values in households and a market system which focuses on a narrow range of exchange values. The chapter also touches upon the stratification of markets, and the implications of monopoly market control for a more diversified and environmentally sensitive utilization of resources.

Chapter 6 explores the adaptive and experimental skills of farmers in coping with and adjusting to changes in the agro-ecosystem and land degradation. Farmers are experimenting with evolving new regenerative technologies. The chapter examines the factors encouraging experimentation in different localities and the implications for the relationship between farmers and formal scientific research and development. It argues for a new structure for research and development which is more exploratory in its approach to problems and diagnosis, and which seeks to strengthen and support the independent research capabilities of farming communities.

Finally, Chapter 7 draws up a critical framework for the analysis of contemporary environmental and development policy. It is argued that this has to examine the structures and modes through which nation states and producers are integrated into the world economy, rather than focusing on abstracted rural producers as the problem. Throughout history the world economy has influenced and redefined the relationship between producers and their environment. What is needed is a political economy approach rooted in historical experience which explores the fundamental contradictions in development policy and integrates a critical policy framework with the objectives of creating popular participation in technology development and development planning. This would provide new models which support the regeneration of environments and districts in accordance with the aspirations of producers.

2

Political Economy of the Frontier in the Ghana Forest Zone

In recent years a growing body of literature has been concerned with documenting folk environmental and agricultural knowledge and the land management systems of local communities. The concept of the local community has often been abstracted from the historical and regional context in which it occurs. The impact of regional and macroeconomic factors on localities has often been neglected. Frequently, isolated village case studies are used to develop models of the rural sector without understanding the location of these settlements in the political and economic life of the region. The relation of settlements to commodity markets, to centres of political power which administer infrastructure and technical support services, and to new frontier areas in which services are concentrated is often critical in determining the characteristics of incorporation into national life.

This chapter explores the historical significance of the concept of the frontier to the rural economy and agricultural policy within the forest areas of Ghana. It develops a historical and regional framework which enables the impact of macroeconomic policies and microeconomic structures to be observed. It examines the interactions between settlement patterns, farming strategies, market incorporation and land degradation. It argues that socio-economic relations and the logic of responses to markets mediate ecological adaptations to the environment and define the ways in which local environmental knowledge is applied. Thus any meaningful understanding of local land management and perceptions of the environment needs to analyse the impact of social and economic conditions on the application of knowledge to land-use strategies.

Frontiers and Margins

Agricultural systems are frequently classified in terms of agro-ecological zones. However this only describes the spatial distribution of cropping systems for one particular moment in time without taking into consideration

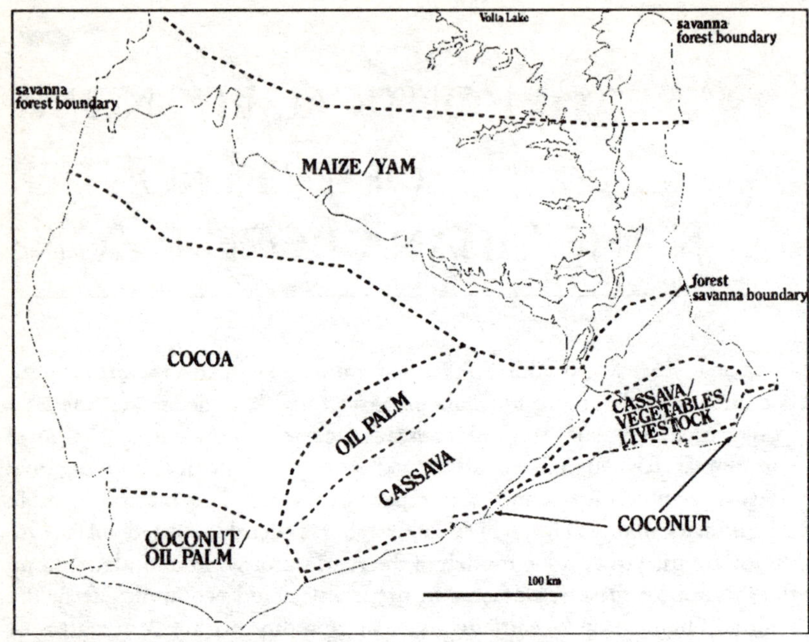

FIGURE 2.1 Cropping systems in the forest area of Ghana
Source: Adapted from Otchinya (1989)

historical patterns of agricultural transformation and the processes which induce variation and change.

Approaches based on agro-ecological zoning characterize a large part of the transitional zone of the Eastern Region of Ghana as belonging to a cassava belt (Otsinya, 1989; see Figure 2.1) without taking into account the history of part of this area as the original pioneer cocoa zone. The history of cocoa and its subsequent decline is important to understanding the present social and economic conditions of production in this area, and accounts for many features of tenurial systems, labour relations and the nature of incorporation into commodity production. This results in quite different social and economic areas from other parts of the cassava belt to the south, in which cocoa and the commoditization of land were never prevalent. Although farmers may grow similar crops in different areas, the history of incorporation into markets may result in quite different agrarian systems with different levels of commoditization. Similarly, a large area of the forest may be classified as the cocoa belt. But different relations of production and relations to the development organs of the state occur in old areas of production where farmers are increasingly turning to food crops, and new frontier areas where the agricultural systems are now being incorporated into the cocoa export market.

The characteristics of the cocoa economy and forest farming in Ghana have been determined by a process of pioneer frontier settlement – the movement of populations into new areas with empty, unsettled agricultural lands. Pioneer frontier settlement in tropical forests is frequently associated with forms of shifting agriculture based upon the development of extensive farming systems to bring about rapid conquest of the wilderness and effect the opening up of potential agricultural land (Richards, 1985; Grandstaff, 1981; Greenland, 1975). Historically, pioneer frontier settlement has involved fierce competition between neighbouring states for control of the forest estate and the development of political forms of organization to facilitate rapid land colonization (Kea, 1982). The expanding frontier has also absorbed a considerable proportion of the growing agricultural population, and led to a dislocation of population from old declining pioneer zones to the new frontier. Old zones of production have frequently been abandoned. Faced with the prospects of declining yields and land fragmentation, a large percentage of the farming populace move to the new frontier. Pioneer frontier settlement is also associated with the utilization of natural resources as a windfall, and a system of extensive farming results which maximizes the advantages of land colonization. As land becomes scarce a reorientation of farming strategies is required, away from the maximization of the cultivated area and towards both the intensification of farming and the rehabilitation and conservation of land.

In the forests of Ghana, frontier farming arose between the sixteenth and nineteenth centuries as a response to the opening up of large areas of sparsely populated land for agricultural colonization. In its early years this process was controlled by district states and their ruling families (Kea, 1982). During the early nineteenth century, pioneer frontier settlement was associated with the development of oil palm production for the export trade (Johnson, 1964; Wolfson, 1953). At the end of the nineteenth century, cocoa became the major crop influencing the development of the frontier (Hill, 1963). During the early twentieth century the Gold Coast emerged as the major world cocoa producer. Cocoa has remained the main agricultural export crop of the forest zone until the present, although the relative production of Ghana on the world market has declined. Pioneer frontier settlement is in its final stages. The last remaining forests in the Central and Western regions have now been opened up for cocoa production.

Frontier development has resulted in complex social relations of production and land tenure systems. It has been important in the alienation of land and labour and has facilitated the process of social differentiation. This has involved the emergence of large landlords, absentee landowners with multiple holdings, and landless labour and smallholder cultivators with insufficient land to farm.

The most successful farmers have continuously invested their profits in purchasing new lands along the frontier and hiring labour (Hill, 1963). Many smallholder farmers have been faced with ruin and impoverishment in the old frontier districts and have been forced to move to the new frontier districts, where they work as labourers and sharecroppers for large landholders. They have migrated to the new frontier districts with great expectations. But many of them fail to gain land, become embroiled in debt, and eventually form a pool of landless labour for large landholders (Arhin, 1985). The degradation of the environment in old frontier districts spells the ruin of the smallholder farmers. Their shortage of land exacerbates degradation as they are forced to overexploit the land they have. But the plight of old frontier smallholder farmers can be the lifeblood of the large landowners and absentee farmers in the new frontier districts, who find themselves presented with the gift of migrant landless labour. This system has profound long-term consequences of impoverishment and environmental degradation.

The development of the new frontier results in the marginalization of old frontier districts. Infrastructural developments, agricultural support services and market traders focus on the new frontier districts. The infrastructure of old frontier districts is not renewed and falls into decay and dilapidation. Since the richest and most politically influential farmers within the old frontier districts have moved to the new frontiers, old frontier districts can rarely form strong lobby groups to demand services from government. The strongest agrarian lobby groups are based in the newer frontier areas.

The decline of old frontier areas has been associated with degradation and crisis in producing cocoa under conditions of environmental stress. Farmers move out of cocoa into food crop production. But central government is committed to the cocoa sector which provides the principal source of levies raised from the agricultural sector. Government has little control over the internal marketing of food crops. As a result, the movement of production from cocoa to food crops is anathema to the state. State policies tend to produce disincentives for food crop production in areas defined as lying within the cocoa belt, and incentives for the rehabilitation of cocoa (Konings, 1986). However, cocoa has declined because of complex environmental and economic factors which are not accounted for by the state. As a consequence, the economic interests of the state compound the marginalization of old frontier districts, while the failure to take the long-term environmental and economic implications of state policy into account may lead to future crisis in the whole forest agrarian sector.

Within the forest area five frontier zones can presently be defined:

- The Eastern Region, with the oldest frontier districts situated in the transitional zone of the south. The frontier developed in the early nineteenth century with the extensive cultivation of palm oil for the

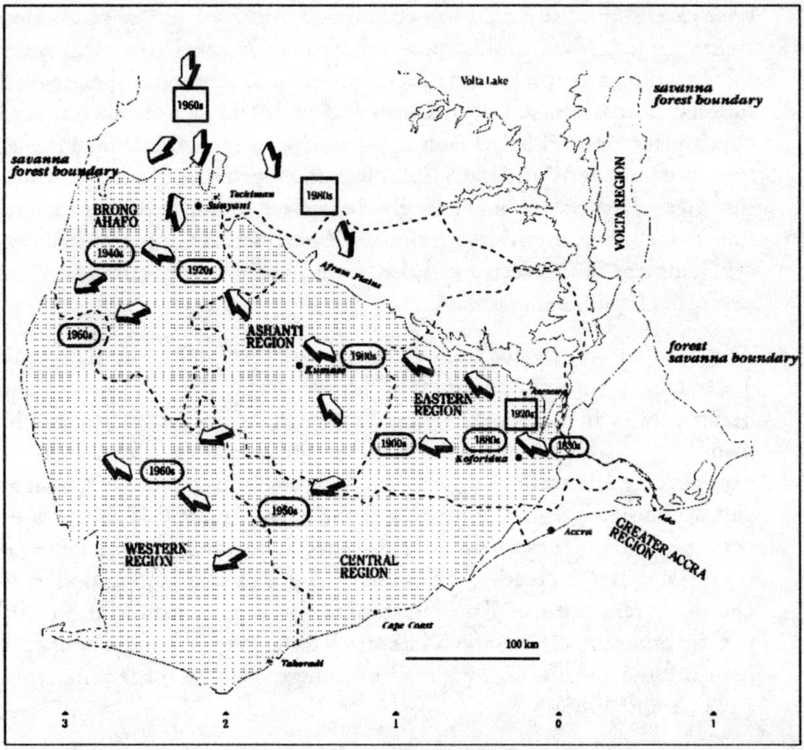

FIGURE 2.2. The frontier in the forest areas. While the cocoa frontier has moved gradually throughout the forest in relation to the development of infrastructure from the coast, the food-producing frontier has been confined mainly to the transitional zone and forest edge. Migrants from the Upper East–Upper West regions are playing important roles in opening up the new food frontiers.

export trade. By the late nineteenth century the zone was transformed into the pioneer cocoa-producing area. By the 1930s cocoa was devastated by swollen shoot disease and was replaced by a food crop farming system centred on maize, cassava, oil palms and vegetables. The area is presently characterized by decline, outmigration and environmental degradation. State policy has tended to focus on the rehabilitation of the cocoa sector in the area under the Eastern Region Cocoa Rehabilitation Project, sponsored by the World Bank. However, much of this area is too dry to support a viable cocoa economy. This is the area in which case material for this study was drawn.

- The middle frontier areas of Ashanti and southern Brong Ahafo, in moist semi-deciduous forest. These areas were opened up from the 1920s, with the expansion of the road transport infrastructure. The Ahafo cocoa belt is an extension of the Ashanti cocoa belt, which was settled by Ashanti cocoa farmers when land became scarce there in the 1940s. This is the most favoured area for cocoa production. In recent years the area has suffered from increased degradation and problems of rehabilitating old cocoa plantations. The Ashanti Region Cocoa Rehabilitation Project, sponsored by the World Bank, subsidizes the replanting of cocoa farms in this area. Farmers are increasingly dependent upon hybrid seeds and inputs, including the widespread use of pesticides. Absentee landowners are dominant in this sector and sharecrop relations prevalent. There are also many smallholder farmers.

- The new cocoa pioneer frontier of the Western and Central regions. These areas were first opened up by farmers during the late 1960s as land became scarce in other areas. They are now the major cocoa area and the main area to which farmers and labourers are migrating. Other areas are experiencing labour shortages as a result of the outmigration of labourers and smallholder farmers. However the soils and ecology of this area are very fragile and the expansion of cultivation is resulting in rapid degradation. Lands are increasingly dominated by absentee landholders who choose to rent it out under sharecropping arrangements. Oil palms and rice are other important crops. The area has the most heterogeneous rural population in Ghana, drawing the land-hungry from all other agricultural areas (Arhin, 1985).

- The northern transition zone in the Brong Ahafo region. This area became the major food-producing zone for the urban markets during the 1970s, displacing the southern transition zone. The main movement of population into this area has been from the northern savanna rather than the south. The main crops include maize, yams, plantain, cassava, vegetables, cowpea, groundnuts and tobacco. Production is mainly carried out on smallholdings, though there are also a number of large mechanized enterprises and state farms which have now collapsed. The area is one of the least densely populated areas in Ghana. Land values are not highly commoditized, unlike other areas of the forest. The area is largely seen as the major food-producing area for the home market in national development plans, and is well served by extension and other support services for food crop development. Migrant farmers from the north are also moving into the Afram Plains to the east, which is developing into the new food frontier.

- The new oil palm belt. This area is situated within the cocoa belt of moist semi-deciduous forest and wet evergreen forest within the Eastern, Central, Western and Ashanti regions. This belt has displaced palm oil production in the drier areas of the old pioneer frontier zone. The zone developed in the 1970s as a result of increasing strains placed on foreign exchange earnings by rising importations of vegetable oils. Policy measures and subsidies were introduced to encourage the development of large agro-industrial oil palm estates. This sector is focused on highly capitalized commercial estates. Smallholder farmers have been coopted into this sector as contract farmers on outgrower schemes. Their lands have often been appropriated to make way for large estates, and then they have been reapportioned blocks to farm. They are provided with hybrid seedlings, inputs, directives on cultural methods and extension support. They are under contract to provide their yields for the large oil mills associated with the estate complexes. The forests are often clear felled to make way for these monocultural plantations and result in intensive degradation of the rainforest environment and decline in local food-producing capabilities (Gyasi, 1988; Gyasi, 1992). This belt does not constitute an ecological frontier but an economic frontier of new technology and capital organization, which involves the expropriation of older frontier producers.

The Forests of Ghana

The forest areas have a bimodal rainfall, with a heavy rainfall season from the end of March to early July, a short dry season in July, a minor rain season in late July and during August and a dry harmattan season from November to March. This enables two harvests to be reaped in a year. The northern savanna, by contrast, has a unimodal rain season from June to September. While the total rainfall of up to 1,000–1,250 mm is comparable with the dry semi-deciduous forests, the length of the dry season and rates of evapotranspiration prevent forest trees from growing and allow only one harvest a year. In the east the forest is bounded by the savanna salient of the Togo–Dahomey gap which reaches the coast on the Accra Plains. This area has a total rainfall of under 750 mm and a rain season of less than six weeks. While a bimodal rainfall pattern is reproduced here, the minor season is unreliable and often fails to materialize. The forest has been the main focus of agricultural activity as a result of the richness of its soils and the moist environment which enables two annual cropping seasons and tropical fruit trees to be grown.

The differentiation of the forests of Ghana and their relation to other ecological niches has also been significant in determining patterns of human settlement. Six main types of forest occur (Hall and Swaine, 1981):

- *South-east outlier forest.* Only 20 square kilometres of this forest type remains today in Ghana. It has a canopy height of 10–15 metres, above which emergents such as *Ceiba pentandra* and *Adansonia digitata* may tower. There is a paucity of species present, never more than forty and frequently less than twenty. Gregariousness is high with one species capable of dominating the canopy and understorey. Characteristic species include *Vepris heterophylla, Ochna ovata, Tiliocora funifera, Uvaria ovata, Ritchiea reflexa* and *Diospyros abyssinica.* Rainfall regimes lie in the range 750– 1,000 mm, representing the driest conditions under which tropical rainforest can grow. Soils are among the most nutrient-rich in the forest. Most of this forest has been destroyed for agricultural purposes and degraded into derived savanna thicket and bush. Nineteenth-century accounts describe these forest areas, which lay 15 km from the coast (Burton 1873; Reindorf, 1895). Many historic settlement patterns can be explained by the boundaries of these outlier forests, such as the line of seventeenth-century administrative and market towns lying 15–20 km from the coast (Kea, 1982).
- *Southern marginal forest.* This forest also occurs in small relics between Cape Coast and Akosombo. It is characterized by an upper canopy of less than 35 m and a dense understorey. A few emergents such as *Ceiba pentandra* and *Antiaris toxicaria* may dot the landscape. Characteristic species include *Hildegardia barteri, Hymenostegia afzelii, Talbotiella gentii, Manilkara obovata Drypetes floribunda* and *Diospyros abyssinica.* It occurs within a rainfall regime of 1,000 to 1,250 mm.
- *Dry semi-deciduous forest.* This has an upper canopy in the range of 35–45 m and a rainfall of 1,000 to 1,250 m. Deciduousness is higher in this forest than in any other type of tropical rainfall, and there is a dense undergrowth of herbaceous plants, climbers, and a dense leaf litter. Under this forest *Antiaris toxicaria* and *Milicia excelsa* achieve their greatest abundance. Other common species include *Triplochiton scleroxylon, Sterculia tragacantha, Diospyros monbuttensis, D. mespiliformis, Celtis zenkeri, Spondias mombin, Afzelia africana, Cola gigantea var. glabrescens, Elaeis guineensis* and *Trichilia prieuriana.* To the north-west a variant of this forest occurs which is characterized by the incidence of natural fires. The fires thin younger trees and this results in the dominance of fire-resistant trees such as *Anogeissus leiocarpus, Celtis africana, Khaya grandifoliola* and *Elaeis guineensis.* Low levels of leaching of soil nutrients and large quantities of leaf litter produce soils which are fertile for agricultural land use. Most of this area is under food crop production and few of the upper canopy species remain. The area is prone to desiccation, invasion by savanna grass species, and bush fires destroying tree growth and promoting 'savannization'. This is the dominant forest in existence in Krobo and in the study area.

- *Moist semi-deciduous forest*. This forest is the area in which historically cocoa has predominated. It has an upper canopy which frequently exceeds 50 m and a dense understorey. Characteristic species include *Celtis mildbraedii*, *Nesogordonia papaverifera*, *Culcasia angolensis*, *Microdesmis puberula*, *Baphia nitida*, *Khaya ivorensis*, *Cola nitida*, *Daniellia ogea*, *Turraeanthus africanus* and *Chytranthus macrobotrys*. Annual rainfall is in the range of 1,200–1,800 mm. This is sufficiently high to allow for leaching and loss of soil nutrients. Plants thus attempt to preserve nutrients in leaf growth and evergreen species make up about half the total species in this type of forest. Cocoa and oil palm cultivation has led to the removal of most of the forest cover of this area. This is the dominant forest in the middle frontier belt and in the north-western Krobo settlements, which were colonized specifically for cocoa farming.
- *Wet evergreen forest*. This forest predominates in the westerly forest areas and is characteristic of the new cocoa frontier area. The canopy rises to about 40 m and predominantly consists of evergreen trees. The forest is highly diverse with low densities of individual trees. The most numerous trees are *Dacryodes klaineana*, *Stromosia glaucescens*, *Diospyros sanzamimika*,

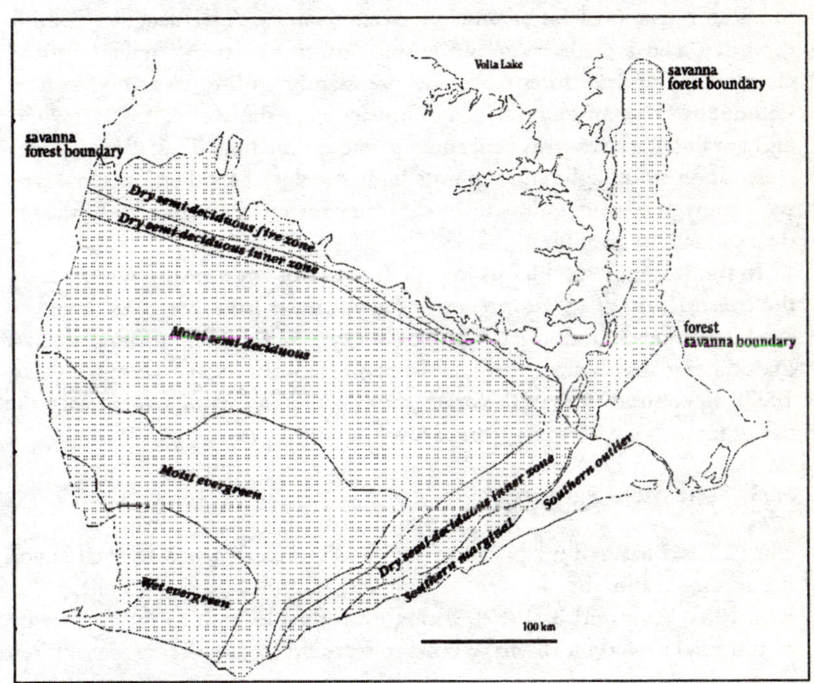

FIGURE 2.3 Forests of Ghana.
Source: After Hall and Swaine (1981)

Dialium aubrevillei. The understorey is sparser than in other forests with the shrub *Scaphopetalum amoenum* frequently dominating many localities to the exclusion of other species. Annual rainfall is in excess of 1,750 mm. Soils suffer from heavy leaching and are acidic. Decomposition rates are high and leaf litter and humus never abundant. Most nutrients are preserved in biomass rather than in the soil or leaf litter. In the past the poor soils have 'repelled the cocoa or food farmer and the population has been low for a forest area' (Hall and Swaine, 1981: 92). Only in recent years, with the alienation of land completed in all the other forest areas and declining soil fertility, has this area been opened up for agriculture. The removal of the forest cover and heavy leaching of the soils may lead to rapid soil degradation.

- *Moist evergeen forest.* This is intermediate between wet evergreen and moist semi-deciduous forest, with characteristic species of both types being present, an upper canopy of under 45m, a large number of evergreen species and soils which are poorer in nutrients than moist semi-deciduous forest.

Historically, the exploitation of the forest zone has tended to move from the drier transitional forests into the wetter forests. Advantages of farming the drier areas include more fertile soils and smaller trees, facilitating land clearance. The drier forests can also withstand a greater clearance of trees without as great an environmental impact as in the wetter forests, where higher rainfall makes farm land more prone to leaching. This allows greater penetration of sunlight and supports higher yields of food crops. However, with more intensive cultivation, the drier forests are prone to bushfires, desiccation and savannization.

In the wet semi-deciduous forest, clearance of large trees often involved the construction of a platform above the buttresses from where the tree was axed. In earlier periods the clearing of this type of forest constituted a major undertaking involving considerable organization of slave labour (Wilks, 1977). In contrast trees in the drier forests could be cleared largely with the use of fire and cut close to ground level.

Early Settlement Patterns

The earliest phases of urbanization in Ghana are associated with societies on the forest-savanna border (Posnansky and McIntosh, 1976; Flight, 1976; Kea, 1981; Anquandah, 1982), dating from the eleventh to the fourteenth centuries. The earliest towns to emerge were situated in the northern forest ecotone, in the Brong area.

The south-east forest ecotone was a major centre in which the state emerged. The wide variety of environments facilitated the development of specialized production niches dependent on each other and encouraged the development of trade. These niches included a coastal salt and fishing sector, riverine fish and irrigated vegetables, livestock on the Accra Plains and food crops in the forest areas (Bosman, 1967; Nathan, 1904; Field, 1941). Within the auriferous forest areas a gold-producing sector also developed, which formed the main commodity integrating the region into the nascent world economy (Kea, 1982).

By the sixteenth century commodity trade had developed and gold formed the main regional currency. The main social formations were characterized by the emergence of classes and the domination of town over country. The towns were the home of a landowning and merchant nobility who controlled retainers, professional soldiers, artisans, and markets. The towns exercised suzerainty over agricultural districts from which they extracted revenues in gold. The farming population was forced to produce surplus for the town markets to raise money to meet their revenue obligations. The peasantry was also dependent upon the town for articles they did not produce, including iron farm implements (Kea, 1982).

These states were small, consisting of a large town surrounded by an agricultural district with a radius of up to 25 km, densely populated by revenue-paying subjects. The town populations were comparatively large, and some towns had between 10,000 and 20,000 people. The nobility claimed control over the land and, deploying their numerous retainers, organized the clearing for cultivation of forest land, which was then released to peasant subjects (Kea, 1982). The limits of the radius of the domain were determined by the need to control the peasantry and market its surplus on the town market. The central towns combined marketing and administrative functions.

By the seventeenth century the old town states were in decline and new imperial states began to emerge. The crisis was associated with increasing social strife, riots, brigandry and land flight of farming people escaping from increasing difficulties in meeting revenue obligations (Kea, 1982). This crisis may have also been related to increasing degradation and failing yields resulting in increasing deprivation. In the period between the sixteenth and the nineteenth centuries agricultural activity resulted in the complete degradation of the outer marginal and southern outlier forests which were transformed into derived savanna.

In the seventeenth century population began to move increasingly out of the outlier forests into dry semi-deciduous forest. By the mid-seventeenth century the major centres of agricultural production lay in dry semi-deciduous forest. During this period wealthy lords (*birempong*) began to move their retainers into semi-deciduous forest and open up new settlements. This process was marked by intense competition, military conflicts and skirmishes between rival groups for control over the land. New political organizations developed in which the *birempong* emerged as the rulers of polities with powers of jurisdiction over new forest lands and settlers (Kea, 1982; Wilks, 1982). Stronger *birempong* subjugated their weaker neighbours and incorporated them into their polities. The subjugated *birempong* retained control over their realms but performed fealty to their overlords, providing tribute and services, including a quota of soldiers for military campaigns. The *levée en masse* was a major political innovation of the period. The strongest *birempong* emerged as the rulers of empires and the weakest as village chiefs (Kea, 1982; Wilks, 1982).

In contrast to the earlier town-based social formations, the imperial states were associated with extensive settlement and the maximum territorial organization of a hierarchically based population. The village gained greater autonomy, the rural-based periodic market emerged as the main node of exchange for rural produce, and craft production (particularly farm implement production) became ruralized. Centralized state revenues were raised from villages as a collective, often in kind, and village rulers were responsible for realizing their collection. This replaced the extraction of monetary rent from individual peasants. This relaxing of central state control over rural social organization facilitated the rapid conquest of the vast wilderness of semi-deciduous forest. Pioneer frontier settlement emerged, focused on extensive colonization of semi-deciduous forest for agricultural purposes.

Intense conflicts for control of land and population acted as a brake on extensive agrarian settlement. Whole areas were depopulated through warfare, flight of the defeated, and the forced expropriation of prisoners of war. These were transported to the centres of empire as slave labour which was absorbed into the peasantry or exported to the Americas (Gold Coast Ministry of Interior 1956; Kea 1980; Atkinson 1980; Wilks 1975). During the late eighteenth century the south-eastern semi-deciduous forest was seriously depopulated. In contrast, areas to the south on more marginal land became densely populated. Conquered peoples from the zones of contention in deciduous forest sought refuge in these more marginal areas. The outer forests became subject to serious land shortage and degradation, which intensified skirmishes between neighbouring peoples for control of land. The successful farming peoples were not those who focused on adapting to land degradation, but those who developed their military potential to defend their lands and encroach into areas of contention. These pressures on settlement encouraged the development of social organizations which would facilitate rapid and extensive land colonization when the opportunity arose.

The pressures on farming peoples in the late eighteenth century, and the environmental consequences of political and socio-economic conflicts, are vividly described by Reindorf, a Gold Coast historian who lived through much of the nineteenth century and documented the oral historical traditions and events of that time:

> After the conquest of the Akras by the Akwamus, cultivation was carried out close to the towns on account of incessant inroads and kidnapping by the latter. By and by those high forests and bushes which attract so many rains were felled for fuel and consumption, and rains became scarce, hence scarcity of food prevailed in June and July every year. This forced the farmers to form small hamlets 2 or 3 miles distant from the towns, such as Ologobi, Tatarawa Kpatshakole, Sowotuom, Abroduafa, Legong, Papao, Hatso, Kwantanang, Ashikuma, etc. The meaning of Ologobi and Sowotuom already show how the farmers fared at the hands of the enemies. The former shows they eluded their kidnappers and escaped home, the latter, their plantations could be made only by holding onto their guns in defence. As they could not make their plantations inland, the harvest in corn was never plentiful (Reindorf, 1895: 274).

During the eighteenth and early nineteenth centuries there was an increasing vacuum in the south-eastern semi-deciduous forest: dominant powers failed to consolidate their control over the area. By the 1740s Asante emerged as the major power in the area, but it was unable to integrate successfully the south-eastern province into its political administration as rebellions spread. By the 1830s the yoke of Asante domination in the south-east was broken. A coalition of south-eastern states allied with British and Danish forces to defeat Asante. These events eventually led to the formation of the Gold Coast Protectorate under British influence. The defeat of Asante and increasing security encouraged the rapid colonization of the south-eastern semi-deciduous forest from the forest fringes, and the growth of British economic interests in the Gold Coast led to the growth of export crop production.

The Colonial Economy and Frontier Settlement

By the middle of the century the most important trade routes in the Gold Coast hinterland were involved in European trade. Manchester cotton and other industrial goods were the main commodities imported into the Gold Coast. Palm oil was the major staple commodity produced for the European market, where it was utilized as an industrial flux and in the manufacture of soap. The major supplier was the Krobo area. Its comparative advantage lay in its vicinity to the Volta River, enabling economies of river transport to the coast. The second largest producer was Akuapem, near Accra, where barrels were rolled down to the coast or headloaded in pots.

The expansion of demand for palm oil intensified pioneer frontier colonization. By mid-century, land purchase became predominant in the south-east forest ecotone. States which had gained large profits from oil palm production offered compensation for expropriated lands and expressed a desire to buy any surplus land offered them. Vendors were found in the forest interior of Akyem. This area was still suffering from the repercussions of centuries of war, reflected in economic decline and poor transport, and the population was unable to to take advantage of the opportunities to reorganize agricultural export production. As a consequence the chiefs sought to gain profits from the export boom by selling land to migrant farmers rather than developing export crop estates. A process of land migration into purchased land in semi-deciduous forest began, which has been well documented (Field, 1943; Hill, 1963; Johnson, 1964, 1965).

By the 1860s and 1870s world palm oil prices declined. This was a result of the discovery of mineral oil as an industrial flux replacing palm oil and the opening of European oil palm plantations in Malaysia and Java. These events led to the ruin of the Gold Coast oil palm industry which could not produce competitively at the then current world market prices. There began a period of experimentation with new crops, including coffee, rubber and cocoa. By the 1890s cocoa emerged as the most profitable crop on the Gold Coast and became the focus of colonial economic policy. Cocoa required minimal outlays in capital and labour, and could be grown on an extensive basis. Cocoa production rapidly spread through the forest, leading to the alienation of most forest land.

While the early cocoa farmers resembled capitalist farmers investing profits in land, labour and infrastructure (Hill, 1963), as the enterprise developed it increasingly became dominated by a landlord economy and speculation in land (Hunter, 1963; Austin, 1987). This was encouraged by colonial policy which sought to transform the more marginal areas of the economy into labour reserves for the mineral export enclaves and the export agricultural sector (Konings, 1986; Howard, 1978). Through introduction of taxation into the north men were forced to migrate southwards seasonally to seek employment to pay revenues. The rationale of this policy is clearly revealed in the *Gold Coast Annual Report 1937/38* which describes northerners as:

> an amiable but backward people useful as soldiers, policemen, and labourers in the mines and cocoa farms, in short fit only to be hewers of wood and drawers of water for their brothers in the Colony and Ashanti (p. 3).

Under the domination of the Asante empire the north had been a major area from which slaves were drawn. Colonial policy sought to maintain the internal structure of labour appropriation while transforming its outer form.

Taxation in money rather than the expropriation of slaves became the major mechanism of ensuring sufficient cheap labour for the export-producing sectors.

This source of migrant labour enabled the landowning families of district states to transform their forest estates into cocoa plantations without alienating the land to cocoa farmers. Sharecropping arrangements came into being in which landless migrant labourers and tenant farmers created cocoa plantations and managed them for landlords in return for a share of the proceeds (Hill, 1956). These arrangements had similarities with pre-capitalist relations in which a dependent peasantry originating from enslavement paid its lords rents in kind (Amanor, 1989). They displaced wage labour which in the late nineteenth and early twentieth centuries was dominant in the cocoa sector (Austin, 1987). In the period 1920–40 the landowner appropriated a third share (*abusa*) of the proceeds of the cocoa harvest or received a third portion of the cocoa farm which was created. In the post-war period, as land became increasingly scarce and expensive, this was increasingly transformed into a half share (*abunu*).

The domination of land by the ruling classes of district polities and by absentee landlords has had important implications for agriculture. Cropping decisions have been made by non-farming landlords who demand that tenants grow cocoa. The interaction of the cultivator with the environment and the agro-ecological system is frequently dictated and mediated by the capital interests controlling the estate. The bringing of land into cultivation has been determined by the narrow interests of absentee landowners and land speculators rather than agro-ecological factors. These interests have involved widespread degradation of forest and alienation of land away from the mass of cultivators. In the Western Region, the expansion of cocoa farming into areas which were little farmed prior to the coming of migrant cocoa farmers in the 1960s has resulted in the rapid commoditization of land. Benneh describes how landowning groups cleared large tracts of land to establish ownership rights:

> The native Wassa were slow in taking up cocoa cultivation; they were, however, interested in granting land to strangers in return for cash or other benefits. This made it necessary for rights over land to be established by the Wassa chiefs and the heads of the kin groups. This was done through encroachment on virgin forest land. Anyone clearing an area of land which has not before been cultivated established his right over that tract of land. This method of acquisition led to ecologically damaging practices. People cleared large tracts of land, felled the trees, and left the land uncultivated, merely in order to establish their rights over it. The holders of such large tracts now lease portions to land-hungry Wassa and

migrant farmers, mainly because of lack of labour and capital to develop such lands (Benneh, 1988: 231).

In the New Suhum area Hunter (1963) records that the activities of the local landowning classes had resulted in land alienation to the extent that 98.6 per cent of land was cultivated by migrant labour. The insufficiency of land available for local farmers ensured the reproduction of land-hungry tenants and labourers for big landowners. In the Western and Central regions Arhin (1985) found that 86 per cent of migrant farmers interviewed had moved from their homeland as a consequence of exhaustion of their original cocoa land and that 63 per cent of the migrants arrived with extremely limited funds of less than ₵100. Most of them ended up working as labourers for big landowners or became heavily embroiled in debt.

Several studies of the cocoa sector reveal marked differentiation in holdings and tonnage of cocoa marketed, with the top 10 per cent of farmers marketing up to 50 per cent of total sales in several instances (Beckett, 1944; Beckman, 1976; Hill, 1956). A few absentee farmers often held substantial holdings, while a large number of farmers had small holdings of under 3 hectares (Hill, 1963). Indebtedness was also characteristic of the small farmer and a large amount of capital was tied up in forward buying and pledging of crops (Nowell Report, 1938; Shephard, 1936; Ghana Ministry of Agriculture, 1957).

The social relations which have developed in the cocoa industry in the twentieth century are not conducive to the practice of agriculture along sound agro-ecological principles. The farmers' knowledge of the agro-ecosystem has been subjugated to the dictates of colonial and world commodity market interests in monocultural production and to the short-term profits of landlordism. The ruin of the mass of smallholder farmers has prevented them from developing and applying their agro-ecological knowledge to the enhancement of the farming craft.

The study of rural environmental knowledge needs to be rooted in the dynamics of the evolving social structure. To root environmental degradation in the practices of smallholder farmers, in the incapacity of shifting agriculture to respond to social change and population growth, as is common in present policy frameworks, is to miss the complexity of the social structure. The roots of degradation lie in the failure of dominant economic interests to take into account the long-term environmental and social consequences of their actions and policy frameworks.

Contemporary Policy Frameworks

The life of a cocoa plantation may extend to 40 or 50 years. As a consequence, by the 1970s–1990s the original cocoa plantations of the middle frontier areas were being phased out and the only remaining frontier area is in the Western Region, now the main centre of cocoa production. The rehabilitation of old cocoa plantations has emerged as a central policy objective for the Ghana cocoa industry.

The rehabilitation of cocoa is a complex problem. It involves considerable outlays of capital in clearing old plantations and replanting. The environmental conditions of the old plantation areas have also changed. The wet moist forests in which cocoa thrives in its early years no longer exist. Declining soil fertility and moisture, and the build-up of pest and weed populations, are also problems in the agro-ecosystem in old cocoa areas. Although there are efforts to improve the environment for cocoa production, by planting agroforestry species such as *Glyricidia sepium*, rehabilitation largely focuses on the planting of new drought-resistant hardy varieties and large outlays in chemical inputs.

The comparative advantage of Ghana as a cocoa producer used to lie in the cheapness of production in new frontier areas. This enabled Ghana to displace other cocoa production areas in the Caribbean and Latin America. With the decline of the frontier in Ghana other new cocoa-producing areas have developed to supplant it, including Côte d'Ivoire and Malaysia. There has been a notable expansion in world cocoa production, resulting in saturated world markets and depressed prices.

The social relations of production which have developed in the cocoa areas have been adapted to conditions for producing cocoa cheaply, with minimal outlays in labour and technical inputs. This production base now faces problems in adapting to the outlays of capital in cocoa rehabilitation and to declining profit margins resulting from depressed international prices. Many cocoa farmers refuse to follow the input recommendations of development projects and extension services. Many farmers in old cocoa areas have converted to food crop production or have moved to the remaining new cocoa frontier areas.

Transformation of production into food within the forest is not in the interest of the state which is dependent upon levies from cocoa and exports to raise revenues and balance its accounts. The northern transitional zone and savanna areas are the main areas targeted for the development of food crop farming. As a result policies have tended to develop incentives for cocoa and disincentives for food production in the forest area. Incentives include subsidies – for cocoa rehabilitation in the old producing area in the Ashanti and Eastern regions, and for new cocoa planting in the Western Region – and increased producer prices for cocoa. In the 1970s disincentives included policies which attempted to fix low control prices for food crops, alongside subsidies for agricultural inputs. These were unsuccessful. During the 1980s, as part of the structural adjustment programme, policies have focused on trade liberalization and the importation of food crops from the EC and South East Asia to bring down prices on the domestic market, although supplier countries are often those with an agricultural sector heavily subsidized by government. The food producer, with minimal technical support services, is expected to compete on the free market against the most technologically advanced agriculture which is also heavily subsidized.

Cheap food is also a central objective of policies which seek to maintain low domestic wages for workers to attract foreign capital investment in manufacturing and agro-industries. The Policy Planning, Monitoring and Evaluation Department of the Ministry of Agriculture continually assesses levels of domestic food production and prices. This enables government not only to import food in the wake of shortages to avert hunger, but also to encourage importation to maintain low food prices. The farmer within the forest area who departs from cocoa production faces the consequences of marginalization.

Problems still exist for the cocoa sector, however. While the decline of cocoa has been averted and production has begun to grow, total government proceeds from cocoa remain static as a result of depressed market prices. Cocoa has been relegated from the major export earner to third place behind gold and timber. As a result, the state is attempting to promote a new range of non-traditional exports, including pineapples, coffee, medicinal plants, cane furniture, scrap metal, etc. (Jebuni *et al.*, 1992). But these are being left to private entrepreneurs to develop. The main policy initiatives in this field consist of tax concessions for exporters. Few linkages have been created which would facilitate diversification of production among forest-zone communities. Little public-sector investment has gone into promoting infrastructural development for diversified production, in contrast with the funds which have been channelled into cocoa rehabilitation and the timber industry. Despite the serious decline in export earnings from cocoa, under structural adjustment the major focus of state agricultural policy still lies in promoting the rehabilitation of cocoa production in agriculture and the maintenance of a monocultural, export-oriented economy.

This marginalization of food crop production is revealed in the allocation of agricultural funding. In 1978 the cocoa sector received over 45 per cent of funding allocated to agriculture, forestry and fishing and provided 17 per cent of agricultural gross domestic product (AgGDP). In contrast the forest staples of cassava, yam, cocoyam and plantain provided almost 60 per cent of AgGDP but only received 5 per cent of time allocated to agricultural research. Research funding as a percentage of AgGDP allocated to agriculture compares favourably with other similarly sized developing countries. But if the cocoa sector is removed from calculations, research funding levels are low. In 1987 0.80 per cent of AgGDP was invested in agricultural research. With removal of the cocoa sector this fell to 0.57 per cent of AgGDP (ISNAR, 1989).

Patterns of marginalization of food crop producers have also been complicated by a commitment of central government to supporting agribusiness and large farmers in the domestic food sector since independence, and a belief that smallholder peasant food producers are backward. This has reinforced the marginalization of smallholder food producers. Yet the peasant farmer sector forms the backbone of the food delivery system providing over 95 per cent of domestic food production (Hansen, 1989; Miracle and Seidman, 1968).

There is growing evidence that the development of the cocoa monoculture has had a major impact on deforestation. Degradation in the Western Region is presently developing at a rapid rate as a consequence of the cultivation of cocoa. However this evidence is being suppressed since it undermines the interests of the state, cocoa commodity research institutes and donor funding for the cocoa industry. While major research efforts focus on replanting of cocoa hybrids, the long-term security of the cocoa sector remains uncertain, given global overproduction and replacement of cocoa by other natural and synthetic substitutes in the confectionery and beverage industries.

The state runs the danger of seriously marginalizing its agricultural research potential through its commitment to the vestiges of the colonial economy and decaying modes of agricultural research; through its failure to develop a critical and radical appraisal of existing agricultural policy; and through its failure to draw upon and appraise the potentials of the diversity within environments and the farming systems of the people.

OLD FRONTIERS, DECLINING DISTRICTS AND DECENTRALIZATION

Many areas which were formerly centres of export crop production lie in decline. This includes the pioneer cocoa area in Akuapem, the Manya Krobo area, and the states around the Volta Gorge. Many decaying towns lie in these areas with large dilapidated houses built in the colonial style, a sad testament to a vibrant but shortsighted era when the energies of the people paved the way for the marvels of early colonial trade. But what of the present, marooned in a futility of purpose? The young are, more often than not, doomed to a life of unemployment and life on the fringes of employment. Agricultural activities in these areas often shift increasingly to cassava and small quantities of other crops with erratic and unreliable yields. These areas lie beyond the frontiers of policy frameworks, which focus on lethargically carrying old modes of colonial economy into new areas and conveniently forget the areas in which this framework has produced disaster. Little has been done to develop policy initiatives which examine the problems of decline within these areas and design concrete frameworks for their regeneration. While international policy frameworks have resulted in the propagation of technologies for sustainable development and environmental objectives at the national level, these are articulated abstractly without specific reference to how they can help to regenerate areas in which environmental decline is closely allied with economic decline.

Recent policies of decentralization may also aggravate the marginalization of these areas. Within Ghana, PNDC Law 207 establishes the structure for decentralization of local government and charges local government with carrying out 86 functions. This includes functions which came under the ministries of Health, Agriculture, Education, Water and Sewerage, Co-operation, the Ghana Highways Authority and the Post and Telecommunications Corporation. Local government is empowered to enact bye-laws in accordance with these functions; to form sub-committees which initiate and implement development plans and coordinate the activities of the various district sectors of the government ministries; and to raise local finances and organize community labour. However, local district assemblies frequently lack the funding to carry out such actions, and lack the competence to organize the various sectors of ministries to work within a coordinated development plan. In reality many of these committees have failed to develop into working bodies. The dominant concern of local government, given the lack of funding, is to raise rates and levies, and enact bye-laws as a means of gaining funds from licence fees and fines. Local environmental policy frequently consists of a series of bye-laws in different sectors which are not integrated and do not reflect a unified perspective of environmental conditions within the district. These laws may encourage activities which degrade the environment, since this provides revenues for the district administration. Thus, a system of licensing of charcoal burning exists to control the extraction of fuelwood. However, many district administrations concentrate on ensuring that charcoal burners pay their licence fees rather than on evaluating and appraising the effect of charcoal production on the environment.

Most districts consist of towns (in which the district administration is situated) surrounded by rural settlements. During the 1960s these towns were centres of infrastructural development, including the provision of roads, markets, lorry parks, health centres, sewerage, schools and, in some cases, pipe-drawn water and electricity. Most councils are now suffering from budgetary crisis, and are struggling to maintain this infrastructure, which in many urban areas is breaking down. In this situation, most district funds are diverted into trying to maintain elements of the existing structure, rather than into providing services to villages or implementing development and environmental plans.

Districts are also charged with utilizing 'popular participation' for their development plans. This involves raising funds within the district for development initiatives and communal labour to carry out public works. However, this is likely to compound the marginalization of the poorer districts where the inhabitants, already suffering from a marked decline in income and capacity to earn a livelihood, are too poor to meet the demand that they raise revenues, and too demoralized to engage enthusiastically in communal labour.

A concept of participatory democracy and devolution of power accompanies decentralization. But district secretaries are not elected by popular franchise within the districts. They are appointed by the government. This in effect means they are accountable to the government and not to the people. Decentralization is in danger of becoming a policy which removes the responsibility for administering local districts from central government and places the burdens of the budgetary crisis of the state onto the backs of the people. This will compound the marginalization of many communities and create unfavourable conditions both for environmental conservation and regeneration and for the promotion of productive activity which takes into account the interests of future generations.

Processes of environmental degradation are intimately associated with frontier expansion. The economic interests which have arisen through the frontier expansionary process also influence the ways in which frontier interests have been integrated into development policy frameworks. The interests of world commodities markets, including the cocoa and forestry sectors, and landlord capital, ensure that policy frameworks do not assess too critically the impact of forms of staple export crop production on the environment. They also ensure that these forms of economy remain dominant despite the great environmental and human waste which has resulted. The decline of old frontier areas, which is a direct consequence of their participation in frontier expansion to meet the needs of staple commodity markets, is further compounded by state and international development policy frameworks. These deliberately marginalize areas within staple export crop regions which attempt to develop a food crop economy. Despite growing evidence, since the commodity markets crisis of the 1970s in Africa, of the shortcomings of over-concentration on export crop production, policy frameworks still direct their main energies to the last new frontiers.

This situation is further exacerbated by structural adjustment measures which seek to rationalize government services within this export-oriented policy framework, and make the people increasingly responsible for funding their own development. In effect, most capital and support is going to lock agricultural production into modes of production which have outlived their usefulness. Communities which have suffered from the fall-out of colonial export trade and are trying to create a new stable productive base are starved of assistance, or directed by assistance to return to the old export crop production base. The policy frameworks of the 1980s and early 1990s have failed to develop a rounded critique of the problems in the agricultural sector, and have implemented reforms which do not address underlying problems of integration into commodity markets and the impact this has on regional economy and the environment. Paradoxically, while these reforms focus on deregulation and allowing free market forces to operate, financial levers and other project levers firmly lock the economy into the production for export of primary commodities, and hinder the emergence of new forms of economic activity.

Conclusion

The relationship between people and the environment has changed through time as a result of structural and political changes in this society and its integration into the world economy. In the early precolonial period densely settled but small city states broke down in the face of mounting production problems and social unrest. This gave rise to new organizations based on extensive colonization of the forest and frontier development. The development of the colonial export crop economy, with its large metropolitan and world market, resulted in an economy based on extensive forms of land colonization allied to the production of monocultural export crops for the demands of the world economy. While production dramatically grew, this was not allied to a significant growth of agricultural and scientific research within the colonies. The large profits which were realized both locally and internationally were not reinvested in agricultural technology but often accrued to mercantile trading firms and landlords as a windfall from nature. This form of economy has taken its toll on the environment. In the present period, faced with the decline of frontier land, there is a crisis of production in many areas and primary producers are now forced to find solutions to mounting problems and to devise new adaptive technologies and farming strategies. State policy, however, is shaped by powerful political interests which represent mercantile trade, world commodity markets, and landlord agricultural capital.

3

THE FRONTIER IN MANYA KROBO DISTRICT

The study of the history of frontier development within a specific district enables micro and macro concerns to be integrated. It discloses present constraints on production, the social and economic dimensions of environmental degradation, the perceptions of farmers of their problems, and the impact of macro policy frameworks on farming systems. It demonstrates that the context of environmental conservation must address issues of the regeneration of rural areas and the radical rethinking of present economic and agricultural policy frameworks.

Manya Krobo, situated in the forest ecotone of the Eastern Region, is one of the oldest pioneer frontier districts in Ghana. It consists of lowland towns situated in derived savanna and farming settlements in the semi-deciduous forest area. By the mid-nineteenth century the Krobo district produced about 60 per cent of total Gold Coast exports of palm oil (Wolfson, 1953). The early development of the frontier in Krobo has resulted in certain peculiarities which distinguish it from other frontier areas. A large infrastructure was developed in food crop marketing by the Manya Krobo for the regional economy prior to export crop production and this has been maintained up to the present, although it is now in crisis.

The Krobo district, in contrast to other areas, was a frontier of both export crop and food crop production. It was able to take advantage of monocrop specialization in cocoa in other districts to become the principal supplier of food to the non-agricultural population in the Gold Coast. It was late to take up cocoa production since considerable overheads were tied up in oil palm production. It was also one of the earliest districts in which cocoa production began to fail and was replaced by a food crop economy. It has a long history of environmental problems. There has been considerable dislocation of production within Krobo throughout the twentieth century. It has suffered from increasing marginalization as a result of the decline of its export crop base and the concentration of political attention on other, newer frontier areas.

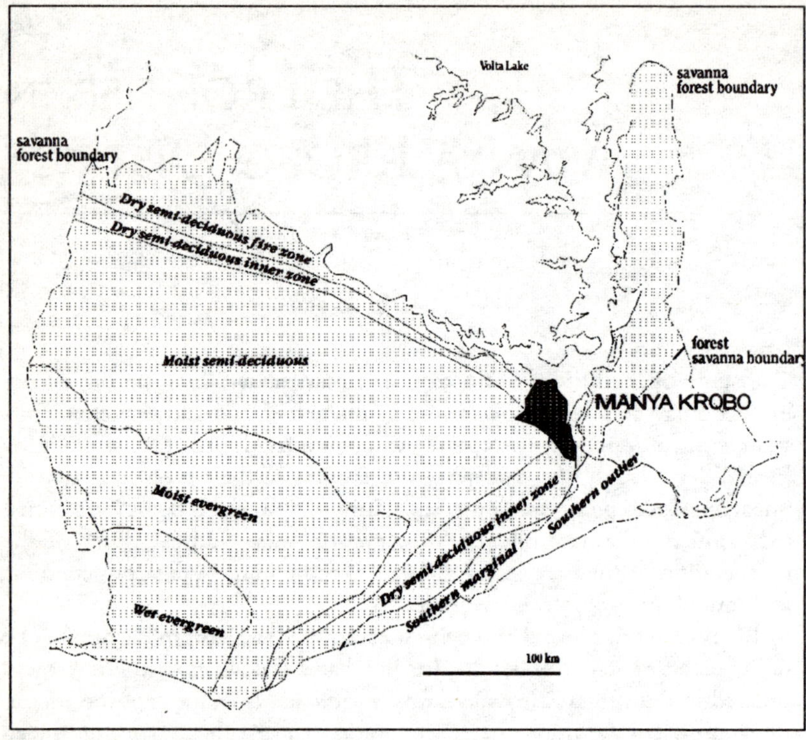

FIGURE 3.1. The Krobo area in relation to the forest.

Early History

During the eighteenth century Krobo was a small backwoods polity situated in the southern outlier forest, on a defensive inselberg known as Krobo Hill. The farmers made their farms on the plains below and retreated to their hill fortress at night. There were no village settlements, just a central polity with several quarters ruled by priests. During the late eighteenth century, as war raged within the semi-deciduous forest districts of Akyem, a large number of Akyem people sought refuge on Krobo Hill. They were escaping from defeat by the Asante, the most powerful empire in the hinterlands, whose zone of political control at its zenith almost corresponded with present-day Ghana (Arhin, 1967; Wilks, 1975). While these émigrés were integrated into Krobo society, they brought traditions of Akan politico-military organization with them. This eventually led to the transformation of Krobo society. Political power was soon captured by a secular authority at the head of the military, based on Akan state culture. By the mid-eighteenth century Krobo had emerged as the main centre of resistance to Asante domination and the home of a coalition of Akyem and Krobo *banditti* who raided the major Volta River trade routes (Kea, 1986). By 1770, the Krobo eventually came under Asante domination, but sporadic rebellions and skirmishes with neighbouring people for control of land continued into the nineteenth century. The emergence of rival factions of politico-military organization, both involved in transforming Krobo society, led to the emergence of two distinct Krobo polities: Manya and Yilɔ (Wilson, 1991).

During the late eighteenth and early nineteenth centuries land hunger was a major problem in Krobo and the politico-military machine was charged with winning new land. The Krobo began to expand into the forested areas of the dry semi-deciduous forest beyond the Okwe River. Thomas Odonkor, a Krobo who lived through much of the nineteenth century, describes this process:

> The Krobo had taken up seriously the question of acquiring land for farming. Unfortunately they got it into their heads that the means of acquisition could be fair or foul – one can imagine the series of conflict and free fight which were common features of this era.
>
> Yilɔ people claimed tracts of land from the Apirede and Adukrom people. The Manya also harassed the Akrade and Kotropeli people. The neighbouring tribes owned the land before the arrival of the Krobos....
>
> These people had been weakened by the wars which caused their southward trek, and so the Kotropeli and the Akrades on the Manya side, could afford no great resistance to the Krobo scramble for land (Odonkor, 1971: 18–19).

Political expansion involved a three-pronged drive: the creation of new administrative centres in the trans-Okwe area to organize and coordinate the expansionary process, the organization of a market infrastructure, and control over the Volta ports of Kpong and Akuse to facilitate participation in regional trade.

During the eighteenth and nineteenth centuries Volta trade flourished. Salaga and Kintampo became the largest markets in the interior of the Gold Coast. The Ada emerged as the largest salt producers, supplying communities as far as the Niger bend (Sutton, 1981). A variety of craft goods came southwards and large numbers of slaves. Kpong lay in the vicinity of dangerous rapids and developed as a transshipment centre where salt was loaded in smaller canoes with specialized canoemen to continue the journey into the upper reaches of the Volta. It was an international town with Ada, Ewe, Ga and Hausa sections (Johnson, 1964). Akuse arose in the mid-nineteenth century, as a major terminus in the oil palm trade, the furthest upriver port which steam launches could reach. Slaves, coming southwards from Salaga, were an important commodity for which there was a ready market in Krobo. They were largely used as agricultural labour to facilitate frontier expansion (Odonkor, 1971). They were not reproduced as slaves but incorporated as household dependants who provided a portion of their farm product to their masters as rent in kind and rendered them services.

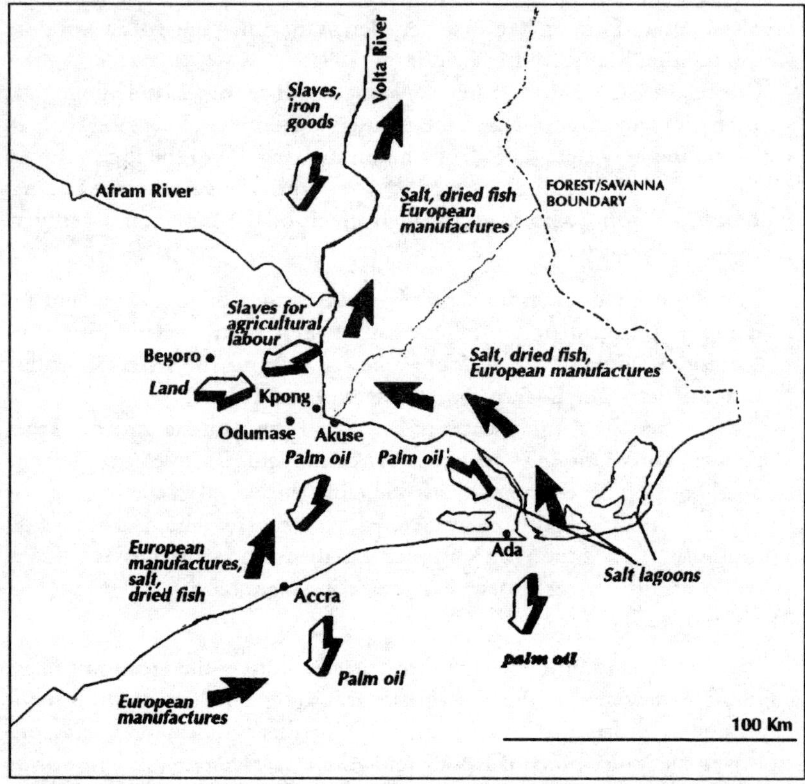

FIGURE 3.2. Krobo participation in Volta and international trade in the early nineteenth century

Land Purchase and Frontier Expansion

With the emergence of Krobo as a major oil palm and food crop producer, insecurity of land ownership and skirmishes with neighbours threatened newfound economic wealth. The Krobo sued for peace with their neighbours, and offered to purchase the lands they had seized:

> During the reign of King Odonkɔ Azu the scramble for land reached a chaotic state. Quarrels and free fights continued to be the common

feature of these undertakings. Indeed there were murders among the Krobo themselves in land disputes. The king therefore made friends with King Bamforo of the Kotropelis and the chief fetish priest of Akrade. On the occasion of the Akrade Mantche fetish festival, Azu regularly gave

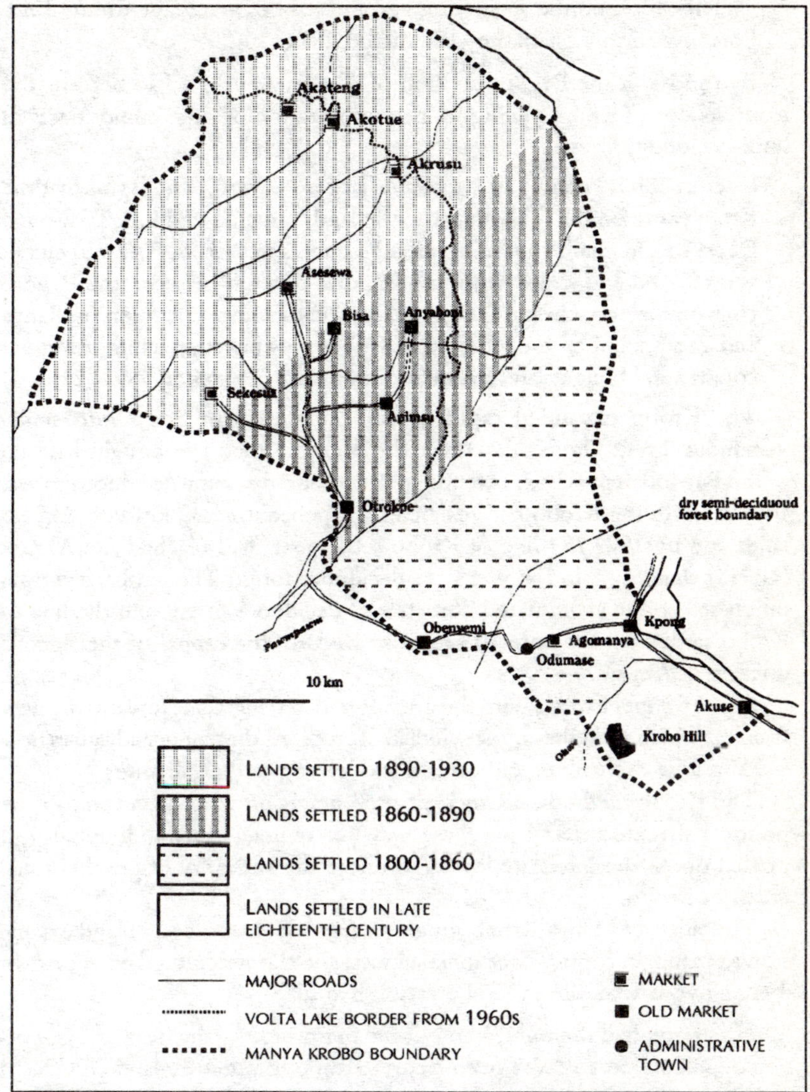

FIGURE 3.3. Frontier expansion and markets in Manya Krobo. As the frontier expands into the interior, traders congregate towards the new frontiers which yield the largest windfall of crops. As the frontier advances new markets arise outflanking old centres and leading to their demise.

> them presents of drinks and rolls of cloth, and was represented by his brother Tei Wayo. At the height of the friendship, Odonkɔ suggested to the Akrades that they should in a fair deal, sell their lands occupied by the Krobos for farming, so as to stop the brawls.
>
> They took up the suggestion and the Krobos were able to buy land. Peace was firmly established (Odonkor, 1971: 10).

By the 1860s the Begoro division of Akyem Abuakwa had become the main vendor of land, opening up the colonization of large empty tracts of semi-deciduous forest:

> Later in 1862, Fenning, the Chief of Begoro (Akan), who heard that the Krobo were on the lookout for fertile land, came down himself, through Dawa to Odumase and Sra to arrange trade agreements. The agreement was affected and sealed with the drinking of fetish between the Begoro chief on the one side and Ologo and Azu on the other [the rulers of Manya and Yilɔ Krobo] on the other. The Krobos now penetrated into the upper country and bought land freely from the Akan (Odonkor, 1971: 21).

The Krobo expanded rapidly over the Akuapem Scarp into semi-deciduous forest. During the 1860s the Manya Krobo had bought land up to the Pawmpawm River, extending 15 km into dry semi-deciduous forest. By the 1890s the Krobo had reached Bisa, penetrating 32 km into Akyem lands and by 1922 the line of Krobo settlements had reached the Akrum River, extending into the wet semi-deciduous forest. The Krobo had now purchased about 110 square kilometres of deciduous forest, and the line of Krobo settlement lay only 10 km from Begoro, the capital of the Begoro division of Akyem.

As the frontier expands into the interior traders congregate towards the new frontiers which yield the largest windfall of crops. As the frontier advances new markets arise outflanking old centres and leading to their demise.

The Krobo methodically incorporated newly purchased lands into their political structure. Land purchase was not transacted by individuals but carried out at the interstate level and under the authority of the divisional chiefs of Krobo.

The rulers of Manya Krobo sought to regulate the process of land expansion to maintain control over their subjects and the agricultural economy. In 1910 a bye-law of Manya Krobo established that:

1 No person had the right, without the permission of the head chief or his councillors, to go away from Manya Krobo to purchase land connected with the Begoro stool.

2 When this permission was given the purchaser had no right to transact the purchase by himself, unless the chief and councillors had appointed persons to accompany him to witness the transaction.

3 The witness should be remunerated with a reasonable sum, according to the dictates of the head chief and his councillors.

4 Those who infringed the bye-law were liable to a fine and prohibited from cultivating the land (Ghana National Archives, ADM 11/313).

A characteristic pattern of land purchase and colonization emerged, known as the *huza* system (Field, 1943; Benneh, 1970). In this system those wishing to purchase land formed a company of buyers. The land purchased consisted of a valley with a stream and slopes up to the summit. A baseline was cut along the tract of land parallel to the stream or valley bottom, and the various plots were measured out along this line. The basic unit of measurement was the *kpa* (rope), consisting of a set number of *gugue* (armspans) which varied from settlement to settlement. Hence, a farmer purchased *x kpa* consisting of *y gugue*. The length of the lands was not measured, but boundaries consisting of lines of *buna* trees (*Dracaena arborea*) were planted parallel to the baseline up the slopes of the hill. This ensured an equitable distribution of the various soil catennas and access to streams.

Farmers did not settle the purchased lands at once and no communal land was set aside for a village site. Houses were built on the plots near the major path. The Krobo farmers live in linear ribbon settlements rather than in nucleated villages. A political official (*zugbanyadalɔ*) from the divisional or paramount political authority was elected to negotiate the purchase of land for the farmers. He was also responsible for the political integration of the settlement into the Manya Krobo state. He was remunerated by the farmers with a plot of land in the settlement, which ensured his continual interest in its affairs.

In 1922, when the Manya Krobo frontier reached the Akrum River and met lands settled by Akyem farmers, the northern boundary of Manya Krobo

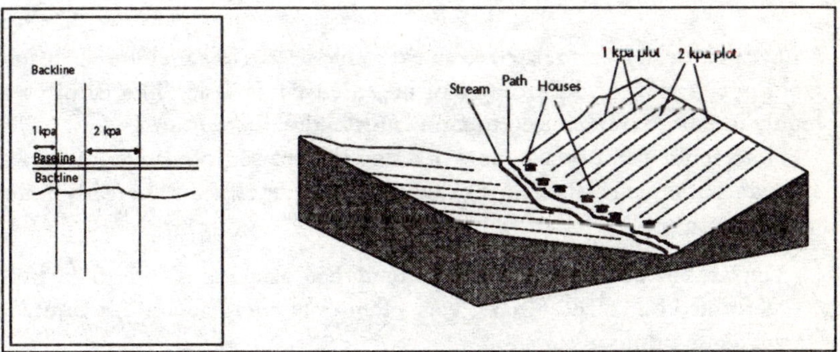

FIGURE 3.4. The *huza* system of the Krobo. Typically, the land purchased comprised a valley with its slopes. These were parcelled out into rectangular strips which were sold according to their breadth. The breadth was measured along a baseline and farmers planted boundary trees throughout their land along the borders of their strips.

became fixed. The Krobo have continued to buy lands beyond the Akrum, but this development has taken place outside the *huza* system. They have bought lands as individuals in areas of mixed population, without the organized patronage of the Manya Krobo state. They have moved into the Akyem, Ashanti, Brong Ahafo, Central and Western regions. From the 1920s Manya Krobo has been characterized by outmigration and the frontier of Krobo farmers has moved beyond its political boundaries.

Considerable controversy surrounds the expansion of the Manya Krobo frontier. In Begoro, two paramount chiefs were destooled for selling lands to the Krobo (Ghana National Archives, ADM 11/457, 1913). Within the borderlands of the Akrum, at such places as Miaweso and Ehiaminkye, violent conflicts have surfaced between Krobo and Begoro farmers in the 1980s as land becomes increasingly scarce and degraded. A dispute has surfaced in the law courts over the Krobo lands beyond the Pawmpawm, with the Begoro ruling families claiming rights of jurisdiction. The political and economic interests behind this claim seek control over market revenues rather than the ejection of the Krobo farmers, however. While claims are being contested on the basis of traditional rights to control over land, whether jurisdiction is 'tribal or territorial' (Gold Coast Ministry of Interior, 1956), the preceding analysis has shown that there is nothing traditional in the history of this area, which since the seventeenth century has been marked by upheaval and radical transformation. Such disputes need to be solved by considering the interests of the farming peoples and the security of agriculture, rather than on the basis of metaphysical conceptions of a tradition which lies above and beyond history.

Frontier Farming

Frontier expansion was related to an extensive system of agriculture to assure rapid penetration of the frontier of unsettled virgin land. The family was highly mobile and organized to farm lands in different locations.

Nineteenth-century accounts describe the sparse population of Krobo agrarian settlements. Reindorf (1895: 307) comments for the early nineteenth century:

> The Krobos who were trying to extend their plantations far into the bush ... formed but small villages, very often only one man and his family in the dense primeval forest.

Johnson (1965: 18) confirms this, citing an account from the *Evangelische Mission Magazine* of 1891:

> Among the numerous oil palms which he cultivates carefully and from whose fruits he gets the palm oil of commerce, hundreds of settlements are scattered. Mostly they are only a single compound, which lie in the palm forest under mango and lemon bushes, and in which one peasant family carries out its existence.

The main ecological principles used in farming were concerned with minimizing labour inputs to assure rapid frontier expansion. The development of a stable fruit-bearing tree component was central to this strategy. The tree component mimicked the forest by creating a canopy which shaded out weeds and undergrowth species, and thereby minimized weeding. The major labour requirement lay in clearing the forest. A cropping component was integrated with the orchard crop/plantation system. This provided a lucrative source of income before the fruit trees matured and shade for the young tree seedlings. It maximized returns from labour on the land, and also from the intensity of cultivation over a number of years. The farms were continually cropped for about five years until the fruit trees (cocoa and oil palms) began to mature and formed a canopy under which food crops could not thrive.

The forests were cleared by fire. Fires were lit under trunks to kill the trees and also to create a large leaf fall which would enhance the fertility of the soil for food crops. The first crops grown when the land was cleared were yams, maize and vegetables (pepper, tomato, okro and garden egg). These were followed by shade crops – including plantain, banana, cocoyam and cassava – under which oil palm and cocoa seedlings were tended. The period is remembered as a time in which food was in plentiful supply. Cassava was not eaten but introduced into the farming system purely as a shade crop. Bananas were also mainly cultivated as a shade crop and bunches were frequently left by the roadside for travellers to consume on their journeys.

Tree crops were gradually extended over the farm plot. When the whole land was under tree crops the farmer moved into new land further along the frontier. If a farmer had no new land and all land had been converted to plantation, land could be hired from neighbouring farmers for food crop cultivation. In exchange for the land the farmer planted cocoa under the food crops for the landowner. All the cocoa belonged to the landowner and all the food crops to the cultivator.

Two different types of farms characterized the Krobo area: forest food plots in the new frontier areas (*hwem*) and mature plantation (*nmonya*) in the older settled districts. Family labour was deployed to maximize frontier expansion. The young men worked in the new frontier districts bringing new land into cultivation and tending to foodcrop cultivation. The old men inhabited the old plantation districts where labour requirements were least.

Mature cocoa and oil palm plantations were considered old men's farms. During the oil palm and cocoa harvesting season younger relatives travelled from the frontier districts to help them. Foodstuffs were also sent from the new frontier to the old relatives in the plantation districts (Field, 1943). Large cooperative labour groups (*noboami* or *yekɛboami*) were also organized within villages for oil palm and cocoa harvesting to achieve economies of labour (Field, 1943; Huber 1963).

The ambitions of most propertied men were to acquire lands for all their sons and to have many sons. During this period women were generally excluded from land ownership. A large part of the proceeds from the land the son worked would accrue to the father, the landowner, but the sons would eventually inherit the land they cultivated.

Frontier expansion also encouraged rapid population growth to provide sufficient labour. In the late nineteenth century labour requirements for frontier expansion were partially met by purchases of slave labour, including women who were brought into the family to increase its fecundity (Huber, 1963). Krobo social institutions have also encouraged rapid population growth and consolidation of the household. Daughters were encouraged to have children early and also outside of wedlock. Such children (*yoobi/kplaabi*) were absorbed into the family as the children of the daughter's father and were given rights of inheritance (Field, 1943; Huber, 1963). Field (1943) has argued that in the 1930s–1940s the Krobo were more prolific than their neighbours, and that deliberate strategies were devised to encourage expansion of the rural population to facilitate rapid frontier colonization.

In addition to direct descendants, family dependants (the descendants of slaves or people who had sought the protection of a wealthy patron) could work as tenants and provided either a share of farm proceeds or labour service to their lords. Family labour could also be supplemented by migrant cropshare tenant farmers. This form of tenancy was based on the *abusa* system.

Market Influences on the Frontier

International and regional markets have influenced the process of frontier development. Unfavourable oil palm prices encouraged a movement into cocoa. This resulted in rapid expansion beyond the Pawmpawm River into wetter semi-deciduous forest for more suitable cocoa land. Bringing new virgin land under cocoa cultivation was simpler and cheaper than converting oil palm to cocoa plantation. As a result, the early frontier oil palm belt became neglected in the early twentieth century and the population moved further into the forest.

The development of motor transport also facilitated frontier penetration, enabling crops and cocoa to be cultivated far into the interior. Since the new frontier areas received bumper yields from the conversion of forest biomass into ash and humus (leaf fall), crops were cheaper and of prime quality. Traders were attracted to these frontier districts and large wholesale markets developed at the termini of roads into the frontier. As the frontier moved further into the interior, away from the wholesale markets, new bulking centres emerged, forming the basis for new markets. Roads were extended to the new frontier areas and new markets arose to eclipse the old. Services relocated to the new markets, leaving behind declining towns (Figure 3.3). The political dynamics of this process have been vividly captured by Grace Djeagbo and Adeline Mate (1962: 37):

> When lorries came to this area, the market for the whole region was at Bisa. Bisa had a flourishing market on the rocks beside the river until other villages sprang up further away near the Kwawu area. These villages found it very difficult to bring their goods all the way to Bisa, so they built a small station at Asesewa to which they could carry their loads and then take them to Bisa. The people at Bisa did not like this idea because as trade was getting away from Bisa, it became less important. There were verbal quarrels over this until 1948, during the lootings.
>
> The local people raided Bisa and looted goods. Those at Asesewa decided that there would be continuous lootings at Bisa market. They even went on to make horrible songs about the poisonous things sold at Bisa market. Only a few people went now to Bisa. But people at Asesewa wanted everybody to trade at Asesewa, so on market day, they marched on to the market at Bisa with sticks and this started the battle of Bisa. This was on Friday, and they fought with hands and sticks. However Asesewa won and you can still hear the saying 'Asesewa gbe Bisa' among the local people. This means 'Asesewa has defeated Bisa'.

Markets provided lucrative tolls for marketing authorities and strong political factions sought to outflank each other by creating new markets in frontier districts beyond the old established markets controlled by other factions (Addo, 1988; Amanor, 1989). Political power was also used to force the closure of markets which threatened dominant economic and political interests. Political disputes between various factions were instrumental in closing down Manya Kpongunor market at the turn of the century (Gold Coast *Route Book*, 1906), Apimsu market in the 1920s, and Bisa in the 1940s (Addo, 1988; Amanor, 1989). Since the 1930s Asesewa and Sekesua have maintained their position as the dominant upland markets since the most northerly extension of the Krobo frontier was reached by this time. Subsequent movements of population within the Krobo area back into the abandoned lowland areas have involved a resurgence of Agomanya as both a provisions market for the lowland towns and a bulking centre for the produce of Lower Manya Krobo. Within Upper Manya Krobo barter markets on the Volta Lake emerged during the 1970s and have grown. This represents an extension of the fishing frontier into the Volta Lake, however, rather than a movement of the farming frontier. The main developments in frontier markets over the last twenty years have been the decline of the Krobo district and its replacement by Techiman in the Brong Ahafo area. Political factors have also played an important role in this process. This includes the development of state farms in the northern Brong Ahafo area and plans to develop it as a major food-producing area. In contrast, Manya Krobo was starved of development funds and its transport infrastructure allowed to decay.

While the market infrastructure facilitated frontier development, monopolistic control and competition tended to compound the decline of old frontier areas. This has resulted in a distorted development in Manya Krobo in which economic activity focuses on the new frontier. Today the frontier has left Manya Krobo behind, forgotten and neglected.

Decline of the Frontier

By 1940 the Krobo district was beset by crisis: the frontier moved out of its environs and degradation began to characterize the now old farm lands. During the 1920s cocoa, usually an evergreen species, began to develop deciduousness in Krobo. This was followed by swollen shoot disease. These ailments were associated with environmental stress (Collingwood, 1972). Cocoa requires considerable moisture. It does not adapt well to the long dry season of dry semi-deciduous forest. The felling of the forest canopy to make way for the establishment of a closed cocoa canopy also led to increased desiccation. Environmental degradation in Upper Manya Krobo in the 1920s is well documented by Moor (1930: 126):

> There is little forest left in the locality but from the evidence of the odd trees this part of the colony was covered with deciduous type of forest of good average height and density and with only a narrow transition belt between itself and the grass savannah.
>
> The present condition is somewhat different. A belt of oil palms, now neglected, created some 50 years ago has replaced the forest east of the Pawmpawm Su, the greater part of the transition belt has been absorbed by the savannah which has now also thrust a wedge up the valley of the river and the rest is a mixture of good and bad cocoa farms, areas of oil palms and sporadic patches of savannah and secondary growth, with here

> and there the remains of the original forest.... This savannah intrusion is quite definitely the result of excessive deforestation.

He also mentions the occurrence of a serious bush fire in the 1927–8 dry season, indicating the extent of degradation and desiccation in the area:

> It was the first known fire on any appreciable scale in the locality and burnt out a semicircular belt a mile wide on a four mile radius destroying several hundred acres of cocoa and severely damaging many thousands of oil palm trees (Moor, 1930: 127).

By the early 1940s cocoa was devastated in the Eastern Region and the colonial authority instigated a policy that enforced the cutting out of diseased trees. In the Krobo area maize and oil palms became the dominant crops. There was limited scope for palm oil to develop as an alternative export crop, however, and prices were depressed on the home market (La Anyane, 1956; Gold Coast Department of Agriculture, 1952). The production of palm wine from the sap of the oil palm trunk and its then illicit distillation into *akpeteshie* spirit gradually grew into the dominant palm product. This enabled thinner densities of oil palms to be cultivated, enabling greater food crop cultivation. Maize emerged as the main cash crop, finding a ready market in the expanding urban areas.

The farming system underwent considerable transformation during this period. With no new lands to move into, farming became more intensive. The demarcation between tree plantation and frontier food crop cultivation, the hallmark of pioneer frontier settlement, broke down as both were integrated into a system of bush fallowing. Food crops were interplanted between oil palms, and oil palms preserved in fallow land.

Fallow periods of medium duration were introduced with rest periods of 3–6 years. Cassava began to be cultivated on a large scale and intercropped with maize. By the 1960s cassava had become a major staple for home consumption, increasingly replacing declining yields of plantain, cocoyam and yam. While degradation was evident in this period, maize yields were relatively good and Krobo food crop markets maintained their position as the largest wholesale markets in Ghana. As Onipayedeh, an old farmer at Odometa Akwenor, commented of the 1950s:

> I used to farm at Pupunya and I alone could clear five *kpa ngwa* [about 4 hectares]. When it came to harvesting I could not harvest all and even the labourers which I employed could not harvest all. I would get about 60 bags of corn. I used to employ six people to help me with weeding and cultivation.

By the 1980s degradation has become more pronounced, resulting in desiccation, unreliable rainfall, infestation of weeds and increasingly marginal yields. Many farmers are experiencing difficulty in meeting their subsistence needs. Patterns of degradation vary between localities. They are most pronounced in the old cocoa lands of Upper Manya Krobo, and less intense in the more recently settled westerly settlements in moist semi-deciduous forest and in the old oil palm frontier zone, which was neglected during the cocoa era.

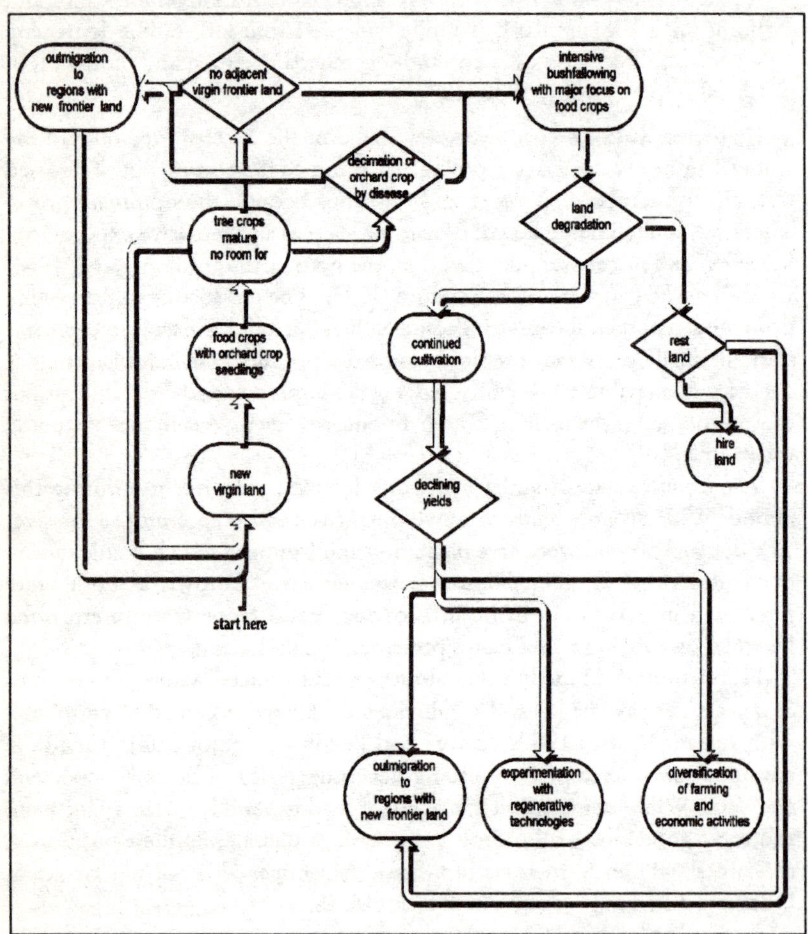

FIGURE 3.5. Conceptual model of the process of frontier settlement in Manya Krobo

The Social and Economic Dimensions of Frontier Decline

The devastation of cocoa production and lack of new available land in Manya Krobo has had complex effects on the social relations of production and settlement patterns.

POPULATION

The decline of the frontier has been aggravated by the creation of the Volta Lake for hydro-electricity in the 1960s, which exacerbated land shortage: over 20 per cent of the semi-deciduous forest area of Manya Krobo was inundated. Changes in population density are difficult to calculate since the boundaries of enumeration areas have changed in the 1960, 1970 and 1980 population censuses. Nevertheless, the overall population density rose from 78 people per square kilometre in 1960 for Manya-Yilo Krobo-Osudoku to 88 people in 1970 and 128 people in 1984 for Manya Krobo. There have been significant outmigrations from Upper Manya Krobo (Benneh, 1970). Migrations have involved movements into newer frontier areas, and into the urban sector within Ghana and other West African countries. Migrant labour has also moved out of the Krobo area into other cocoa-producing areas.

Within Manya Krobo there has been a reallocation of population. There has been a movement out of the *huzas* into the lowland towns and from the former cocoa districts of Upper Manya Krobo into the old oil palm pioneer zone below the river Pawmpawm, which was neglected and undercultivated during the cocoa era. The population of the lowland towns grew by 43 per cent between 1960 and 1970 and a further 43 per cent between 1970 and 1984. The population of the old palm oil belt grew by 40 per cent between 1970 and 1984. In contrast the population of Upper Manya Krobo grew by 8.5 per cent between 1960 and 1970 and declined by 3 per cent between 1970 and 1984.

Despite outmigration, land shortage is still a pressing problem in Upper Manya Krobo. Outmigration has not eased land pressures, but only made more land available for hiring and sharecropping. It has consolidated absentee ownership.

LAND, LABOUR, SHARECROPPING AND THE HOUSEHOLD

The position of the family and household in farm production has been redefined. The farming family was originally a highly mobile unit organized to manage lands in different localities and deploy labour along the expanding frontier. With the decline of the frontier the descendants of households cannot be deployed in adjacent new lands. They either migrate outside the Krobo area (beyond the organization of the Krobo farming enterprise), remain on existing household lands, or hire land. Lands have been fragmented and divided among various sons and sometimes daughters on inheritance (Benneh, 1970).

Contemporary production is oriented towards a specific farm plot and towards the autonomy of the resident farming household and individual farm management. Production is intensive. Extended family labour no longer has any significant role in agriculture. In the 1950s Pogucki noted the disappearance of extended family labour:

> In some areas collective work consists solely of the clearing of vegetation and initial hoeing. But in many areas the custom of working farms of ascendants has completely died out. And one may meet expositions of that custom worded in detail only to be followed by the mournful phrase 'but they don't do it any more' (Pogucki, 1955: 8 fn).

The decline of extended family labour is partly conditioned by the constraints of intensive food crop production under bush-fallowing, which requires large inputs of timely labour during the cropping season. The basis for extended cooperation has been eroded by a shortage of labour for weeding, which has become a major bottleneck in crop production. Farmers are preoccupied by the problems on their own farm plots.

Land shortage also undermines extended family labour. The young members of households frequently migrate to other areas since there is insufficient land to farm, or they seek plot tenancies in neighbouring farms and areas. This results in the withdrawal of their labour from the household. Hired migrant labour is also scarce since labourers have migrated to other frontier areas. Migrant labourers prefer cocoa plantations to food crop farms or oil palm estates since labour requirements on the former are less arduous and remuneration higher (La Anyane, 1956).

During the 1950s a major restructuring of labour relations occurred in Krobo, in which local hired labour replaced migrant hired labour. Farmers with insufficient land hired land from neighbours on a monetary or cropshare basis, or hired out their labour to supplement the insufficient incomes they could raise from their small plots. Absentee landowners and landholders with insufficient household labour to farm sought local tenants and labour to hire. This has resulted in increasing commoditization of the factors of production, with significant expenditures being allocated to land and labour hire.

Low levels of capital accumulation and the insecurity of agriculture result in the dominance of land tenancies based on sharecropping. Tenants generally prefer to hire land on a monetary basis but often lack the means. With a large demand for land and increasing shortage, landowners are able to charge monopoly rents: sharecropping arrangements are now based on a half share of the food crops. Half cropping has replaced earlier arrangements in which the tenant took two thirds of the crop. In the cocoa era the tenant took two thirds of the cocoa and was able to cultivate food crops freely. While the relative share of the tenant has declined, the absolute share has decreased even more dramatically because of declining yields. Land degradation also results in the decline of the rent realized by landlords.

Crop tenancies are agreed on a short-term basis, usually of one cropping cycle. Landlords are reluctant to release land for longer-term tenures, because they fear the land will be badly degraded. Given the dominant bush-fallowing cycle, landowners are anxious to protect their land from ruin under continuous cultivation by tenants with no long-term interest in the land. Since land hiring and sharecropping are dominant relations in production, the fact that tenants lack long-term interest in the land acts as an impediment to the development of regenerative technologies.

The capitalization of the means of production has eroded forms of cooperative and communal labour. The smallholder youth, the main suppliers of labour, are drawn into production either as land hirers or labourers, away from their household land. Lack of household labour forces the heads of household lands to hire labour or cropshare, reinforcing the process of commoditization of the means of production. This commoditization of the means of production is not reflected in a growth of technological components or of technological support services. It takes place in a declining agricultural economy in which degradation is a serious problem and standards of living are being eroded. Degradation itself results in increasing labour expenditure as exotic and savanna weeds invade former forest fallows, and more marginal returns for this labour. Thus the interaction of the rationale of the production system and degradation results in high costs of entry into production.

The commoditization of production has enabled women to play an increasing role in agricultural production and farm in their own right on hired land. Insufficiency of family land to meet the requirements of the household results in a relaxing of the control of husbands over the labour of their wives, and encouragement of wives and unmarried daughters to hire land for crop production. However, the participation of women in agricultural production is increasingly determined by large outlays of capital in land hire and labour, and by insecurity of tenure.

MARGINALIZATION

Marginalization is deeply felt by farmers in Upper Manya Krobo. As one farmer, Dademantse Madjate of Odometa Akwenor, commented during an interview:

> The government only helps the cocoa farmer. Maize is like our cocoa, yet the proceeds from what we sell in a year will not even buy a bundle of corrugated iron roofing sheets. When they make the government budget, we find that the price for maize compares unfavourably with commodities we buy. This is what troubles us farmers without cocoa. We the food farmers are looking after the nation. We need help for all farmers, not only for the cocoa farmers alone.

Marginalization is reflected in the decline of investments in infrastructure, agricultural services which do not reflect the problems and aspirations of the farmers, the lack of viable credit facilities, and unstable prices for agricultural commodities.

During the early part of the century, the Krobo district received much attention from government agricultural services. It was generally considered to be the best agricultural district in the colonial era and was the main area in which the government launched the cooperative movement, the main initiative of the colonial agricultural services during the 1920s and 1930s (*Gold Coast Farmer*, 6, 1932).

With the decline of cocoa the needs of the Krobo district have been forgotten. While cocoa has not been an important crop in the Asesewa district since the 1940s, until the mid-1980s the cocoa services continued to enjoy considerably more resources than any other agricultural service, with a full-time staff of over ten officers, between 50 and 100 part-time and full-time labourers, and nursery facilities. In contrast the agricultural extension services had a staff of two and no transport facilities, despite the fact that they were responsible for farmers in 34 settlements within the district. During the mid-1980s the cocoa services were reorganized and offices in Asesewa closed down.

At present the agricultural extension services consist of two divisions: Extension, and Plant Protection Regulatory Services. Each division has a staff of two. One of the extension officers is a representative from Global 2000. Global 2000 is a private foundation, under the patronage of Norman Borlaugh, architect of the Green Revolution, Jimmy Carter and the Sasakawa Foundation of Japan. It seeks to promote a Green Revolution in several African countries by making loans of prescribed high-yielding varieties (HYVs) and chemical inputs available to farmers (Martinez *et al.*, 1989). Global 2000 works within the existing extension services, allocating its officers to extension offices. Its activities are extended very thinly among farmers, however, and are mainly concentrated on educated farmers and salary earners engaged in part-time farming, largely to ensure that loans can be collected. Major difficulties in collecting loans for agricultural inputs in all parts of the country resulted in a crisis in the organization's operations. The main focus of extension work is on promoting modern varieties, row planting, fertilizers and pesticides. These inputs are not adapted to the conditions of the small farmer and there is no system of diagnosing farmer problems and designing extension programmes to solve specific problems encountered in the locality. The technologies promoted by extension do not cater for the serious problems of degradation farmers are facing, nor do they systematically collect data on these problems to feed back to research centres. Within the whole district the extension services have about 180 contact farmers.

The veterinary service has a staff of two and no transport facilities. Its main aims are to promote preventive treatment of livestock and to treat sick animals. The staff do not have any extension programme, however, and do not develop contacts with farmers. They rely on farmers to visit them. The cost of vaccinations is high in comparison to the price livestock fetch at market, so farmers rarely use their services.

Credit and loan facilities for farmers in the Asesewa district are extremely limited. The Rural Banks are supposed to concentrate surplus savings for development initiatives within their area of operation and to give loans to farmers for agricultural development. However, they do not cater for small food crop farmers. They are instructed to give loans only to cocoa farmers who sell their produce to the Cocoa Purchasing Division, to salaried employers or to large traders. The crops and lands of food crop farmers are not recognized as sources of collateral. Since there are very few cocoa farmers in the district, this policy in effect means that farmers are largely excluded from gaining loans. It also announces the government policy of support for cocoa farmers and non-support for small-scale food farmers in forest areas.

In Upper Manya Krobo the rural transport infrastructure has been in crisis. Until the end of 1992 there had been no renovation of the road linking Asesewa to the major nodes of transport on the national marketing network for nearly twenty years. For many years this road could only be traversed by the sturdiest of vehicles. A journey of 48 km took three to four hours and imposed great wear and tear on vehicles. The road has now been repaired between Koforidua and Asesewa, and is being extended to the Afram Plains. This seems to be designed to meet the needs of the Afram Plains, the new food-producing frontier in the transitional zone, rather than those of Upper Manya Krobo. The road from Upper Manya Krobo to the lowland Manya Krobo towns, major commercial and social centres for all Krobo farmers, has not been repaired. Feeder roads have also declined and in some cases are now closed to lorry transport. Hand-pulled carts and headloading have replaced lorries on some feeder roads as the main form of transport. With this paucity of transport facilities the cost of transport to market is often high.

The recent history of poor infrastructure has resulted in the decline of the Asesewa market. Many traders are reluctant to visit Asesewa. The few traders now visiting the market are able to command a monopoly price and the real prices of foodstuffs have declined while the cost of production has increased.

Farmers have attempted to circumvent what they consider to be the traders' monopoly over market outlets and prices. A series of barter markets came into existence from the late 1970s on the Volta Lake, at settlements such as Akrusu Saisi, Akateng and Akotue. These markets focus on exchange between farmers and fishermen working on the Volta Lake. Originally, farmers bartered food crops directly against fish, but barter is now on the decline. As these markets developed, wholesale traders moved in to dominate the fish trade. Fishermen need to sell their fish in bulk, since it is highly perishable. Thus, farmers' attempts to escape from monopoly control have had limited success.

Wholesale food price insecurity has also been exacerbated by government policies of improving cocoa prices in relation to food crops and by the liberalization of food imports. Farmers are highly vulnerable to monopoly pressures, since with no control over transport and little access to market information it is difficult for them to diversify production. There have been recent attempts to diversify into cowpea and, along the Volta lakeshore, into sweet potato production.

Marginalization also results in a declining range of crops for which there is a market. Until the 1960s the Manya Krobo area was the heart of the oil palm belt (La Anyane, 1961). The oil palm belt has since moved into wetter forest areas, where higher rainfall produces heavy yields. Production in this area is increasingly mechanized (Gyasi, 1988, 1992). In contrast, within the Krobo area palm oil is largely produced in individual households using laborious pestle and mortar pounding techniques. While Krobo palm oil is reputed to be of very high quality, it cannot compete with prices established in the new oil palm belt.

Farmers are further marginalized by degradation which results in increasing insecurity and poor quality of yields, and the failure of particular crops to yield, which further reinforces their weak position on the market. It is difficult for them to make projections on their future yields, to hold out for better prices, to move into better priced crops and to form producers' associations. The insecurity of food prices and the predicament of the food cultivator is illustrated by the response of a Rural Bank official to the question why loans were not given to farmers: 'If the rain fails and maize yields are bad the farmers have no money to repay loans, and if yields are good prices are so low that they cannot afford to repay.'

The emphasis on decentralization in present policy frameworks also compounds marginalization, since impoverished villages have a lower capacity to undertake development activities. At the village of Odometa in Upper Manya Krobo an attempt to rebuild the dilapidated local school failed to raise the necessary funds. An attempt to get three boreholes dug with outside assistance met with serious problems, since the community found it difficult to raise the necessary financial contribution of ₵100,000 for the maintenance of each borehole. The wells were locked for some time by the implementing agency as a punitive action, despite the fact that the people had contributed labour.

A large number of farmers are spending more time working on their farms, coping with weeds and gaining diminishing returns for their efforts.

They are increasingly dependent upon land hiring and sharecropping. These factors serve to demoralize farmers from engaging in self-help initiatives. Communal labour may appear as an unnecessary imposition from political structures which have not seriously attempted to solve the problems of farmers.

Farmer Organization

Within the forest areas of Ghana there are long traditions of farmer and rural community organization, which are rooted in pre-capitalist socio-political administration. Community organization, such as *asafo* companies, have historically been important for defence of the community, for raising taxes and levies for central government, and also for the maintenance of the social and physical infrastructure. In the modern period these organizations have played important roles in purchasing frontier land for cocoa cultivation, building and maintaining roads and markets, organizing public works campaigns and communicating information from central government. Under colonial rule these organizations were used to ensure free labour for infrastructural development, within policy frameworks which emphasized that colonies should pay their own way. This was articulated in the ideology of 'indirect rule', an alliance between colonial government and pre-capitalist rulers which protected the privileges of traditional authorities to levy labour service, tributes and taxes from their subjects, provided this was carried out in collaboration with the objectives of the colonial mission. During the 1980s community organizations and chiefs have assumed greater importance and their power has been revived and 'reinvented' as policy frameworks have become preoccupied with decentralization and community self-help. Popular mass organizations are often informed by command structures and directives reflecting domination in hierarchically based social formations.

Rural cooperatives have also been important organizations from the 1930s when the agricultural department organized the cooperative movement as a means to circumvent the control of large cocoa merchants and brokers over the internal marketing of cocoa. Large merchants also organized farmer marketing organizations to circumvent the low prices paid by expatriate trading houses (Holmes, 1972; Howard, 1978: Nowell Report, 1938; *Gold Coast Farmer*, 1932).

During the early 1980s a resurgence of local farmer organization took place under the umbrella of the Federation of Cooperative Societies. The main objectives of this organization were to circumvent the shortage of commodities in rural markets, and to challenge the monopoly control of traders over food prices. The main aims of the cooperatives were to gain direct access to commodities from parastatal organizations through registration, and also to organize the direct barter of food crops against manufactured commodities. With the adoption of the structural adjustment programme in 1983, the introduction of trade liberalization, and the widespread availability of industrial produce, the rationale for cooperatives has disappeared and they have waned.

A third important source of organization is village and town development associations, which seek to raise funds for developing infrastructural projects in home towns. These associations often have urban branches. In the recent past they have become closely associated with NGOs and also with government-controlled mass movements such as the 31st December Women's Movement. In 1991 there were over 350 registered NGOs, of which many were village development associations (Fowler *et al.*, 1991).

These organizations are frequently dominated by traders, clerks and schoolteachers who have different outlooks to farmers. The interests of the small farmers are rarely articulated in these organizations since small farmers have difficulty in interfacing with sector agencies. Farmers are not literate, sometimes they speak different languages to those that are dominant in the ministries, and they do not know where to find sector agencies or how to lobby them. Without traditions of independent struggle in the modern period, peasants look for patrons to represent them. Small farmers look to the educated members of the community and to non-farming elements whose livelihoods have resulted in greater mobility and greater familiarity with the outside world. This stratum of the local community often takes upon itself the role of representing the community, and of projecting its own interests – often rooted in petty trade rather than agriculture – as those of the community.

In 1983, the Upper Manya Krobo Federation of Cooperative Societies was formed. Its executive was dominated by traders, clerks and teachers. This was reflected in its programme. The main short-term objective was to collect grain from members which was to be bulked and exchanged on a barter basis with manufacturing corporations for industrial commodities. This reflected the marginalization of the district, the shortage of commodities during that period, and the monopoly control exerted by traders over the pricing and distribution of manufactures. The principal long-term objective was to raise funds from farmers to purchase a tractor. This tractor was not going to be used for local farming purposes, since everyone knew it was unsuitable for tilling forest soils. It was to be hired out to farmers on the Afram Plains, as a commercial income-generating project. Thus local farm production problems were subjugated to merchant interests. However, these merchant interests also reflected the problems of marginalization which were felt by farmers.

In the present period local organizations are more concerned with development projects, which include environmental projects focused around woodlot and community forestry programmes for income generation. However, these projects do not necessarily reflect specific environmental conditions experienced by farmers, or build upon the environmental experiences and awareness of the people. They are still largely dominated by the clerks, traders and schoolteachers, who now perceive that development agencies are throwing large amounts of capital into rural areas for environmental projects, and that access to this capital through organizing village environmental associations forms one of the most promising avenues for realizing capital for their commercial aspirations. In this case, village organization based on the formation of community woodlot programmes is the mode through which marginalization is addressed. The farmers are assured that their marginalization will end if they follow the prescriptions of the state and development agencies. However, this environmentalism consists of agroforestry and woodlot commodity package technology, which does not necessarily address specific environmental problems within a locality. The serious business of organizing to end specific forms of marginalization has been replaced by the illusion of boundless manna flowing from Europe and America. Global environmentalism stands in danger of reconstructing the cargo cults of Melanesia.

This meets with full encouragement of the state which is anxious to show international donors that it is serious about the environment, is mobilizing the people to take up environmental concerns, and deserves more loans, grants and aid. These developments may in reality result in the subordination of local development and environmental initiatives to the aid packages of global environmentalism. This may create increasing problems for local people to organize independently for their own interests, since they are continuously being coopted into organizing according to the priorities of the state and the donor community.

Conclusion

Current environmental paradigms tend to argue for the soundness of traditional forms of land management, but stress their breakdown in the modern period faced with social change and population growth. In contrast, this analysis has stressed that the present environmental crisis has long historical roots related to the integration of the Ghanaian forests into the world economy and the articulation of regional social and economic class formations with world commodity production.

Environmental degradation or conservation does not necessarily reflect environmental awareness, but the application of knowledge, which is defined by socio-economic and political factors. In the past, there were few incentives to utilize this knowledge for environmental protection, since the frontier of uncolonized land was vast. Environmental knowledge was harnessed for the conquest of the wilderness and for the penetration of human settlement into the forest. The nature of this colonization of the frontier was also determined by political developments and the competition between hierarchically organized polities for control over the forest estate. Under colonial rule forest colonization was determined by the colonial prerequisites of staple monocrop exports. This mode of economic organization facilitated rapid deforestation, colonization of new frontier areas, and marginalization of old areas, unable to produce crops at optimal production costs. Marginalization has resulted in failure to rehabilitate old frontier districts. It is only now, with the decline of the new frontier, that environmental conservation is being taken seriously. Favourable perceptions exist for environmental conservation among farming peoples, based on reflections on their experiences of cultivation. But socio-economic relations expressed in land tenure contracts, which are the historic bequest of the cocoa era, create major obstacles among a large percentage of farming people to long-term access to sufficient land – a necessary prerequisite for the task of environmental regeneration.

A systems analysis rooted in the relationship between environment, technology and population misses many dimensions of the dynamics of environmental degradation and its interaction with the political economy. Environmental policy frameworks need to be informed by critical research which develops an analysis of the economic and social dimensions of degradation, an awareness of the historical impact of social formations on the environment, and a regional framework of the organization of production and its interaction with the environment. This enables the impact of macro policy on the micro level and the political factors affecting policy frameworks to be discerned.

The history of environmental degradation is intimately connected with the marginalization of old frontier districts. A meaningful programme of environmental conservation needs to be conceptualized in terms of regenerating declining districts which have fallen out of export crop production owing to the contradictions in this form of economy. The organization and integration of world commodity markets and the subjugation of the national interests of developing nations to the economic performance of these markets need to be critically evaluated and reassessed as principles on which development is based.

4

Conditions of Agricultural Production

People's access to resources and their relationship to the factors of production are important in determining their farming strategies and their modes of managing the environment. This chapter examines access to land, labour, capital, agricultural technology and technical services among farmers in Upper Manya Krobo. It looks at the impact of the decline of the frontier, of population growth, and of migration on agricultural production. It also investigates the effects of different patterns of degradation in distinct micro-environments on the social relations of production. The analysis is based on a survey questionnaire carried out in a line of settlements in the forest ecotone area of Upper Manya Krobo.

Upper Manya Krobo Survey

Upper Manya Krobo is the district which is mainly served by the Asesewa market. This area was largely settled in the period 1900–20. It was essentially colonized for cocoa cultivation. It was the main food-producing area in Ghana between 1920 and 1970. The area extends from the edge of the forest on its north-eastern perimeter, through dry semi-deciduous forest and into moist semi-deciduous forest west of Asesewa. As one proceeds in a westerly direction the environment becomes progressively wetter and more thickly forested. The most westerly settlements are also more thickly forested because they were the last areas in Krobo to be settled. During the 1920s and 1930s the easterly settlements were known for their agricultural riches. *Huzas* such as Awoweso, Akrusu and Sesiamang were highly productive agricultural settlements. Their vast wealth in the old frontier days is often recounted like a legend, with an air of resignation and disbelief at the present predicament. In official agricultural circles these settlements were often held up as model agrarian settlements for the Gold Coast (La Anyane, 1956). Today these *huzas* are beset by ecological crisis. The land has become severely degraded. The former forest cover has been transformed into savanna scrub. The rainfall is erratic and the environment parched. Cultivation is increasingly unproductive and farmers are suffering from marginal yields and hunger.

From east to west a series of distinct micro-environmental belts runs from pure grassland in the east to forest fallows in the west. Many forest species have disappeared from the westerly settlements – particularly after the severe bushfires of 1983, when all of Ghana's forests went up in a blaze. Yet these settlements still have the countenance of a forest area, with tall forest species dotted all over the landscape, forming shady groves here and there. In contrast, the easterly settlements have the appearance of more open land, with an abundance of grass, small tree species and few stands of true forest trees. Yet vestiges of the forest seed bank still remain, and rare forest trees can often be found standing incongruously in savanna scrub.

RESEARCH METHODOLOGY

These micro-environmental belts are particularly striking since the Krobo live in 'lines' on *huzas*. These lines tend to follow the valleys of rivers which move in a westerly direction, draining into the Afram River basin which is now part of the Volta Lake. The main paths of the *huzas* east of Asesewa move in an easterly direction to the Volta Lake, gradually becoming less and less forested. For survey purposes it was decided to use one of these paths and sample people living along the *huzas* in areas where there were pronounced changes in the vegetation. The line chosen ran from Odometa, immediately west of Asesewa, through various *huzas* of Awoweso to Akrusu Saisi on the banks of the Volta Lake. The length of this line is about 20 km. Awoweso, the largest settlement on the line, is 11 km long. Five localities were sampled along these lines. These consisted of Odometa, Awoweso Kpeti (Middle Awoweso), Awoweso Adome, Awoweso Sisi (Lower Awoweso), and Akrusu Saisi. Awoweso Kpeti consisted of three lower-level *huzas* (Piengwa, Nuaso, and Agomanya) representing different sections of the Manya Krobo people. While each maintains separate political authority, they all come together to form one section represented by a council of elders and farming chiefs (*dademantse*).

The environment at Odometa is characterized by predominant forest bush, with many large forest trees and a herbaceous undergrowth dominated by *Chromolaena odorata*. Grasslands only occur in patches. In the upper reaches of Awoweso forest trees occur less densely: *Cassia siamea*, a fast-growing exotic tree originating from Burma, is the dominant tree. In the lower reaches of Awoweso savanna grassland becomes the dominant vegetation. At Akrusu Saisi neem trees (another imported fast-growing

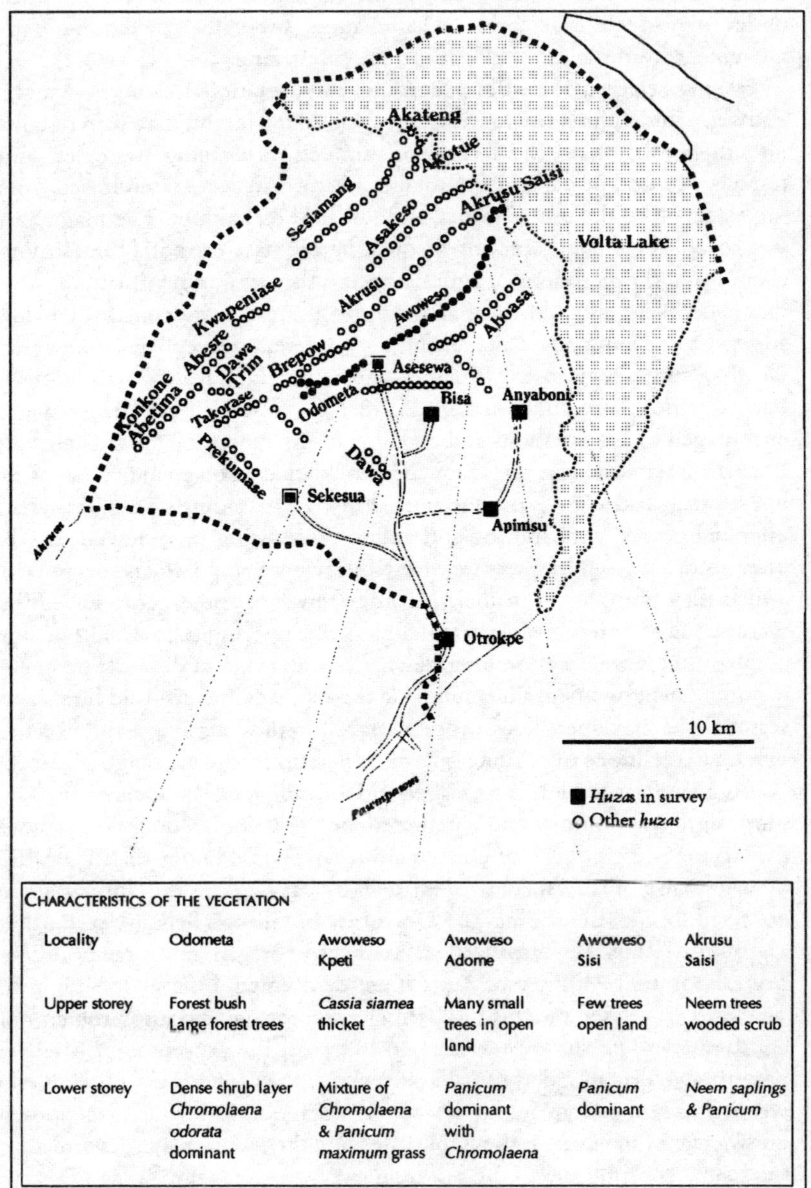

CHARACTERISTICS OF THE VEGETATION

Locality	Odometa	Awoweso Kpeti	Awoweso Adome	Awoweso Sisi	Akrusu Saisi
Upper storey	Forest bush Large forest trees	*Cassia siamea* thicket	Many small trees in open land	Few trees open land	Neem trees wooded scrub
Lower storey	Dense shrub layer *Chromolaena odorata* dominant	Mixture of *Chromolaena* & *Panicum maximum* grass	*Panicum* dominant with *Chromolaena*	*Panicum* dominant	*Neem saplings & Panicum*

FIGURE 4.1. The line of *huzas* surveyed in Upper Manya Krobo.

exotic from Asia) and grass species are dominant. The vegetation gradually changes into derived savanna, despite the fact that all these areas were once under semi-deciduous forest. The changes generally correspond with movement from the forest interior to the forest fringe (see Figure 4.1).

Having selected localities according to vegetational changes, a large number of individuals were interviewed within the localities, to gain insights into their relation to the factors of production, farming strategies, and responses to land degradation. A total of 172 farmers were interviewed. The survey involved the use of formal and informal techniques. The major aim was to collect a large amount of quantitative data on both the farming economy and perceptions of agriculture and the environment. But qualitative issues were also addressed and the questionnaire was constantly being adapted to accommodate the nuances of different perceptual frameworks which occurred in changing localities, and new insights provided by farmers. Each questionnaire ended in an informal discussion where farmers were encouraged to ask questions and add any information they felt was missing from the interview. The questionnaire was conducted on an individual basis, but it usually had a group flavour, with many farmers sitting through sessions, querying points, contributing and aiding those being interviewed. It was often found that under pressure of the interview many farmers forgot facts which they brought up in the next interview. On some occasions efforts were made to interview several people from one household. The major emphasis, however, was on interviewing a wide range of different people – including men, women, the young and the old, landowners, land hirers and seasonal sharecroppers – in order to gain a representative sample of the different conditions of production which pertain on a wide range of farms.

About 200 farms plots were visited and soil samples taken for analysis. The most significant information gathered on new innovations and fallow management techniques originated from farm visits rather than from the questionnaire. Plant species identified by farmers in the survey were collected for identification at the University of Ghana's herbarium. Finally, a group meeting was organized at Awoweso with an agroforestry officer from the nearest Ministry of Agriculture demonstration farm at Huhunya, which also provided insights into farmers' perceptions and into problems of agroforestry. The survey was carried out with the assistance of Michael Kwabla Odjidja, an elderly smallholder farmer at Odometa, who formerly worked as a nurseryman in the cocoa services. He has an exceptional knowledge of the flora in the Krobo area and the uses of plants, and made a substantial contribution to the research.

In analysing the data two different criteria were used in defining populations. In analysing data related to specific ecological adaptations to environment, the population was divided according to the localities represented in the lower half of Figure 4.1. This representation provides the criteria used in comparing localities in Chapters 5 and 6. While this method clearly shows responses to the changing environment as one proceeds down 'the line', it has the disadvantage of resulting in some small sample clusters in the lower reaches of Awoweso which is no longer densely settled. In analysing socio-economic data Awoweso is divided into two clusters – Upper Awoweso, consisting of Awoweso Kpeti and Lower Awoweso comprising Awoweso Adome and Awoweso Sisi. This enables commensurate populations to be compared and simplifies the analysis. The division also reflects the dominant social differences in Awoweso, which relate to larger holdings and less population in the lower reaches and a higher population density and smaller holdings in the upper reaches. The two dominant interests in analysis of field data concern specific adaptations to differential rates of degradation and the impact of differing land shortage problems on farming strategies. These two factors are related since increasing degradation can result in higher rates of outmigration and more available land within a locality.

The dominant population of the survey are Dangme-speaking Krobo. At Odometa a small settlement of Kyerepong-speaking Apirede people from Akuapem exist, who settled independently of the Krobo. At Akrusu Saisi there is a small community of Ewe people from Volo who have intermarried with the Krobo. All these peoples, however, have similar social institutions, material culture, and farming systems, and their settlements and ways of life are integrated.

THE SAMPLE

The various categories of farmer in the survey are shown in Figure 4.2. These categories reflect different conditions of access to land, related to position in the household, gender and other factors. They represent farmers' conceptions of their association with the resource base. A 'wife of an owner' may also be a 'daughter of an owner', but her relationship to the land she resides on and the resources of the land which she exploits on a regular basis (for farming, firewood, etc.) is conditioned by her position as a wife. A 'wife' will be classified as an 'owner', however, if her use of the land is determined by her ownership status rather than that of her husband. 'Wife of owner' and 'son or daughter of owner' are intermediate ownership categories. In these contexts the farmer may have limited use of the household land, and may be forced to hire out land or sharecrop as a result of insufficient family land and low rank in the priority of allocation of land. The aim of this classification is to understand how land shortage affects different groupings of people within and across households. It does not represent social differentiation in the context of social classes since some socio-economic groups, such as absentee owners, are missing. The survey examines conditions of production among working farmers.

Figure 4.2 and Table 4.1 show that the 51 per cent of the survey are owners of land. Sixty-six per cent of men and 13 per cent of women are owners of land. Access to land for the majority of women (54 per cent) is determined by their status as wife. The percentage of landless people is small: only 5 per cent of the sample are either caretakers, who look after the land of absentee landlords, or are landless and rely completely on the seasonal hiring and sharecropping of land for farming. Twenty-three per cent of males and 17 per cent of females are children of owners. Their access to land depends upon the availability of their fathers' or mothers' land and the number of people farming it. 'Wife of owner' and 'children of owner' are intermediate categories, who frequently have to hire or sharecrop farmland to supplement their use of family land.

Table 4.2 provides an age breakdown of the various categories of land users. This shows that most owners in the survey sample were above the age of 35. Thirty-six per cent of the sample were also over 50 years old. This reflects the migration of young people away from rural areas as a result of shortage of land and limited local opportunities. In some localities, such as Odometa Apirede where insufficiency of land is particularly pronounced, the population consists of the elderly and young children. All the youth old enough to pursue an independent livelihood have migrated.

TABLE 4.1. Categories of land user

Land user	Frequency	%
Owner (male)	75	43.6
Owner (female)	13	7.6
Son of owner	27	15.7
Daughter of owner	10	5.8
Wife of owner	32	18.6
Caretaker (male)	6	3.5
Landless seasonal tenant (male)	5	2.9
Landless seasonal tenant (female)	4	2.3
Total	172	100

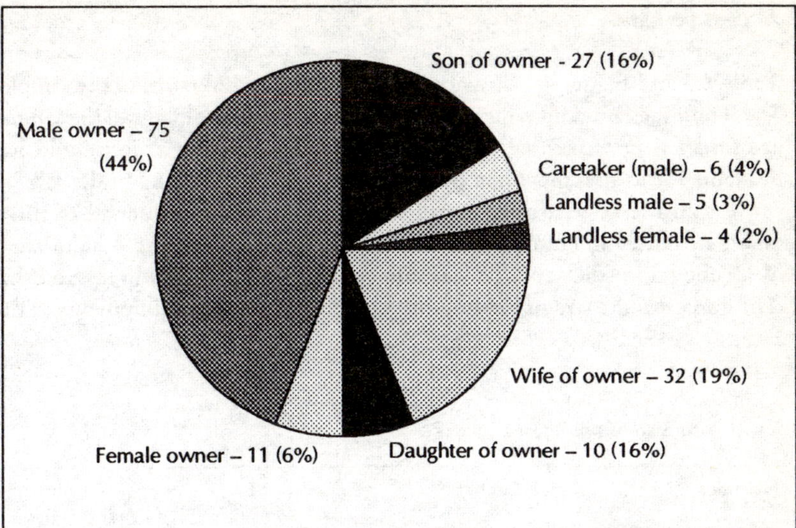

FIGURE 4.2. Categories of land user

TABLE 4.2. Age and sex composition of the sample

Age	< 25	25-35	35-50	>50	Total
owner (male)	1	13	19	42	75
	(1.3%)	(17.3%)	(25.3%)	(56.1%)	(100%)
owner (female)	1	–	4	8	13
	(7.7%)		(30.8%)	(61.5%)	(100%)
son of owner	7	14	6	–	27
	(25.9%)	(51.9%)	(22.2%)	–	(100%)
daughter of owner	4	3	3	–	10
	(40.0%)	30.0%)	(30.0%)		(100%)
wife of owner	3	3	17	9	32
	(9.4%)	(9.4%)	(53.1%)	(28.1%)	(100%)
caretaker (male)	1	2	3	–	6
	(16.7%)	(33.3%)	(50.0%)		(100%)
no land (male)	1	2	1	1	5
	(20.0%)	(40.0%)	(20.0%)	(20.0%)	(100%)
no land (female)	–	–	2	2	4
			(50.0%)	(50.0%)	(100%)

Access to Land

Table 4.3 and Figure 4.3 show sizes of holdings for 128 farms in the sample. Small holdings are dominant. Seventy-five per cent of holdings in the sample are under 6 hectares (ha). This is the total area of land a household has available for its use, including both land under crops and land under fallow.

Within the system of bush-fallowing, given a fallow interval of three years, a household cultivating 1 ha per annum would require 4 ha of land. With the same fallow period a family cultivating 2 ha would require 8 ha. This indicates the size of holdings in relation to the land requirements of the farming system.

TABLE 4.3. Size of holdings (hectares)

Hectares	Frequency	%	Cumulative %
< 2	9	7.1	7.1
2-4	54	42.5	49.6
4-6	32	25.2	74.8
6-8	4	3.1	78.0
8-10	11	8.7	86.6
10-12	5	3.9	90.6
12-14	3	2.4	92.9
14-16	4	3.1	96.1
16-18	3	2.4	98.4
> 18	2	1.6	100
Total	127	100	

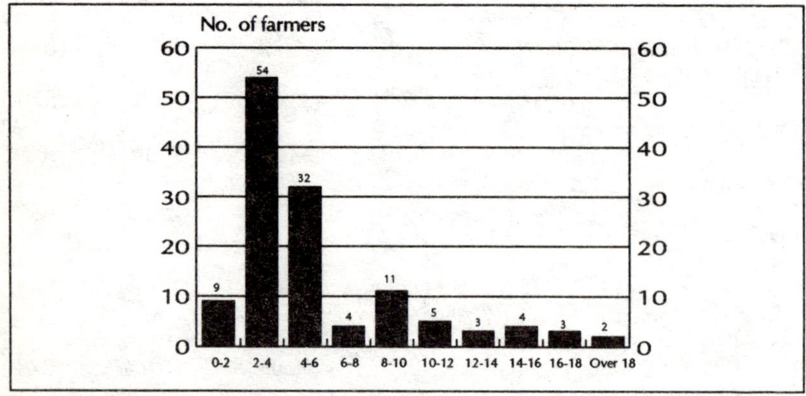

FIGURE 4.3. Size of holdings (hectares)

Tables 4.4 and 4.5 and Figure 4.4 reveal significant differences in the distribution of holdings between the three settlements. At Upper Awoweso the least variation in holding sizes occurs, with all farms lying in the range of 2–10 ha. Eighty-five per cent of lands lie in the range 2–6 ha. At Odometa there is a preponderance of small holdings: 67 per cent of holdings are under 4 ha and 89 per cent under 6 ha. In addition to these small holdings, however, there are a few large holdings. This reflects the history of land purchase at Odometa. The largest share of land was purchased by the *konor* (paramount chief) of Manya Krobo and parcelled out to relatives and servants. Close relatives were given large tracts of land. Those who had served him well, as state functionaries or labourers on his cocoa estate at Dawa, were rewarded with small parcels of land. At Lower Awoweso and Akrusu Saisi land was individually acquired by a 'company' of purchasers and holdings tend to be larger than at Odometa.

The history of settlement and land purchase are important influences on patterns of land distribution and differentiation of holdings. Patterns of land distribution may also reflect environmental factors. The size of holding in the survey increases in more degraded settlements: the smallest holdings occur in the less degraded settlements. This may be an accident of the particular configuration of settlements chosen for the survey. It may also reflect a process where more family members migrate from the more degraded lands, resulting in less population pressure and larger *per capita* holdings. More family members will congregate on the better family land and claim rights in it, eventually leading to fragmentation and subdivision into smaller holdings.

TABLE 4.4. Summary data on distribution of land in the survey settlements

Settlement	Mean (ha)	Minimum holding (ha)	Maximum holding (ha)	Std
Odometa	4.9	1.3	22.3	4.1
Upper Awoweso	4.9	2.5	9.8	1.9
Lower Awoweso	6.8	1.5	23.5	5.2
Akrusu Saisi	9.1	2.6	16.2	5.0

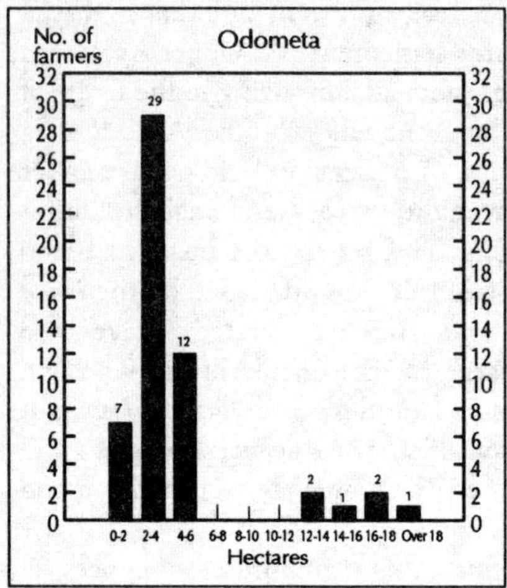

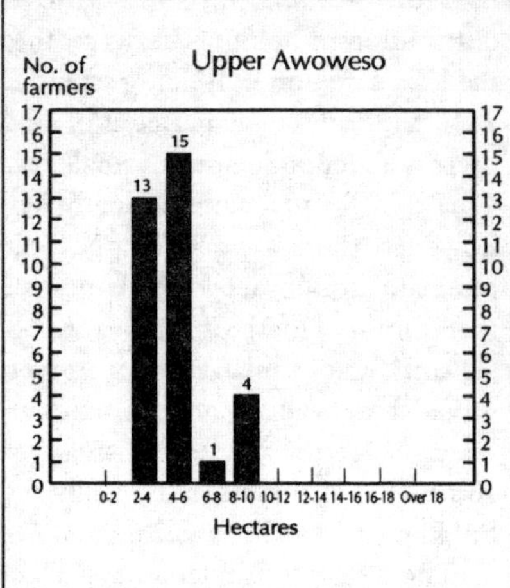

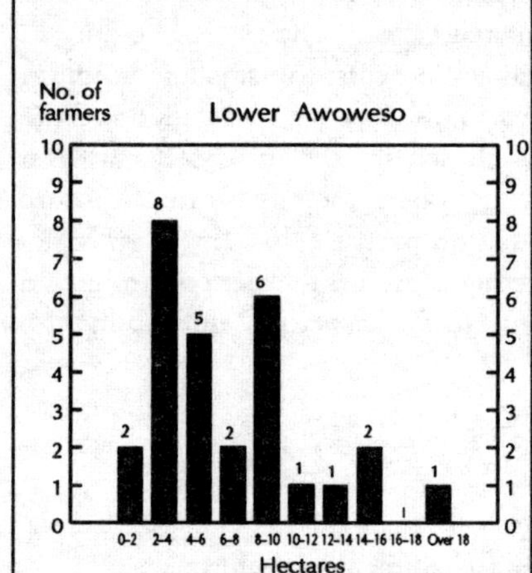

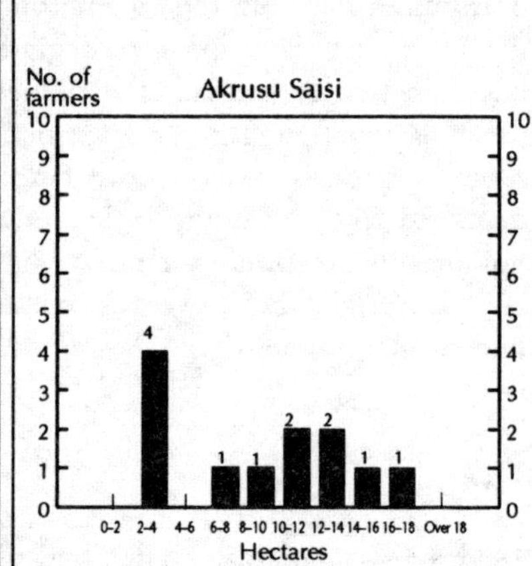

FIGURE 4.4. Land distribution in the survey settlements

TABLE 4.5. Land distribution in the survey settlements

Size of holding (hectares)	Odometa		Upper Awoweso		Lower Awoweso		Akrusu Saisi	
	No.	%	No.	%	No.	%	No.	%
< 2	7	10.3	–	–	2	5.3	–	–
2–4	29	42.6	13	30.2	8	21.1	4	17.4
4–6	12	17.6	15	34.9	5	13.2	–	–
6–8	–	–	1	2.3	2	5.3	1	4.3
8–10	–	–	4	9.3	6	15.8	1	4.3
10–12	2	2.9	–	–	1	2.6	2	8.7
12–14	1	1.5	–	–	1	2.6	2	8.7
14–16	1	1.5	–	–	2	5.3	1	4.3
16–18	2	2.9	–	–	–	–	1	4.3
> 18	1	1.5	–	–	1	2.6	–	–

TABLE 4.6. Multiple ownership of lands

No. of other lands owned	Frequency	%	Cumulative %
0	103	59.9	59.1
1	57	33.1	93
2	9	5.2	98.3
3	3	1.7	100

Landowners have frequently purchased many holdings in different areas of the forest (Macmillan, 1940; Hill, 1963). This has been associated with continual investment in land on the new frontier. Table 4.6 shows multiple ownership of land among farmers. Sixty per cent of farmers do not own any land other than that covered by the survey. Of the 40 per cent who own 'other land', 7 per cent own more than one other farm. 'Other lands' are usually given out to children and close relatives to farm or placed under a caretaker. In a few cases the land has been deliberately left uncultivated to regenerate. The locations of other farm lands vary considerably. Sometimes they are situated in the forest interior and developed for cocoa farming by wealthier farmers. In other instances they are located on some of the worst degraded land.

Fifty-eight per cent of farmers considered that they had sufficient land to meet their farming requirements while 42 per cent considered they did not have enough land. However, within the category of those who felt they had enough land, 29 per cent regularly hired land and 25 per cent regularly sharecropped. This shows the extent of land shortage in the area: insufficiency of land is being assessed by a large number of people according to their ability to hire land or sharecrop rather than by their access to family land.

HIRING AND SHARECROPPING OF LAND

Data were collected on 419 cultivated plots cleared in 1990, with a total area of 425 *kpa ngwa*. A *kpa ngwa* is the basic unit size of a food plot, ideally measuring 48 x 48 armspans. In practice it varies from 0.4 to 0.8 ha, since the *kpa ngwa* is only relatively uniform. Farms are frequently less than 48 armspans wide. To overcome problems of measuring a *kpa ngwa* the surplus of the width of the *kpa ngwa* is added to the length, to achieve an outer perimeter of 96 armspans along two sides. This results in different areas for different *kpa ngwa*, however, with declining areas for less wide *kpa ngwa* (Figure 4.5).[1]

---

1 The *kpa ngwa* originated in the late 1950s when the increasing incidence of hiring of land and labour required some standard aerial criteria for land. The uniform distance of 48 armspans was originally measured from two telegraph poles outside the house of a man called Dawa Kofi. Hence the *kpa ngwa* is also known as the *Dawa Kofi*.

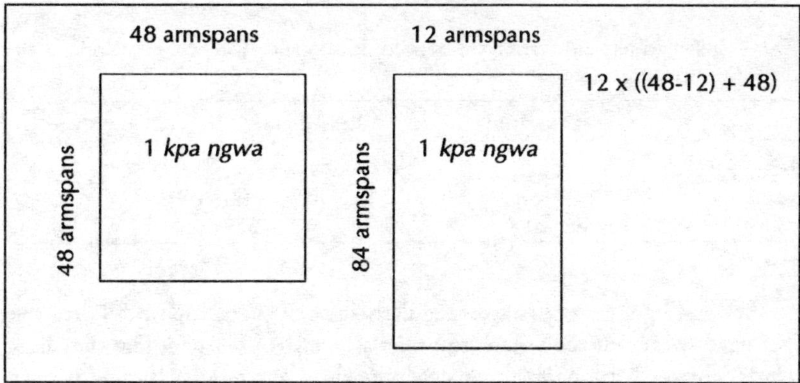

FIGURE 4.5. Different methods of measuring a *kpa ngwa*

Table 4.7 provides data on patterns of access to land. About 40 per cent of land is either leased for monetary payment or sharecropped. Sharecropping is more prevalent than hiring of land. The column 'Plots (*kpa ngwa*)' records the estimated total area in the sample cultivated for owned, hired and sharecropped land in 1991. It is a more accurate reflection of the significance of patterns of land usage than the number of plots cultivated, since some farmers may cultivate several small plots of 0.5 *kpa ngwa*.

In a sample of 492 plots farmed by 169 farmers in the neighbouring Akuapem district of the Mampong Valley, Gyasi (1991) records that 25.8 per cent of land was leased and 33.5 per cent sharecropped.

TABLE 4.7. Hiring and sharecropping of land in the 1990/91 cropping season

Plot type	Plots (*kpa ngwa*)	%	No. of plots	%
Household land	260	61	269	64
Hired land	72	17	62	15
Crop share	93	22	88	21
Total	425	100	419	100

Table 4.8 also shows the number and percentage of farmers who cultivated household, leased and sharecropped land in the 1990/91 farming season. Twenty per cent of farmers cultivated leased plots and 30 per cent contracted plots on a sharecrop tenancy. Twenty per cent of cultivators did not make farms on their own household land and were totally dependent upon hired or sharecropped land for their crop-farming activities.

TABLE 4.8. Farmers cultivating household, leased and sharecropped land for the 1990/91 cropping season

	Own land	Leased plot	Crop share
Total farmers	137	34	55
%	79.1	19.8	32.0

About 45 per cent of farmers regularly lease or sharecrop land. Forty-five per cent claim that they sharecrop regularly and 44 per cent that they lease land regularly. Most people sharecropping also claim to lease land. However, in any one year the proportion of people leasing land is significantly lower than those sharecropping (Table 4.8). Farmers generally prefer to lease land, but shortage of land for leasing or shortage of money results in sharecropping predominating over leasing. A significant proportion of farmers are not annual sharecroppers, but sharecrop at least once within every three-year period. Here sharecropping is a response to insufficiency of land to maintain a viable fallowing system: farmers hire land to enable their plots to recuperate.

LAND HIRING AND SHARECROPPING IN DIFFERENT LOCALITIES

Significant variations in patterns of land hiring for the 1990 cropping season occurred between the settlements in the sample (Table 4.9). At Odometa only 68 per cent of farmers cultivated their own land as compared to 78 per cent in Akrusu Saisi and 88–90 per cent in Awoweso. At Odometa only 13 per cent of farmers leased land as compared to 49 per cent in Akrusu, 14 per cent in Upper Awoweso and 21 per cent in Lower Awoweso. Fifty per cent of farmers at Odometa sharecropped, 43 per cent at Akrusu and only 13–14 per cent at Awoweso.

TABLE 4.9. Percentage of farmers cultivating household, leased and sharecropped land in different settlements

Settlement	Own land %	Leased plot %	Crop share %	Total no.
Odometa	67.7	13.2	50.0	68
Upper	88.4	14.0	14.0	43
Lower	89.5	21.1	13.2	38
Akrusu Saisi	78.3	47.8	43.5	23

These differences are related to a complex set of factors. At Odometa there is a more pronounced land shortage among small farmers and a more marked differentiation of holdings – there are a small number of farmers with large holdings and a few farmers with large holdings. Fewer farmers have sufficient land to meet their requirements, but there is more scope for them to engage in sharecropping and leasing. High demand for land and the expense of hiring at Odometa results in a lower incidence of land leasing, since farmers frequently cannot afford to hire land and landowners with surplus land also prefer to release it for sharecropping, from which they get higher returns. They may also 'play the market' with their share of the proceeds, waiting for the lean season when food prices rise sharply to release their foodstuffs.

In contrast, at Awoweso and Akrusu the mass of farmers have more land available and need not rely as much on hiring land as at Odometa. The cost of leasing land is cheaper at Awoweso than at Odometa, which is related both to the fact that it is more marginal and yields less than at Odometa, and also to lower demand. Since yields are lower than at Odometa, sharecropping provides much lower returns to both the landowner and the cultivator than leasing. Yields are also erratic. This makes it difficult for land hiring costs to be worked out, or for landowners to gain a stable source of rent from sharecropping. Since few large landowners exist at Awoweso, the rationale for releasing land to tenants relates more to shortage of money and the need to raise capital than to the expropriating of surplus labour through sharecropping. In degraded environments large landowners may be impoverished by crop failure, and may be forced to hire land, their only valuable resource, to raise funds. Thus at Awoweso hiring of land is more dominant than sharecropping, but both sharecropping and land leasing are less important than at Odometa.

At Akrusu Saisi land is not generally short, although there are more people with no land, but there is a high incidence of both hiring and sharecropping. This is related to both the intense nature of degradation in the locality and adaptation to specialized niches in this environment. Akrusu Saisi suffers the most from desiccation and unreliable rainfall. Farmers can no longer rely on their traditional modes of staple production. Crisis in production has resulted in innovation and experimentation and a number of successful adaptations have arisen which focus on particular micro-environments which have arisen through environmental change. These *adaptive environments* have become the centres of agricultural activity. Farmers are increasingly focusing on two environments: the Volta lakeshore and *Panicum maximum* grassland which mainly occurs on the borders between Akrusu and Awoweso Sisi. On the banks of the Volta Lake farmers have introduced innovatory forms of floodwater retreat cultivation which have been adapted for growing sweet potato, tomato and cassava. On lands dominated by *Panicum maximum* farmers have successfully developed cowpea cultivation. Sweet potato and cowpea are now the major cash crops in Akrusu Saisi, and provide the most stable yields. Farmers without lands bordering the Volta Lake or *Panicum* grassland are increasingly turning to hiring land from others to gain a viable livelihood. As a result of increasing demands for land in these two micro-environments, prices have increased and sharecropping has become important. During the period of research, sharecropping was replacing land leasing as the dominant form of land hire, and land leasing prices were increasing. Land is not scarce at Akrusu, but owing to patterns of degradation the quality of land is crucial. Scarcity of good land results in increasing leasing and sharecropping.

These findings are substantiated by an examination of the mean areas of cultivated plots on household, leased and sharecropped land (Table 4.10). This shows that average areas of plots cultivated on farmers' own household land are lowest at Odometa, where farmers supplement their land most by sharecropping. Mean areas for leased land are highest at Akrusu and lowest at Odometa. Farmers at Akrusu cultivate the largest plots, and supplement household land with leased and sharecropped land. Farmers at Lower Awoweso cultivate the largest areas of land on their own household land, but make less use of hired and sharecropped land than farmers at Odometa or Akrusu Saisi. At Upper Awoweso, where holdings are small and where no successful adaptations to the degradation of the land have as yet been achieved, farming is depressed by poor and risky yields. As a consequence, farmers cultivate the least areas of land and hire less land.

TABLE 4.10. Mean cultivated areas on household, leased and sharecropped land in different settlements (all areas in *kpa ngwa*)

Settlement	Household land	Leased land	Crop share	Total area cultivated
Odometa	1.3	.25	.9	2.5
Upper Awoweso	1.6	.3	.2	2.1
Lower Awoweso	1.8	.5	.2	2.6
Akrusu Saisi	1.6	.9	.6	3.0

An examination of patterns of land hiring among landowners in the survey area further substantiates the above findings (Table 4.11). This shows that in the better-endowed environment of Odometa land hiring occurs among those with smaller holdings. It is a response to shortage of land. But in the more degraded environments where larger holdings prevail, hiring of land is also important among landowners with sufficient land and is a response to quality of land and the need for land in specialized niches. While the sample of Akrusu Saisi farmers is small and weighted towards larger holdings of over 6 ha, this does not alter the conclusion that farmers with surplus land at Akrusu are hiring land, and large farmers at Odometa have no need to lease land.

TABLE 4.11. Patterns of land leasing and sharecropping among landowners in different settlements

Settlement	No. of landowners	Landowners hiring or sharecropping land		Landowners with under 6 ha hiring or sharecropping		Landowners with over 6 ha hiring or sharecropping	
		No.	%	No.	%	No.	%
Odometa	38	4	10.5	4	100	.	.
Upper Awoweso	19	2	10.5	2	100	.	.
Lower Awoweso	21	3	14.3	1	33.3	2	66.6
Akrusu Saisi	9	6	66.7	1	16.6	5	83.3

The Household in Production

The survey sought to assess the effects of household size on the use of land. The household in Krobo, however, is a complex entity to define. Historically it has been a highly mobile unit and with increasing land shortage it has become even more migratory. Attempts were made to determine the size of households in relation to the total number of people dependent upon the land, the number of personal dependants, and the number of people cultivating the household land. This was not really successful, since informants used different criteria to assess these factors. Some people defined the household ('total farm dependants') in terms of all people associated with the household, including those residing in urban areas and other rural areas who rarely visited the farm. Other farmers defined the household in terms of those constantly residing on the farm. The 'number of people cultivating land' was sometimes designated to exclude those residing on the farm who sharecropped and leased land elsewhere. In other instances sharecropping and land-hiring household kin were included in farmers' assessments of the number of cultivators of the land.

These problems reflect objective conditions: the household is a constantly changing entity, in which some members leave to attempt to make a livelihood elsewhere and others return as a result of redundancy, retirement or difficulties encountered in settling in new frontier regions. Some families have systems of rotational cultivation: in one year one brother may make a farm on the land and hire land the following year, while another brother or other relative cultivates the land. On occasions family members who reside elsewhere come to make farms during the cropping season or help their fathers, mothers and siblings, and then return to their residences. Since the household is a highly fluid unit, the number of personal dependants thus becomes the most stable measurement of farm residential population. But this does not reflect the actual composition of households, which may be aggregates or subgroups of different groups of personal dependants. Figures

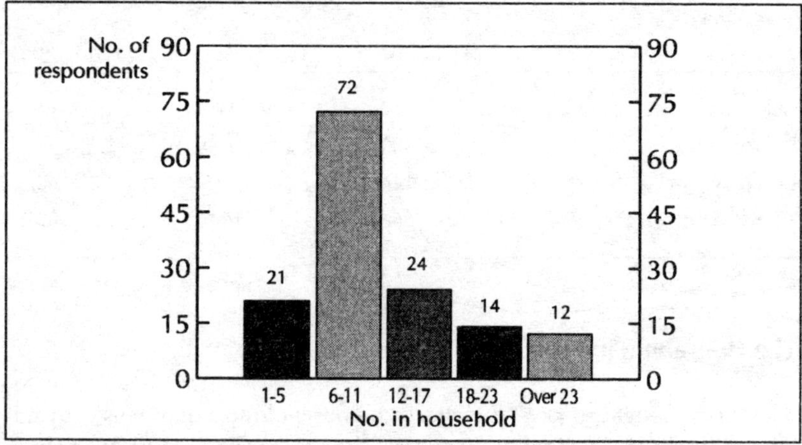

FIGURE 4.6. Total number of household members dependent upon the land

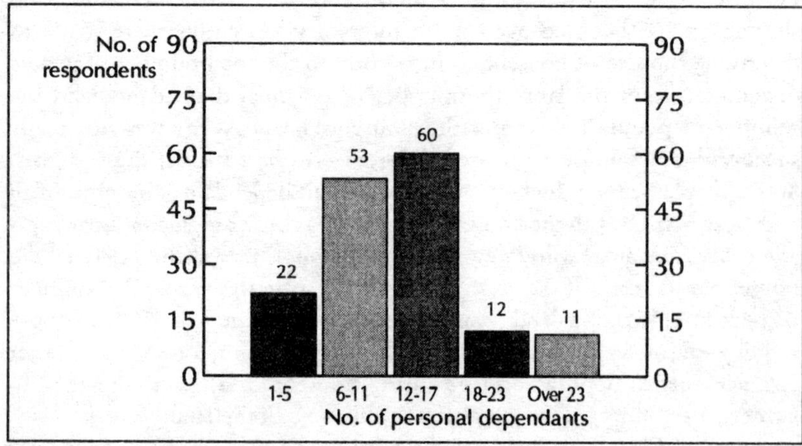

FIGURE 4.7. Total number of personal dependants of farmers

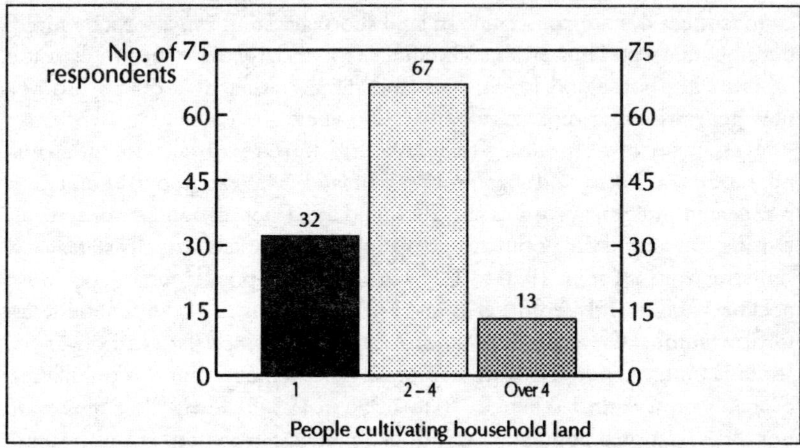

FIGURE 4.8. Number of people cultivating the household farm

4.6, 4.7, and 4.8 represent the responses to questions on household size and number of people working on the household land.

In the course of the survey we found a lively debate among farmers at Odometa about population and household size. One elderly farmer, experiencing difficulty in feeding his family, bemoaned his circumstances and declared that he had now come round to accepting what the 'white man' said about limiting family size. Another young man, with two young children, farming a small plot of land by himself, said he had heard on the radio that the government said people should limit the number of children they have. He did not know why the government was saying this, but he declared he had come to a similar conclusion since if he had many children there would not be enough land for them. Other farmers on small lands, however, had decided to maximize labour rather than land, and it was considered the norm for all household members to hire or sharecrop land. At Odometa Apirede, where landholdings were particularly small, many of the farmers claimed to have unusually large numbers of children (fifteen and over). Yet hardly any of them were living at Odometa, and most of them migrated as soon as they reached their late teens. It seems that under conditions of very small holdings, migration encourages large families, since the parents have to reproduce a new generation to carry out the household chores ascribed to children (sweeping the compound, carrying water, helping with cooking, helping on the farm, running errands, etc.). Since very small holdings cannot support existing family members, shortage of land does not act as a constraint on large family size, since the reproduction of the household is already dependent upon utilization of hired land. The heavy labour requirements of the household can provide incentives to reproduce large families despite constraints of land shortage. Land can always be hired, but not children. Thus on small holdings farmers may place the emphasis on reproducing household labour and land hirers, rather than on nurturing a new generation of prospective petty landowners.

Responses of households to increasing shortage of land include outmigration and hiring and sharecropping of land. The extent of outmigration is reflected in comparisons of the 1970 and 1984 population census returns. During this period the population of Odometa remained virtually stationary, growing from 1,136 in 1970 to 1,179 in 1984. The population of Awoweso declined significantly from 1,898 in 1970 to 1,057 in 1984. Difficulties exist in determining the exact borders of Akrusu Saisi, since the creation of the Volta Dam has resulted in a myriad of small settlements, but this population probably grew from 1,096 in 1970 to 1,356 in 1984. Clearly these figures do not reflect national population trends (a 3 per cent growth in population per annum) and are the result of outmigration.

Comparisons of the population profile of Odometa and Awoweso confirm the above analysis. The population density of Odometa in 1984 was 118 people per square kilometre, while that of Awoweso was 53 people. Odometa is a densely populated settlement in which scarcity of land prevails. In contrast, Awoweso has a low density of population which is falling. Outmigration and land hiring at Odometa are conditioned by scarcity of land. Land at Awoweso is not scarce and outmigration is influenced by degradation and unreliable rainfall and yields. At Akrusu Saisi population patterns are complicated by the influx of Ewe fishermen exploiting the Volta Lake and its subsequent development as a wholesale fish market.

GENDER RELATIONS

Differences in patterns of cultivation of land in relation to gender are shown in Table 4.12. This suggests that fewer women cultivated their own land or leased land and that more women sharecrop.

An examination of the distribution of land by gender within the settlements reveals that where land is scarce women have significantly less household land for their own use and resort to leasing and sharecropping more than men. Table 4.13 shows that at Odometa only 55 per cent of women cultivate their own household land as compared with 74 per cent of men. At Awoweso (where land is not so scarce) 81 per cent of women cultivate household land and at Akrusu Saisi all women cultivate household land. At Odometa considerably more women than men hire and sharecrop land, but at Awoweso more males than women hire and sharecrop land. At Akrusu slightly more men than women hire land and more women than men sharecrop.

TABLE 4.12. Distribution of different types of cultivated plots by gender

Gender	Own plot	Leased plot	Crop share
Male (no.)	92	22	35
%	81.4	19.5	31.0
Female (no.)	44	12	20
%	74.6	20.3	33.9

TABLE 4.13. Percentage of females and males using own household, leased and sharecropped land in different settlements

Settlement	Own plot		Leased plot		Crop share	
	Fem	Male	Fem	Male	Fem	Male
Odometa	54.5	73.9	22.7	8.7	63.6	43.5
Upper Awoweso	84.2	91.7	15.8	12.5	5.3	20.8
Lower Awoweso	81.8	92.6	9.1	25.9	9.1	14.8
Akrusu Saisi	100	91.7	42.9	50.0	57.1	37.5

TABLE 4.14. Mean areas of land cultivated by men and women in different settlements

Type of land	Odometa		Upper Awoweso		Lower Awoweso		Akrusu Saisi	
	Fem	Male	Fem	Male	Fem	Male	Fem	Male
Own	0.8	1.5	1.2	1.9	1.4	1.9	1.4	1.7
Leased	0.6	0.1	0.3	0.4	0.2	0.3	0.3	1.2
Crop share	1.0	0.9	0.1	0.3	0.1	0.3	0.2	0.7
Total	2.6	2.5	1.6	2.6	1.7	2.9	1.9	3.6

Table 4.14 shows the mean areas of different types of land cultivated by women and men in the sample settlements. This reveals that women at Odometa cultivate less of their own household land than women in other settlements. But when hired and sharecropped land are taken into consideration, they cultivate considerably larger areas of land than the other women. In contrast, men in the other settlements' cultivate as much as or more land than men at Odometa. While women at Odometa cultivate equal areas to men, women in the other settlements cultivate significantly less land than the men. Thus women at Odometa are engaged more heavily in agricultural

production than women in the other settlements, and hiring and sharecropping of land are important avenues through which they participate in agricultural production in their own right.

The differences in areas of lands cultivated by women in different settlements may result from a range of factors: the marginality of land in the more degraded settlements; labour bottlenecks in weeding large areas of land or increased labour requirements of weeding degraded land which may result in more women's time being devoted to their husbands' land; inability or unwillingness of husbands to clear land for women as a result of increased labour; lack of capital (related to poor yields) to hire labour; and the low returns from sharecropping marginal land.

As a result of lack of ownership of land, women have fewer rights in trees than men. In the past women were allowed to cut down forest trees for firewood but they had no rights to plant trees. In the present period their position is ambivalent. According to the survey 43 per cent of women believed that they had no rights in trees, 35 per cent thought that they could plant and own trees (because they owned the land or their father or husband would not object), and 22 per cent believed they could exercise rights over fruit trees but not oil palms.

Women often combine farming with trading, investing the proceeds from their farm in trading and using the profits from trading to farm. Eighty-three per cent of women claimed that their main income came from farming, 12 per cent indicated trading and 5 per cent said that they yielded an equal income or complemented each other.

ACCESS OF HOUSEHOLD MEMBERS TO LAND

Table 4.15 examines the nature of access to land of different household members. This shows that wives of owners (the most numerous female category) have least access to their own household land and lease and sharecrop more land than other household members. Sons and daughters also

TABLE 4.15. Access of household members to land

Household category	Own land		Leased		Crop	
	No.	%	No.	%	No.	%
Owner (male)	62	92	13	17	17	23
Owner (fem.)	13	100	2	15	1	8
Wife of owner	22	69	7	22	13	41
Daughter of owner	9	90	1	10	4	40
Son of owner	23	85	6	22	8	30

need to lease and sharecrop significant areas of land for their farming requirements. As would be expected, the access of wives, sons and daughters to household land is least where land is scarce (Odometa), and sharecropping becomes an important means of access to farm land (Table 4.16).

TABLE 4.16. A comparison of access to land for household members in different settlements

	Odometa		Upper		Lower		Akrusu	
	No.	%	No.	%	No.	%	No.	%
Owner (male)	28	85	16	100	17	94	8	100
Owner (fem)	5	100	3	100	3	100	2	100
Wife of owner	5	46	9	82	5	71	3	100
Daughter of owner	2	67	4	100	1	100	2	100
Son of owner	6	75	6	86	8	89	3	100
Sharecropped land								
Owner (male)	12	36	3	19	2	17	.	.
Owner (female)	1	20	.	.	.	.	.	.
Wife of owner	9	82	1	9	1	14	2	67
Daughter of owner	2	67	.	.	.	.	2	100
Son of owner	3	38	1	14	2	22	2	67
Leased land								
Owner (male)	3	9.1	2	13	3	17	1	14
Owner (female)	1	20	.	.	.	.	1	50
Wife of owner	3	27	2	18	1	14	1	33
Daughter of owner	.	.	.	.	.	.	1	33
Son of owner	1	13	1	14	4	44	.	.

At Odometa only 46 per cent of wives utilized the household land for making farms, 82 per cent sharecropped and 27 per cent hired land. In contrast, at Awoweso 70–80 per cent of wives made farms on the household land, 9–14 per cent sharecropped and 14–18 per cent hired land. At Odometa 75 per cent of sons of owners made farms on their household land and 67 per cent of daughters of owners. Caution needs to be exercised in interpreting these data, since when broken down into these categories the number of values in some cells are very low. Nevertheless the data suggests that wives of owners have least preferential access to land, and depend on sharecropping and land hiring to a large extent.

Landleasing and Sharecropping

Complete landlessness is rare. Only 3 per cent of the total survey were caretakers looking after the land of absentee landowners. Only 4 per cent of the sample had no household land of their own and depended upon the annual hiring or sharecropping of land. Four women and five men were completely landless. All the men were situated at Akrusu. They had either lost their land as a result of its appropriation for the construction of the Volta Lake, or were Ewe migrants from Volo, moving in to take advantage of fishing opportunities created by the lake and engaging in supplementary agriculture. In the case of the women, landlessness was associated with membership of households with the smallest holdings. This precluded them getting rights in land since the existing land could not satisfy the household head, and they were wholly dependent upon hiring and sharecropping land.

Landlessness is often disguised. Many families are dependent upon the hiring and sharecropping of land to reproduce their households and suffer from a partial form of landlessness. Many sons, daughters and wives of owners must hire or sharecrop land on a yearly basis. The degree of landlessness is also disguised by outmigration, with many young people leaving because of insufficient land. There is, however, no polarization of the agricultural economy into a large landlord class and an increasingly proletarianized class of smallholders in the process of transformation into labourers for large landowners. There are no *latifundias*.

Large landowners are often absentee owners. They have invested their profits in the purchase of lands elsewhere in new frontier districts where they are now farming, or have invested in the urban sector.

The rural social structure is characterised by economic depression and the dominance of smallholder agriculture, increasingly struggling to make a livelihood. The local economy has a limited capacity to absorb landless labour, and many young people are faced with the choice of pursuing marginal forms of agriculture (which are really forms of quasi-unemployment) or migrating. There is increasing frustration with the agrarian way of life, particularly among young people, who are acutely aware of the economic and social decay of the settlements in which they live.

LAND-LEASING ARRANGEMENTS

The terms under which land is leased (*pa zubga /haya zugba*) vary quite considerably between settlements and within individual settlements, reflecting shortage of land, quality of land, and the need of the landowner for cash. At Odometa the least variation occurred in land-leasing conditions. Prices ranged between ₵4,000 and ₵8,000[2] per *kpa ngwa* for one-year leases.

2 In 1992 ₵600 = US$1. The cedi is being devalued constantly and has dropped from ₵2.75 = $1 in 1981 and ₵30 = $1 in 1984.

Landowners at Odometa were reluctant to lease land for more than a year. They considered that longer leases would result in continuous cultivation by the land hirer which would degrade the land. At Upper Awoweso prices ranged from ₵5,000 to ₵8,000 for a three-year to ₵2,000 for a single-year lease. At Lower Awoweso they varied from ₵3,200 to ₵6,000 for a two-year to ₵1,000 for a single-year lease. At Akrusu Saisi variations in price were at their most complex. Prices for three-year leases were in the range ₵2,000–₵11,000 and single-year leases in the range ₵3,000–10,000. Grassland for cowpea cultivation commanded rates of ₵8,000-10,000, well-grown bush for corn and cassava ₵5,000, and poorly regenerated corn and cassava bush cost ₵3,000 per *kpa ngwa*. Lakeshore sweet potato land commanded rates of ₵2,400 for 12x12 armspans. Here prices reflect the various micro-environments, with highest premiums for lakeshore land and pure grassland for cowpea cultivation. Within the more degraded lands, where the forest bush environment has been replaced by grassland, longer leases may be arranged: the threat of degrading secondary forest bush into grassland has already become a reality, and the grassy environment is less sensitive to subsequent degradation. The large labour outlays involved in clearing grassland often lead to longer periods of cultivation, which may involve crop rotation systems. Three years represents the maximum period of continuous cultivation before soils become exhausted, and diminishing yields make further planting uneconomic.

SHARECROPPING ARRANGEMENTS

The main sharecropping (*hu ne agba / pe ne agba*) arrangements were a half share system in which landlord and tenant receive equal divisions of the crop, and a third share system in which the tenant received two-thirds and the landlord one-third of the yield. Two intermediate sharecrop arrangements were also found:

1 the tenant took one bag of maize and the remainder of the yield was divided 50:50;

2 maize was divided two-thirds to the tenant and one-third to the landlord, and cassava into half shares.

In recent years half cropping has become increasingly predominant. In the sample it accounted for 70 per cent of all sharecropping arrangements. Sharecropping arrangements vary in relation to quality of land, different degrees of degradation, and market demand. Thus at Odometa 92 per cent of crop share tenancies were based on a half share as compared with 33 per cent in Lower Awoweso and 25 per cent at Akrusu Saisi (Table 4.17). In 1991 sharecropping terms began to be revised at Akrusu Saisi. With the successful development of sweet potato cultivation on the lakeshore and its

TABLE 4.17. Sharecropping arrangements

Settlement	Half share	Two-thirds to tenant	One bag corn to tenant then half share	Two-thirds to tenant & cassava half share
All settlements	69.2%	24.6%	3.1%	3.1%
Odometa	92.1%	7.9%	–	–
Upper Awoweso	46.2%	46.2%	7.6%	–
Lower Awoweso	33.3%	50.0%	16.7%	–
Akrusu Saisi	25.0%	50.0%	–	25.0%

popularity among farmers, lakeshore landowners were now demanding a half share for the 1991/2 season. At Odometa the third share arrangement was usually enjoyed by caretakers, who are allowed a greater part of the proceeds for looking after the whole land; and by farmers who undertook to market the proceeds for the landowner.

Sharecropping tenancies are short and usually end after a year, when the cassava crop in the maize–cassava intercrop has matured and is harvested. Tenants can often interplant minor crops such as yams among the main crops and keep the proceeds for themselves. Major crops (maize, cassava, vegetables, cowpea, sweet potatoes) are divided in several ways:

1 Each party is apportioned a share of the land from which they take the crops.

2 The corn yield is divided into two heaps which are shared out and the two parties allocated a portion of land from which they can reap the cassava.

3 The tenant is responsible for the marketing and gives the landlord a third share of the proceeds – this is common with perishable vegetables and sweet potatoes (the extra labour in marketing accounts for a larger share for the tenant).

Landowners who release land for sharecropping to tenants include those with surplus land, absentee landowners, old farmers who cannot cultivate large areas, and farmers who have debts or need to raise short-term capital.

Labour

Table 4.18 shows the survey's findings on the main forms of labour relations for clearing (preparation of bush/land for cultivation) and weeding, the two

TABLE 4.18. Types of labour used in clearing and weeding

Type of labour used	Clearing		Weeding	
	No.	%	No.	%
Alone	70	40.7	23	13.4
Spouse	10	5.8	30	17.4
Family labour	16	9.3	70	41.3
Hired labour	70	40.7	44	25.6
Katsu	6	3.5	5	2.3

major labouring activities. These consist of:

1 farmers working alone;

2 with their spouse;

3 with close family relatives including combinations of spouse, children, parents, and siblings;

4 with hired labour;

5 *katsu* ('working together'), a form of small-scale collective reciprocal labour in which a group of four or five men (usually young men without families) undertake to clear and weed each other's farms together.

The data show the importance of hired labour, with 41 per cent of farmers frequently hiring labour to clear farms and 26 per cent hiring labour for weeding. The use of family labour is prevalent in weeding, accounting for 41 per cent of the labour used, but in the clearing of land 41 per cent of farmers work alone. For a large proportion of the sample clearing is largely an individual activity which is carried out over months and determines the area the farmer is going to cultivate, after which negotiations on cooperation with other family members for the critical tasks of weeding can be agreed.

Patterns of land clearing are also associated with gender. Table 4.19 gives a breakdown of type of labour by gender. This shows that while the majority of men (58 per cent) clear by themselves, 60 per cent of women depend on hired labour for land clearing. Only 9 per cent of women clear their own land and 17 per cent rely on their husband to clear land for them. With weeding, family labour is the most important supplementary source for both men and women, but 32 per cent of women and 22 per cent of men depend on hired labour to augment their own efforts. This suggests that women depend more upon hired labour than men.

TABLE 4.19. Types of labour used by men and women for clearing and weeding

Type of labour	Clearing		Weeding	
	Male (%)	Female (%)	Male (%)	Female (%)
Alone	57.5	8.5	15.0	10.2
Spouse	–	16.9	18.6	15.3
Family	6.2	15.3	40.7	42.4
Hired	31.0	59.3	22.1	32.2
Katsu	5.3	–	3.5	–

Hired labour has been important in enabling women to participate more in the agricultural economy in their own right. In the past women's role in agriculture was more marginal. Their entry into agriculture was constrained by the arduous task of clearing the forest or bush, which is still unpopular with women. Huber (1963) records that during the colonial period their main agricultural role was in weeding the land of their husbands. Women still help to weed their husbands' land, but in recent times they have been able to take advantage of the growth of hired labour and hired land to clear their own individual farms in addition to those of their husbands. Several women commented: 'in the past we only used to weed our husbands' farms, but now we do everything that men do'. Table 4.20 suggests that women who use hired labour for clearing and weeding are able to cultivate twice as much land as those who weed and clear alone. Close cooperation with husbands in farming also appears to bear dividends with those whose husbands cleared land for them or helped them in weeding able to cultivate equally large areas of land as those hiring labour. For men, reliance on family labour (wife, children, siblings) and hiring is associated with the highest mean areas cultivated. Nevertheless, farming is increasingly an individual enterprise in which hired labour is of growing importance.

TABLE 4.20. Mean areas cultivated by men and women in relation to types of labour used for clearing and weeding

Type of labour used	Clearing (*kpa ngwa*)		Weeding (*kpa ngwa*)	
	Female	Male	Female	Male
Alone	1.1	2.4	1.1	2.0
Spouse	2.0	–	2.0	2.5
Family	1.5	3.9	1.7	2.7
Hired	2.0	2.9	2.0	3.0
Katsu	–	2.4	–	2.4

Table 4.21 presents data on the use of hired labour in the survey settlements. This appears to be greatest at Akrusu Saisi. Hired labour in weeding is used least at Odometa. Factors which may affect use of hired labour include the nature of weed associations and weeding requirements, availability of land and the commercial opportunities afforded by expanded production. At Odometa, with vestiges of a forest environment, weeding and clearing requirements are likely to be less than in the more degraded grassland settlements. Scarcity of land at Odometa also limits the potential to use hired labour for expanded production. The greater use of hired labour at Akrusu Saisi may reflect availability of land, larger farms, and difficulty of weeding grass.

TABLE 4.21. Use of hired labour in different settlements

Type of hired labour	Odometa	Upper Awoweso	Lower Awoweso	Akrusu Saisi
Clearing	36.8%	39.5%	34.2%	65.2%
Weeding	19.1%	23.3%	28.9%	43.5%

The cost of hiring labour for clearing and weeding varies according to the nature of the flora. Plots with numerous irritating plants, thorns or grass species command a higher price than secondary regenerating forest land which is easier to clear and weed. Hired labour is more expensive in degraded environments. At Odometa costs for clearing 1 *kpa ngwa* were in the range ₵4,000–6,000 and at Upper Awoweso in the range ₵4,000–5,000. At Lower Awoweso costs varied more dramatically between ₵5,000 and ₵12,000; and at Akrusu Saisi between ₵4,000 and ₵10,000 per *kpa ngwa* and ₵1,000 for 12x12 armspans of lakeshore land. At Lower Awoweso and Akrusu Saisi the highest prices were for pure grassland for cowpea cultivation.

Labour for weeding is usually hired on a daily or casual 'job lot' basis. The cost of weeding varied between ₵400 and ₵600 for a day's work. Labour may also be hired to weed by the *kpa ngwa*. At Akrusu Saisi weeding costs varied in the range ₵2,500–4,000 per *kpa ngwa*. At Odometa and Awoweso weeding costs per *kpa ngwa* were ₵3,000.

There is no specific class of labourers. Labourers are usually smallholder farmers who are short of cash. Labour is essentially hired on a casual basis, by day or by job.

OFF-FARM INCOMES

Fifty-five per cent of the sample claimed to have sources of off-farm income, including 57 per cent of women and 54 per cent of men. In the case of women 98 per cent of the off-farm incomes were based on trading. Fifty-four per cent of women traded in farm products (food, cooked food, charcoal, and *akpeteshie* gin or distilled palm wine), 10 per cent in fish and 2 per cent in industrial manufactures. Seven per cent of women sold cooked food. In the case of men 27 per cent of off-farm incomes originated in palm wine tapping and distilling, and 6 per cent in fishing (at Akrusu Saisi). Other off-farm work included carpentry, wood sawing, bricklaying, masonry, driving, tailoring, trading, and preparation and the selling of herbal remedies. These occupations reflect the proximity of these settlements to Asesewa, a major market town. However, as a result of economic decline, many men practising other occupations have had to fall back on farming as their basic economic activity. With the exception of palm wine distilling there is a notable lack of a craft sector which processes farm produce.

Agricultural Inputs, Services and Credits

In contrast with the high capitalization of land and labour, farmer investment in modern technical factors of production is very limited. The main interventions by agricultural services in the local economy consist of the promotion of fertilizers, pesticides, high-yielding varieties (HYVs) and methods of row planting, and the provision of credits in chemical inputs (Global 2000) or loans for farming ventures (Rural Banks). Investments in modern agricultural technology and the extent of the support facilities provided by agricultural development services for farmers can be charted by examining the extent of use of these technologies and services.

The use of all these factors was extremely limited in the survey area. Only 9 per cent of farmers had ever used fertilizer and only 10 per cent had tried pesticides. Only 4 per cent of farmers had ever purchased HYVs. Purchased seedlings included oil palms, citrus and pepper. Modern maize varieties were not purchased by farmers. Yet the production of modern maize varieties is one of the major areas of agricultural research and development in Ghana in which a comparative advantage has been identified by the state.

All farmers admitted that they experienced shortage of capital. But only 2 per cent of cultivators had ever received a loan from formal agricultural institutions. The main sources through which farmers gained loans were relatives, traders, money lenders and rotating credit associations (*susu*).[3] Farmers frequently engaged in specific off-farm activities to raise capital

3 A rotating credit association is a savings club where members give contributions at regular intervals. The contributions raised at each meeting are given in turn to a different member to use as capital.

when in need, such as selling livestock, felling oil palm trees for palm wine tapping, working as a palm wine tapper's mate, trading, labouring and preparing foodstuffs or charcoal for sale.

The low usage of agricultural inputs reflects the marginalization of farmers, the unwillingness of agencies to provide credit for them, and lack of capital to purchase inputs. This has become very marked in recent years with the removal of subsidies on agricultural inputs. Prices of agricultural inputs have risen dramatically, with fertilizers increasing from ₵1,500 to ₵5,000 per bag in five years, without any proportionate increase in the prices of foodstuffs. Where fertilizers are used farmers rarely follow recommendations: they may use one bag on 2–3 ha. The main use of fertilizers is in growing vegetables (garden egg and tomato). Farmers claim that these crops no longer grow well without fertilizer. As a result of the rising cost of fertilizer in recent years, fewer farmers are now growing vegetables.

Apart from the cost, farmers do not use agricultural services inputs because they do not find them adapted to their needs, to their farming system and their style of farming. Their main concerns are with weeding bottlenecks and unreliable rain, and these issues have not been addressed in the development of extension packages.

None of the farmers in the survey was a client of Global 2000, but at Akrusu Saisi some farmers were familiar with the agency and described the encounter with amusement. They claimed Global 2000 was only interested in planting maize in lines with fertilizers, not in cassava, or any other crop. They came to plant some maize, but when the maize failed because of lack of rain they lost interest and never came back. Global 2000 claimed that they had given loans to farmers at Akrusu for high-input farming, that the farmers had absconded with the money and they were unable to get their loans back. Nevertheless, they admitted that unreliable rainfall was a problem at Akrusu. Until factors of rainfall and cost of inputs are addressed, investment in extension-promoted technologies will be highly risky for small-scale farmers.

Investment by farmers in other facets of farm technology is minimal. The main farm implements used are cutlasses and hoes, yet many farmers complained that they were too expensive and that they could not afford to replace their cutlasses when they were beginning to suffer from wear and tear. Farmers lack protective farm clothing and often farm barefooted. Injuries to hands and feet are common, resulting in the loss of many work days.

In response to the question 'If given a loan how would you invest it?', 92 per cent of respondents gave an answer which included hiring labour and 84 per cent replied that they would invest all the loan in hired labour. Eighty-seven per cent also identified labour (weeding and clearing) as the major problem they faced on the farm, and 7 per cent pinpointed capital to hire labour.

Labour is the largest problem cultivators face in working on the farm, and a large proportion of surplus capital is invested in labour. This leaves little capital for investment in inputs. Within the prevailing conditions, farmers consider returns to investment in labour to be higher than investment in agricultural services package technology. This suggests that the present priorities of agricultural services do not reflect the immediate needs of the vast majority of farmers, and that research into cheap forms of labour-saving technology for weeding and clearing would be more appreciated by the majority of small-scale cultivators than concerns with raising yield per hectare.

Conclusion

The cost of production within Upper Manya Krobo is high and many farmers depend on hiring land, sharecropping, and hiring labour to gain entry into agricultural production. Hiring of labour has resulted from the decline of household and extended family labour, which is also a reflection of the failure of the household to provide stable sources of land for all its members. Young household members are now forced to find land elsewhere rather than farm in cooperation with other household members on household land. Agriculture has increasingly become an individual enterprise, in which success depends on ability to hire land and labour. Degradation and invasion of the land by exotic and savanna weed species have resulted in rising weeding requirements and hiring of labour is particularly important on more degraded land where timely weeding and clearing are major bottlenecks.

The capitalization of factors of production have allowed women and other landless categories of people to participate to a larger extent in agriculture, but the cost of this participation is high. Forty-nine per cent of women as compared to 19 per cent of men hire land and labour for clearing on a regular basis. Nineteen per cent of women as compared to 8 per cent of men hire land and labour for clearing and weeding. The cost of hired land and labour is high since yields are marginal. A large proportion of capital is expended on the factors of production, and if rains fail – as is frequently the case – this capital investment is lost. Marginal yields and impoverishment also create a large pool of casual labourers who need to generate income from other sources to supplement their own farming activities.

Sharecropping and land-leasing contracts are short. This has important ramifications for the development of regenerative technologies. Constraints of short periodic access to land are going to prevent a large percentage of women, young people and the poorest section of men from experimenting with utilizing regenerative technologies, and will confine this practice to a small section of the population. This will defeat the objective of promoting environmental regenerative technologies. Studies of agroforestry in the Eastern Region have identified land tenure as one of the major obstacles to the wide-scale adoption of agroforestry techniques (Gyasi, 1991; Owusu, 1990).

Land degradation and responses to declining environments involve complex interaction between environment, production, land tenure, household parameters, population, labour, economic adaptation and markets. This suggests that concepts of the carrying capacity of land may not reflect the complex social and economic interactions which characterize degradation. This includes processes of household mobility, diversified incomes, responses to market factors, commoditization, and outmigration.

Sharecropping and hiring of labour have been important from the early twentieth century in the process of frontier settlement. In recent years these institutions have been transformed to reflect conditions of land shortage, small-scale production, and increasing labour requirements caused by invasion of the fallow by gregarious weeds and small-scale production. Hiring of labour is particularly important in the more degraded settlements where clearing and timely weeding are often major bottlenecks.

This commoditization of the productive factors has introduced some flexibility into the farming system. It enables those without land to participate in production and allows those without much land to supplement their production and ease pressure on their own land. However, land hiring and sharecropping are contractually arranged on a short-term basis, and these tenurial arrangements present difficulties for long-term land conservation. The high cost of production and short-term nature of hiring and sharecropping agreements act as major socio-economic constraints on a more sustained management of the environment and the introduction of regenerative technologies.

Farmers can respond to intensified land degradation and unfavourable production costs by confining production or abandoning agriculture. The increasing cost of land for hire may result in migration. This may in turn ease the pressure on the land which leads to a fall in land rental and sharecropping terms. Land prices are set both by demand and by the productivity of land. High prices for degraded land lead to outmigration as the cost of production is not reflected in yields. With declining demand, land rents fall to reflect the degraded state of the land. Outmigration may further lead to less intense population pressure on the land which may enable longer fallow intervals to take place and allow the land to regenerate to a certain degree. Individual production may recede in degraded environments as the risks of production and the uncertainty of yield deter investment in expanded production, hired labour and hired or sharecropped land. Production falls to a neo-subsistence level, and those without land seek hired land in better-endowed settlements. The effect of degradation is to increase the energy requirement of the farming system, which in a market-integrated economy leads to high costs of production yet declining and unreliable yields.

Farmers may also work out adaptations to land degradation in particular micro-environments. They may create new agrarian activities with promising market potentials, which will further intensify the capitalization of the factors of production. Land then becomes more scarce as farmers extend cultivation, hire more labour, and population may return to the area. Under these conditions degradation may itself become capitalized, as the cost of land reflects demand, transformation of production, and the market potential of crops rather than the quality of the land. Social differentiation of the population may become more pronounced as some farmers fail to meet the cost of producing in a highly degraded environment which has managed to capitalize on and adapt to degradation.

Paradoxically, as the farming system becomes increasingly marginalized and yields decline, the factors of production are increasingly commoditized. Under certain conditions this could lead to a transformation of the agrarian structure, to the migration of small farmers away from agriculture, the appropriation of their land and the development of mechanized large-scale agriculture dependent upon chemical inputs. The increasing cost of production may force those who are unable to adapt to leave. This will release land for those who are able to adapt successfully to the new conditions, leading to the development of new forms of agrarian capitalism. With a lack of viable economic avenues elsewhere, however, degradation can become a way of life, continually eroding both the economic livelihood of the population and the productivity of the environment. Returns to agriculture fall to a near subsistence level within a highly capitalized economy characterized by land and labour scarcity, high costs of production and diminishing yields.

This phenomenon has been interpreted from an ecological perspective as *involution* (Geertz, 1963), a process of land degradation through which producers are forced to intensify labour and other inputs and innovate more intricate forms of labour without leading to increased productivity. From a political economy perspective it has been interpreted as a *reproduction squeeze* (Bernstein, 1979) in which the impact of commoditization results in increasing costs of production, decreasing returns to labour and deteriorating terms of exchange for peasant-produced commodities. Bernstein suggests that the reproduction squeeze acts as a mechanism through which labour in the peasant household is intensified to maintain or increase the supply of cheap farm commodities for capital. However, this capitalization of the costs of production can also be a product of a process of marginalization in which rural areas are consumed by capital and then forgotten as economic and ecological problems become pronounced and attention focuses on new frontier areas. These areas are marginalized because the state and capitalism do not have simple solutions to the problems within the parameters which characterize the process of the commoditization of agricultural research and integration of producers into commodity markets. The farmers operate within an economy in which land and labour are highly commoditized, but the technical means of production and reproduction are not highly commoditized, and production is still largely determined by direct interaction with the environment. The cultivators resist modern agricultural input technology because it does not reflect the conditions of production: the modern agricultural sector marginalizes the farmer because their commodity packages have little relevance to the prevailing conditions. Agricultural development policy searches for more productive areas on the new frontier with greater potential for cooption.

5
Adapting to Changing Environments

Changing patterns of natural resource usage among farmers reveal much about perceptions of the environment and the impact of degradation on economic life. In recent years a number of studies have drawn attention to a wide range of plants which are utilized within households and transacted in markets but which have not been accounted for in mainstream economic analysis (Falconer, 1990; Abbiw, 1990; de Beer and McDermont, 1989; Okafor, 1983; Okigbo, 1977). In Ghana there is a long tradition of work by botanists and foresters which traces the uses of plants in the forest (Irvine, 1930, 1961; Dalziel, 1948; Taylor 1960; Ayensu, 1978; Abbiw, 1990). These works, however, have tended to focus on the plants and the products they yield rather than on the overall patterns of resource utilization. The impact of environmental degradation and integration into world commodity markets on patterns of natural resource utilization has not received much attention. It is often assumed that increasing degradation leads to a decline in the diversity of resources which communities use, without a detailed analysis of the processes of change and its impact on natural resource utilization. It is also inferred that the commoditization of new and minor forest products will lead to a more sustainable development, without examining the reverberations of the commoditization of these products on communities and their relationship to the environment. This chapter aims to develop these two themes by relating natural resource utilization to conditions of production in particular localities. A comparison of the utilization of natural resources in the various localities of the survey, in settlements which 50 years ago had common stocks of knowledge and farming styles, enables the effects of land degradation on economic production to be charted.

Most folk cultures utilize a wide range of natural products which are consumed in their raw state or processed into conserves, herbal remedies, beverages, wines, etc. These are often produced as use values rather than as commodities and often have little commercial value. Within rural communities in West Africa three patterns of natural resource utilization can be discerned: exploitation for export markets, for national markets, and for the household.

In Ghana natural forest resources which have become important staple export crops have included rubber and oil palms. With intense competition in world markets, however, natural resources which were originally collected in a semi-wild form tend to be cultivated on plantations or become marginal. In Ghana oil palms and rubber gathered in semi-wild states lost out in competitiveness to modern industrial plantations in South East Asia. Recent developments in the oil palm industry are based on large-scale plantations of exotic hybrid varieties, which often replace the natural diverse environment with an intensive monoculture. The remaining vestiges of forests are often clear felled to make way for evenly spaced rows of oil palms. Timber is also a product which is felled in a wild state but increasingly grown on plantations. In recent years high extraction rates for export have contributed to the rise in Gross Domestic Product (GDP) but resulted in the decline of many forest areas. Production focused on the demands of the world market and on monocultural export crop production often leads to the rapid depletion of natural resources or their cultivation on plantations which come to replace and threaten natural environments. Some forest products which exist in a semi-wild state have also been important in regional export trade, such as the trade of cola nuts from the forests to the Sahel. Away from the competitiveness of world commodity markets these products have managed to retain stable outlets, which raise considerable sources of value without promoting excessive land degradation.

Other forest products are important in national markets, including timber, spices and condiments, wild fruits, canes, honey, chewing sticks, fuelwood, etc. In this context they are often exploited by specialized gatherers, crafts people and traders, who focus on certain products, and range over a wide area of forest reserves and farming communities. Farmers sometimes provide these commodities to traders and sell them on a part-time basis in markets to supplement their incomes. Some households may specialize in collecting firewood and in processing charcoal. While this exploitation of resources often lies within the control of individuals within local communities or traders with links with local communities these commodities are exploited as exchange values. Those that are marketable are often the prime commodities in their category. Selective exploitation of these resources often leads to their rapid depletion. Many prime tree species exploited for timber, charcoal, firewood, chewing sticks and pestles and mortars have become scarce.

The third pattern of resource utilization involves households using a wide array of wild products for personal consumption in their day-to-day existence. This is the dominant pattern in rural farming communities, and involves these products being exploited as use values rather than exchange values. This sector is often the most experimental. It is here that a large number of new use values are being found and evaluated from existing stocks of plants, that use values are found for newly colonizing plants, and replacement plants are found for old plants which have become rapidly depleted. Frequently, innovation within the household use value sector provides the information which leads to the exploitation of natural resources as exchange values in local district and international markets. The household sphere also suffers from the fall-out of over-exploitation of resources in the market sector, and is left to face the consequences of finding alternative resources for everyday use to replace diminishing sources of established natural resources. In contrast, traders and crafts people often move to other areas when resources become exhausted in a locality.

Within frontier societies the exploitation of a wide variety of natural resources is important. The wide variety of resources provided by nature forms part of the windfall of the frontier, enabling households to achieve savings and to be autonomous. This self-reliance is crucial during early stages of frontier colonization when the frontier lies beyond the realm of markets and transport facilities, and when pioneer settlers must rely on provisions of nature to furnish their needs. This leads to autarky, where producers seek to be as self-reliant as possible, and complement the production of exchange values with the consumption of use values for the household. Farmers often utilize a wide array of fallow produce which are peripheral to agriculture but important in household consumption. These strategies run counter to the expansion of the world market and development programmes which seek to integrate primary producers into markets and which seek to appropriate the commons with all their diversity of natural resources. The expansion of the world market and increasing commoditization results in a decline in material goods or use values which are freely acquired from nature and to increasing dependence on market purchases.

This chapter charts the ways in which natural resources are used in households and the pressures of markets and state development plans on these patterns of utilization. This includes products which are gathered from the fallow, and those which are cultivated and nurtured in the agro-ecosystem. Only a few of the environmental resources utilized within a locality enter the market. The contrast between the diversity of local resource usage and the narrow ranges of commodities entering the market reveals constraints which prevent commercial markets building upon biodiversity.

Natural Resources and Human Thought

Natural resources are important to humans in that they have shaped and trained the mind, itself a product of nature. Natural environments afford humans the options of adaptation and experimentation in the quest to satisfy their needs, and of reflection on the natural world and on human interventions. As a result people develop an aesthetic and intellectual interest in the environment and its forces, often personifying nature in stories and building up classificatory systems of nature. In Krobo there are songs which personify plants according to aesthetic traits:

Dede Meseki lɛ	As for Dede Meseki
e wa kɛ	she is fully mature
se e piɛ e kami kɛ e bɔmi	but for her height and her size

Dede Meseki (oldest daughter Meseki, old lady Meseki) is *Elytraria marginata,* a small herbaceous plant growing to a height of about 10 cm with an elegant posture, found under tall forest trees.

I ya ba dɛ ɛ	I have come up
ma tsɛ nyu	I will call water
imitsɛ a tsɛ mi Zozongmo	they call me Zozongmo
i gbowe	I won't die
ha pu la	let the sun burn

Zozongmo is *Portulaca quadrifida,* a tiny prostrate creeping herb with numerous small leaves which root at their nodes. While most plants suffer from stress during the dry harmattan season, becoming yellow or deciduous, *Zozongmo* remains a deep green, looking as if it was growing in lush meadows in the rainy season.

This personification of nature extends into assigning supernatural powers to nature and plants. Sometimes calabashes of water are placed in branches of trees for their spirits to drink. Other plants are revered. *Kpangwa* (*Spiropetalum heterophyllum*), a large woody climber which winds around tall forest trees but is as thick as a human at its base and exudes a deep red sap like blood, is supposed to have a supernatural human form. If one cuts its stem or leaves, without first making an offering of spirit and eggs, it will come to haunt the offender in the night begging and screaming to be let free. Others tell stories about people who were farming and by mistake cut *kpangwa* with their cutlasses, only to find that their arms had also been slashed through.

Stories also abound on how people learn about the powers of nature from animals:

> People found out about leaves which were antidotes to snake venom by watching snakes fighting. One snake inflicted a lethal bite on the other and went away triumphant. The injured snake managed to make its way

> to a certain leaf which it ingested and which relieved the poisonous venom of the other snake. A hunter who had hid himself and watched the fight now knew this leaf was an antidote to the venom of the triumphant snake.

Other tales recount how people have learnt from animal pharmacopoeia, – for example, being led to medicinal plants by sick wild pigs who were digging up the roots to treat their ailments.

This image of nature contrasts with the Judaeo-Christian image of a placid and static nature created by God to serve man and his platter. This is a nature of forces, sometimes in harmony and sometimes in conflict, which can be harnessed by people but which may be dangerous and full of unexpected and unforeseen consequences. Every plant has its use, the problem being to find that use. The quest for the uses of plants involves people in a direct relationship with the environment which is adaptive, experimental, observational, and based on classifying, reclassifying and thinking about the attributes of the environment. While this may fetishize nature as elemental forces and powers, it recognizes interactions which are only beginning to be realized by ecologists in their struggle against the fetishism of the environment as a compendium of isolated commodities.

Increasing commercialization and decline of species diversity through degradation may serve to erode this popular environmental knowledge, resulting in a declining appreciation of the interactions within tropical forests. Most members of the younger generation in Krobo have never seen many of the plants their grandparents talk about, which have become part of the folk legends of the old frontier days.

Economic Uses of Fallow Land

The various resources provided by the forest and fallow flora include:

1 direct benefits, products which can be harvested to provide commodities and use values;

2 indirect benefits, the effects of plants in ameliorating the environment of the locality in relation to the climate, soil protection and enhancement of soil fertility.

Perceptions of the processes of interaction of the various species which constitute the farm and fallow, and their effect in ameliorating the environment, form the subject of the next chapter. This chapter focuses on the use values which can be ascribed to particular plants by the local farming population. Figure 5.1 provides a classification of these various uses.

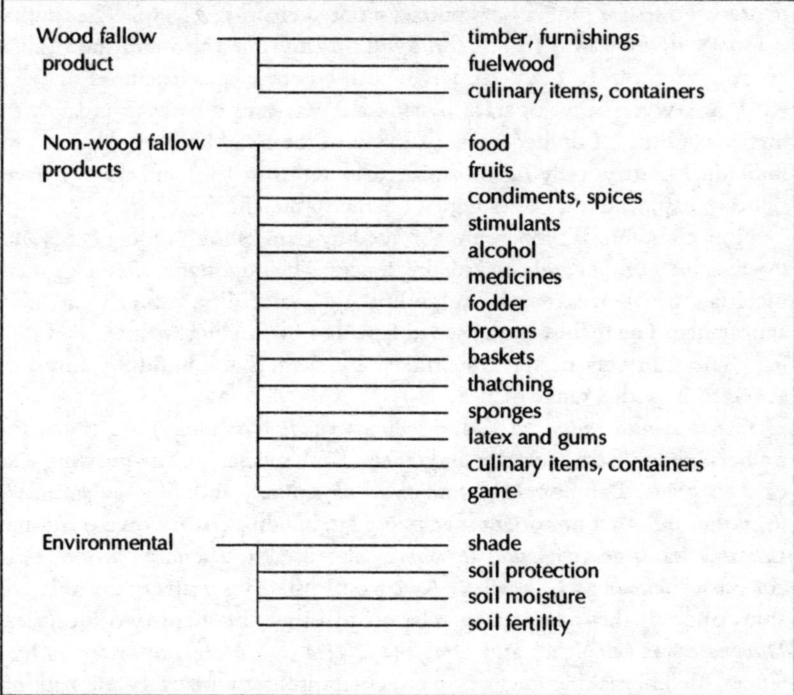

FIGURE 5.1. Fallow resources

Timber Products: Construction Wood and Utensils

Trees from the fallow are used for construction purposes around the house and for fashioning implements. They are also exploited by commercial timber operators. As a result of the market few prime timber trees remain.

TIMBER, FENCING AND POLEWOODS

Little commercial timber remains in the Asesewa area. The main timbers which have been exploited commercially in the past include *Milicia excelsa* (*odum*), *Khaya grandifoliola* (*mahogany*), *Triplochiton scleroxylon* (*otra*), *Piptadeniastrum africanum* (*odahoma*), *Terminalia ivorensis* (*amle*) and *Terminalia superba* (*afram*). They are now rare. In the sample only 13 per cent of farmers admitted having felled commercial timber species in the last six years. The remaining 87 per cent of farmers could not cite when they had last felled a tree, or had inherited land without remaining timber trees. The main timber species felled was *Milicia excelsa* (trade name: *iroko*). Most farmers do not cut their own trees for timber but contract it out to chain-saw gangs. The timber is usually divided into shares: the owner taking one third and the timber operator two thirds. Local farmers who own chain-saw machines or who work as sawyers now operate outside the Asesewa district in areas with higher densities of timber trees. In many of the neighbouring Akan areas, individual farmers only have usufructuary rights in land and do not have rights to exploit timber trees which belong to the chiefs.

Non-commercial timbers are also used by farmers for building barns and sheds, ceiling timber and constructing fences. The important criteria for such materials are their strength, durability and availability, rather than their appearance. The main woods used in fencing and building are listed in Table 5.1. The numbers of species utilized by farmers for building purposes averaged 2, with a range of 1–8.

Cassia siamea (*kasiatso*) and *Azadirachta indica* (*sabolatso*) are the main timbers used in farm buildings and fences. Both species are fast-growing and easy to plant. Bamboo (*Oxytenanthera abyssinica*), and *Newbouldia laevis* (*nyabatso*) are other important species used in building. At Awoweso Adome *Leucaena leucocephala* (*glauca*) (*tɛbone*) is also used as a fencing wood, as is *Anogeissus leiocarpus* (*sakane*) at Awoweso Sisi. This reflects the relative abundance of these species in relation to others in these two localities. *Jatropha curcas* (*kitiblɛtso*) and *Dracaena arborea* (*buna*) are important as live fences, used in making livestock pens, enclosures for pit latrines and bathing areas. A line of interspersed *Dracaena arborea* is also used to mark the boundaries between farm strips (*zugbas*).

FURNISHINGS AND UTENSILS

In addition to fencing and building poles, other woods are fashioned into home-made furnishings and utensils. *Oxytenanthera abyssinica* (bamboo or *pamploo*) and *Holarrhena floribunda* (*osese*) are used for constructing home-made stools and chairs. Most home furniture, however, is purchased from carpenters, who use *Milicia excelsa* (*odum*) and *Triplochiton scleroxylon* (*otra*). Pestles for pounding fufu[1] and palm nuts are made from *Dialium guineense* (*mielɛtso*), *Nesogordonia papaverifera* (*bano*), *Baphia nitida* (*tutso*), *Diospyros canaliculata* (*tɛtso*), *Celtis mildbraedi*/*C. zenkeri* (*papao*), and neem trees (*sabolatso: Azadirachta indica*). Large mortars are made from *Morus mesozygia* (*odongma*), *Milicia excelsa* (*odum*), large *Nesogordonia papaverifera* trees, *mahogany* (*Khaya grandifoliola*), *Afzelia africana* (*gblɛtso*), and occasionally *Hildegardia barteri* (*okpɔtso*) and large neem trees. *Holarrhena floribunda* (*osɛsɛ*), *Dialium guineense* and *Hildegardia barteri* are also important in fashioning culinary utensils, such as ladles and small grinding pestles.

1 A staple food made from combinations of boiled plaintain, cocoyam and cassava, which are pounded in a large mortar.

TABLE 5.1. Species used for on-farm building and fencing (% of farmers using)

Scientific name	Krobo name	Odometa	Awoweso Kpeti	Awoweso Adome	Awoweso Sisi	Akrusu Saisi	Total
Cassia siamea[2]	Kasiatso	74.5	97.7	10.0	85.7	83.3	87.0
Azadirachta indica[2]	Sabolɛtso	3.9	14.0	66.7	50.0	10.0	37.7
Oxytenanthera abyssinica[2]	Pamploo	25.5	34.9	37.5	7.1	3.3	24.1
Newbouldia laevis[1]	Nyabatso	3.9	14.0	20.8	–	3.3	8.6
Leucaena leucocephala (glauca)[2]	Tɛbone	–	4.7	29.2	–	–	5.6
Jatropha curcas[2]	Kitiblɛtso	15.7	–	–	–	3.3	5.6
Dracaena arborea[1]	Buna	7.8	2.3	4.2	–	3.3	4.3
Elaeis guineensis[1]	Ta	3.9	2.3	8.3	–	3.3	3.7
Baphia pubescens[1]	Tutsɔ	3.9	2.3	8.3	–	–	3.1
Thevetia peruviana[2]	Mɔkɔtso	7.8	–	–	–	–	2.5
Trichilia monadelpha[1]	Gbagblabata	–	–	12.5	–	–	1.9
Anogeissus leiocarpus[3]	Sakane	–	2.3	–	14.3	–	1.9
Markhamia lutea[1]	Mɔmɔtso	–	–	–	–	6.7	1.2
Dialium guineense[1]	Mielɛtso	2.0	2.3	–	–	–	1.2
Nesogordonia papaverifera[1]	Banɔ	2.0	–	–	7.1	–	1.2
Milicia excelsa[1]	Odum	3.9	–	–	–	–	1.2
Holarrhena floribunda[1]	Osese	3.9	–	–	–	–	1.2
Albizia adianthifolia[1] / *Albizia zygia*[1]	Papa	3.9	–	4.2	–	–	1.8
Vernonia amygdalina[4]	Abgatso	2.0	–	–	–	–	0.6
Antiaris toxicaria[1]	Hatsɔ	2.0	–	–	–	–	0.6
Spondias mombin[2]	Akole	–	2.3	–	–	–	0.6
No. of farmers		51	43	24	14	30	162

1 = forest tree; 2 = exotic tree; 3 = tree associated with savanna orchard bush; 4 = shrub found in savanna and open forest country

TABLE 5.2. Percentage of farmers using various fuelwood species

Scientific name	Krobo name	Odometa	Awoweso Kpeti	Awoweso Adome	Awoweso Sisi	Akrusu Saisi	Total
Cassia siamea[2]	Kasiatso	64.7	90.7	100.0	50.0	90.0	80.2
Albizia adianthifolia /A.zygia[1]	Papa/papaku	68.6	74.4	79.2	57.1	16.7	61.1
Azadirachta indica[2]	Sabolatso	2.0	41.9	100.0	28.6	100.0	47.5
Newbouldia laevis[1]	Nyabatso	51.0	20.9	75.0	7.1	6.7	34.6
Elaeis guineensis[1]	Kikle	54.9	23.3	33.3	7.1	10.0	30.9
Trichilia monadelpha[1]	Gbagblabata	7.8	32.6	45.8	28.6	10.0	22.2
Holarrhena floribunda[1]	Osɛsɛ	17.6	25.6	29.2	14.3	13.3	20.4
Baphia pubescens[1]	Tutso	19.6	23.3	29.2	14.3	10.0	19.8
Dialium guineense[1]	Miɛlɛtso	3.9	16.3	29.2	7.1	6.7	11.7
Ficus exasperata[1]	Slabatso	31.4	2.3	8.3	–	–	11.7
Nesogordonia papaverifera[1]	Bano	7.8	2.3	20.8	–	10.0	8.0
Ceiba pentandra[1]	Lɛno	2.0	11.6	12.5	7.1	6.7	7.4
Leucaena leucocephala (glauca)[2]	Tɛbone	2.0	7.0	29.2	–	–	6.8
Sterculia tragacantha[1]	Togɔjɔ	–	11.6	12.5	7.1	3.3	6.2
Antiaris toxicaria[1]	Hatso	5.9	11.6	–	–	–	4.9
Chromolaena odorata[5]	Acheampong	7.8	–	8.3	–	3.3	4.3
Landolphia owariensis[1]	Kiakia	7.8	2.3	–	–	–	3.1
Milicia excelsa[1]	Odum	–	9.3	–	–	3.3	3.1
Blighia sapida[1]	Kingatso	3.9	2.3	8.3	–	–	3.1
Manihot esculenta[6]	Agbili	3.9	–	–	–	10.0	3.1
Mangifera indica[2]	Mango	5.9	–	4.2	–	3.3	3.1
Cola gigantea var. glabrescens[1]	Ovuga	5.9	2.3	–	–	–	2.5
Celtis zenkeri[1]	Papao	5.9	–	4.2	–	–	2.5
Markhamia lutea[1]	Mɔmɔtso	–	–	–	7.1	6.7	1.9

TABLE 5.2. CONT. Percentage of farmers using various fuelwood species

Scientific name	Krobo name	Odometa	Awoweso Kpeti	Awoweso Adome	Awoweso Sisi	Akrusu Saisi	Total
Triplochiton scleroxylon[1]	Otra	–	–	4.2	–	6.7	1.9
Spathodea campanulata[1]	Votso	–	2.3	8.3	–	–	1.9
Psychotria calva[4]	Apɔtɔtso	5.9	–	–	–	–	1.9
Solanum verbascifolium[5]	Agbafro	–	2.3	4.2	–	–	1.2
Blighia unijugata[1]	Aklokingatso	–	–	8.3	–	–	1.2
Oxytenanthera abyssinica[2]	Pamploo	3.9	–	–	–	–	1.2
Citrus species[2]	Akututso	3.9	–	–	–	–	1.2
Psidium guajava[2]	Agowa	2.0	–	–	–	–	0.6
Ricinodendron heudelotii[1]	Awama	–	–	4.2	–	–	0.6
Bombax buonopozense[1]	Mangosiedu	–	–	4.2	–	–	0.6
Mallotus oppositifolius[4]	Satwetso	–	–	–	–	3.3	0.6
Ricinus communis[5]	Kumelo	–	–	–	–	3.3	0.6
Trichilia prieuriana[1]	Okummadue	2.0	–	–	–	–	0.6
Anogeissus leiocarpus[3]	Sakane	–	–	–	7.1	–	0.6
Zea mays[6]	Blefo	–	2.3	–	–	–	0.6
Persea americana[2]	Paya	2.0	–	–	–	–	0.6
Jatropha curcas[2]	Kitibletso	–	–	4.2	–	–	0.6
Alchornea cordifolia[4]	Boblo	2.0	–	–	–	–	0.6
Musanga cecropioides[1]	Ojima	–	2.3	–	–	–	0.6
miscellaneous:	lake trees[7]	–	–	–	–	20.0	3.7
No. of farmers		51	43	24	14	30	162

1 = forest trees; 2 = exotic trees; 3 = trees associated with savanna orchard bush; 4 = forest shrubs; 5 = exotic shrubs; 6 = food crops; 7 = dead trees inside the Volta Lake, which were submerged during the formation of the lake – they are harvested by some farmers as fuelwood.

ALCOHOL STILLS

Until the early 1980s tree trunks were used as condensers in the distillation of alcoholic spirit (*akpeteshie*) from palm wine. The trunks were hollowed out, then filled with water, and copper tubes carrying the distillate ran through them. The most common tree used was *Ceiba pentandra* (*lɛno*), a large, soft-wooded tree with little use as timber until very recently. With increasing scarcity of large trees, stills made from tree trunks have been replaced with new designs fashioned from aluminium roofing sheets. A detailed account of palm wine tapping appears below.

Fuelwood

Fuelwood forms the main energy source for cooking. Fuelwoods are obtained from deadwood in the fallow, from woods cut in clearing the fallow for the new farm, from species specifically cultivated or preserved for firewood, and from branches lopped and pruned from large trees. Women are largely responsible for collection of firewood and its utilization in cooking. However, collection of firewood is a shared responsibility, and men frequently bring fuelwood home when returning from work on the farm plot.

Forty-four fuelwood species of variable quality were identified in use in the survey area (see Table 5.2). Follow-up questions revealed another seven species which were considered good-quality firewood, including *Anacardium occidentale* (cashew nut: *atia*), *Talbotiella gentii* (*blɛtso*), *Parkia clappertoniana* (West African locust bean: *dudue*), *Pachystela brevipes* (*siatomamitso*), *Synsepalum dulcificum* (*atamami*), *Gardenia ternifolia* (*peteplɛbi*) and *Theobroma cacao* (cocoa). The most frequently used firewood species included *Cassia siamea* (*kasiatso*), *Albizia adianthifolia* (*papa*) and *A. zygia* (*papaku*), *Azadirachta indica* (*sabolatso*), *Newbouldia laevis* (*nyabatso*), oil palm branches (*kikle*), *Trichilia monadelpha* (*gbagblabata*), *Holarrhena floribunda* (*osɛsɛ*), *Baphia pubescens* (*tutso*), *Dialium guineense* (*miɛlɛtso*) and *Ficus exasperata* (*slabatso*). At Awoweso Adome, *Leucaena leucocephala* (*glauca*) (*tɛbone*) was also an important firewood species. The main species used for preparing charcoal include *Cassia siamea* (*kasiatso*), *Azadirachta indica* (*sabolatso*), *Albizia adianthifolia* (*papa*) and *A. zygia* (*papaku/ papa*). In the use of firewood there has been a distinct shift from utilization of mature forest species to pioneer forest species (*Albizia adianthifolia, A. zygia, Newbouldia laevis, Trichilia monadelpha, Holarrhena floribunda, Baphia pubescens, Dialium guineense, Ficus exasperata*) and the introduction of small, fast-growing exotic trees (*Cassia siamea* and *Azadirachta indica*).

High-grade firewood has the qualities of burning easily, slowly and without creating a lot of smoke. The best firewood species are considered to include *Celtis zenkeri* (*papao*), citrus species (*akutu*), *Pachystela brevipes* (*siatomamitso*), *Azadirachta indica* (*sabolatso*), *Synsepalum dulcificum* (*atamami*), *Baphia pubescens* (*tutso*), *Nesogordonia papaverifera* (*bano*), *Trichilia monadelpha* (*gbagblabata*), *Milicia excelsa* (*odum*), *Khaya grandifoliola* (*mahogany*), *Trichilia prieuriana* (*okumnadue*), *Gardenia ternifolia* (*peteplebi*), *Baphia sapida* (*kingatso*), *Mangifera indica* (*mango*), and *Theobroma cacao* (cocoa). Many of these species are not in common use as fuelwoods either because they are scarce (*Celtis zenkeri, Pachystela brevipes, Trichilia prieuriana*), or have other important uses such as fruits (mango, cocoa, citrus, *Baphia sapida*) or wood (*odum, mahogany*). Most farmers make a compromise between quality of firewood and availability, or rely on fast-growing exotic species.

Poor firewood species used in the survey area included oil palm branches (*kikle*), *Ceiba pentandra* (*leno*), *Bombax buonopozense* (*mangosiedu*) *Markhamia lutea* (*mɔmɔtso*), *Sterculia tragacantha* (*togɔjɔ*), *Jatropha curcas* (*kitibletso*) *and Ricinodendron heudelotii* (*awama*). The worst species used, indicative of serious fuelwood shortage, include *Mallotus oppositifolius* (*satwetso*), *Chromolaena odorata* (*acheampong*), cassava sticks, and maize stalks.

Twenty-four per cent of farmers interviewed claimed they supplemented fuelwood collected from the fallow with purchases on the market. Sixty-six per cent of farmers claimed they were now spending longer in collecting and searching for firewood and 67 per cent were now using poorer-quality fuelwoods. Seventy-two per cent of informants thought they were economizing more and more on the use of fuelwood. While farmers generally felt fuelwood was becoming more scarce, only 6 per cent claimed to plant trees for firewood. Forty-eight per cent stated that they actively preserved firewood species through such activities as weeding around young saplings. Thirty-seven per cent of the farmers sold firewood or charcoal.

Table 5.3 summarizes farmer perceptions of the availability and use of fuelwood in different localities. Paradoxically, at Awoweso Sisi, the settlement with the least tree covering and most grass, more farmers than in the other localities claimed to sell fuelwood on a regular basis, and a larger percentage felt that they were self-sufficient in the production of fuelwood. In contrast, farmers at Odometa, the settlement with the most developed secondary forest bush, sold by far the least fuelwood, economized more on the use of fuelwood, and considered they were spending longer in collecting firewood and using poorer-quality woods. Shortage of firewood was particularly noticeable on smaller plots at Odometa. Vestiges of the former forest vegetation, existence of a few large trees covering a large area, and fewer introduced exotic fuelwood species (*Cassia siamea* and *Azadirachta indica*) may contribute to fuelwood shortage at Odometa. On the other hand, increasing desiccation and bushfires may have halted the successional regeneration of high forest species in the more degraded settlements. These

TABLE 5.3. Farmer perceptions on firewood problems

% of farmers	Odometa	Awoweso Kpeti	Awoweso Adome	Awoweso Sisi	Akrusu Saisi	Total
Unable to meet fuelwood requirements	21.6	21.4	29.2	9.1	33.3	24.1
Spend longer in collecting fuelwood	68.6	71.4	66.7	58.3	56.7	66.0
Use poor quality fuelwood	80.4	61.9	62.5	58.3	56.7	66.7
Economize on fuelwood	82.4	71.4	70.8	58.3	60.0	71.7
Plant trees for fuelwood	4.0	0.0	25.0	8.3	3.3	6.4
Sell woodfuel/charcoal	11.8	40.5	45.8	42.9	66.7	45.9
No. of farmers	51	43	24	14	30	162

are replaced by numerous fast-growing robust and fire-resistant trees, which have excellent fuelwood properties, such as *Albizia adianthifolia* and *Anogeissus leiocarpus*. In Ghana the main charcoal-producing areas tend to lie in the transitional zone and in savanna orchard bush, rather than in the high forest. Under conditions of stress, introduced exotic fuelwood species may also be able to compete much more successfully for space, light and soil nutrients than mature forest species, and may prevent their regeneration. The numerousness of these trees and their excellence as firewood is reflected in their high usage by farmers: *Cassia siamea* and *Azadirachta indica* achieve 100 per cent use as a fuelwood in some localities.

At Awoweso Adome, where many farmers complained of fuelwood shortage, a significant number had responded by planting firewood species, unlike in the other settlements. At Akrusu Saisi higher percentages of farmers were selling fuelwood and charcoal than in other localities, but more farmers also complained of not being able to meet their firewood requirements. Those that claimed to experience fuelwood shortage may have been exaggerating, and may have based this on the fact that they were harvesting dead trees on the Volta Lake from canoes,[2] rather than on purchases of

2 When the Volta Lake was created the original vegetation was flooded, leaving tree trunks standing submerged in the river. The dead wood from these trunks is collected by farmer-fishermen and used as fuelwood, and sometimes for building purposes.

fuelwood. Throughout Akrusu Saisi the dominant vegetation is the neem tree (*Azadirachta indica*), an excellent fuelwood species.

Low levels of sale of fuelwood at Odometa may not only reflect a lack of suitable trees, but also a preference to invest labour in other activities. Collection of firewood for sale by women at Odometa was not a popular activity, but one associated with poverty. The price of ₵200 for a headload of firewood was considered unattractive in relation to the exertion of carrying the load to market. In contrast, in the more degraded settlements firewood formed an important source of income given the insecurity of crops, and had become so established that trucks came to purchase the firewood at the farmgate. Table 5.4 shows percentages of farmers selling firewood in 1990–1.

TABLE 5.4. Percentage of farmers selling firewood and charcoal in 1990–1

	Krobo name	Odometa	Awoweso Kpeti	Awoweso Adome	Awoweso Sisi	Akrusu Saisi	Total
Charcoal	ha	–	18.6	16.7	14.3	21.7	11.3
Firewood	lɛ	1.6	14.0	25.0	–	17.4	10.1
No. of farmers		64	43	24	14	23	168

Housekeeping Provisions

A number of fibres, leaves and tree saps are processed to yield products used around the household as soft furnishings, culinary items, for personal hygiene and in craft industries.

FIBRES: BROOMS, BASKETS, MATS AND SPONGES

A variety of fibres produced from the fallow are processed and used for household purposes. Brooms are made from the ribs of oil palms fronds (*kuɔm*). Where oil palms (*Elaeis guineensis*) are scarce, as in Awoweso Sisi and Awoweso, farmers are forced to buy brooms or to make undesirable brooms from various twigs.

Baskets are woven from longitudinal cut sections of oil palm rachis (*kikle*) or from the raffia palm, *Raphia vinifera* (*lɔwetso*). Those fashioned from the oil palm produce a fine attractive green and white basket, and those from the Raphia palm a slightly more coarse and larger red and white basket. There is a local demand for baskets at Asesewa market, and some farmers gain important supplementary incomes from basket weaving. At Akrusu Saisi rough-hewn baskets are also produced from the branches of neem trees for farmhouse use.

Sleeping mats are usually purchased at market, but may also be woven from oil palm fronds and from *Imperata cylindrica* (*henyu*). The floss of *Ceiba pentandra* (*leno*), *Bombax buonopozense* (*mangosiedu*) and *Gossypium* species (*dote*) is used to stuff pillows and mattresses. Mattresses may also be stuffed with *Imperata cylindrica* (*henyu*) and *Cynodon dactylon* (*gli glas*: 'green grass') collected from school playing fields.

In the past, bark cloth (*tso bo*) was produced from *Antiaris toxicaria* (*hatso*), and last used during the Second World War when cloth was scarce. Cloth is no longer produced locally, although cotton plants are suited to the Krobo area. In the nineteenth century production of 'country cloth' was an important industry in the main Krobo towns (Kirby, 1882), but has now declined.

Sponges for bathing, washing culinary items and scrubbing are produced from the stems of *Momordica angustisepala* (*kutsakpa*). Purchased bathing sponges woven like fishnets from synthetic fibres are, however, increasingly replacing natural sponge fibres.

CONTAINERS AND WRAPPERS

The gourds of *Lagenaria siceraria* (*tsimi/tɔtso*) and *Crescentia cujete* (*tsimitso*) provide containers for holding liquids and other produce. Plantain (*madaa*), banana (*kɔdu*), *Sarcophrynium brachystachys* (*ngoba*), *Marantochloa cuspidata* (*kafaba*) and *Marantochloa leucantha* (*sibli*) leaves are used for wrapping produce and cooked foods. Maize husks are used for wrapping and cooking kenkey.

LATEX AND GUMS

Several trees exude latex and gums for which farmers have developed uses. However, none of these are of commercial importance today. *Landolphia owariensis* (*kiakia*) yields a rubber latex. During the late nineteenth century this was exported as a rubber staple alongside *Funtumia elastica* (*fruntum*) before the opening up of *para* rubber plantations in South East Asia. Mahogany (*Khaya grandifoliola*) yields a gum which farmers sometimes use as glue. Birdlime (sticky latex painted onto trees to catch birds) was also prepared from *obiagale* (unidentified), now a scarce tree.

SOAPS

Soaps are produced from low-grade palm oil and the ashes of cocoa pods, plantain peels or *Jatropha curcas* (*kitibletso*), but most soap is purchased from market. During the crisis years of the early 1980s, when there was a shortage of commercially produced soap, household soap-making activities flourished. They have declined in recent years in the face of competition, particularly from large-scale industrial soap manufacturers such as Lever Brothers. But they may grow again as their quality improves, and as more people come to appreciate their soft lather and purchase them in preference to industrial soaps.

CHEWING STICKS

Chewing sticks form the main teeth cleaners used in the rural areas. Irvine (1961) lists 106 species of chewing sticks used in Ghana. In a survey of villages, towns and cities in southern Ghana, Adu-Tutu *et al.* (1978) record 28 species utilized as chewing sticks. The most important were *Garcinia afzelii, G. epunctata, G. kola, Acacia kamerunsis, A. pentagona, Teclea verdoorniana* and *Dialium guineense.* The favoured chewing stick in the Krobo area, as in the whole forest area of Ghana, is the split stem of *Garcinia epunctata* (*sokodua*). This tree has largely disappeared from fallows as a result of overutilization, and a wide array of trees and shrubs have replaced it. Table 5.5 shows the main chewing sticks used in the survey area.

The main species used for chewing sticks include *Azadirachta indica* (*sabolatso*), *Dialium guineense* (*mieletso*), *Baphia pubescens* (*tutso*), *Nesogordonia papaverifera* (*bano*), *Mallotus oppositifolius* (*satwetso*) and *Griffonia simplicifolia* (*totolimo*). Increasing degradation is reflected in the lack of mature forest species utilized as chewing sticks. The most commonly used species are introduced drought-resistant trees such as *Azadirachta indica*, species associated with the transition zone and savanna areas such as *Dialium guineense*, small, hardy pioneer forest species such as *Baphia pubescens*, and shrubs such as *Griffonia simplicifolia* (*totolimo*) and *Mallotus oppositifolius* (*satwetso*). Species used as chewing sticks also reflect differences in environment, with neem (*Azadirachta indica*) assuming dominance in the more degraded settlements and *Baphia pubescens* at Odometa. Citrus twigs and *Gardenia ternifolia* (*peteplebi*) are also more important at Odometa than at other settlements. Neem trees are little utilized at Odometa.

Numbers of chewing sticks used by individuals varied in the range 0–8. Twenty-one per cent of the sample used one species of chewing stick, 29 per cent two species, 30 per cent three species, and 11 per cent more than three. Ten per cent of farmers relied solely on purchases of chewing sticks from market. Thirty-one of the sample bought chewing sticks from time to time on an irregular basis, including 39 per cent of the farmers at Odometa, 45 per cent at Awoweso Kpeti, 30 per cent at Awoweso Adome, 29 per cent at Awoweso Sisi and 3 per cent at Akrusu. Twenty per cent of farmers at Odometa relied completely on purchased chewing sticks, 5 per cent at Awoweso Kpeti, 8 per cent at Awoweso Adome, and no farmers at Awoweso Sisi or Akrusu Saisi. Purchase of chewing sticks is not related to lack of potential chewing sticks in fallow land, but personal preference for

TABLE 5.5. Popular chewing stick species (% of farmers using)

	Krobo name	Odometa	Awoweso Kpeti	Awoweso Adome	Awoweso Sisi	Akrusu Saisi	Total
Azadirachta indica[2]	Sabolatso	9.8	53.5	79.2	85.7	86.7	52.5
Dialium guineense[1]	Mieletso	25.5	55.8	37.5	50.0	36.7	39.5
Baphia pubescens[1]	Tutso	60.8	23.3	33.3	21.4	23.3	36.4
Nesogordonia papaverifera[1]	Bano	21.6	34.9	54.2	21.4	43.3	34.0
Mallotus oppositifolius[4]	Satwetso	9.8	9.3	16.7	7.1	6.7	9.9
Griffonia simplicifolia[4]	Totolimo	5.9	–	8.3	14.3	16.7	7.4
Gardenia ternifolia[3]	Peteplebi	9.8	–	–	–	–	3.1
Synsepalum dulcificum[4]	Atamami	5.9	2.3	4.2	–	–	3.1
Carpolobia lutea[1]	Opiongo	3.9	–	8.3	–	–	2.5
Citrus species[2]	Akutu	7.8	–	–	–	–	2.5
Trichilia monadelpha[1]	Gbagblabata	2.0	–	4.2	7.1	–	1.9
Antiaris toxicaria[1]	Hatso	3.9	–	–	–	–	1.2
Tamarindus indica[2]	Odompo	–	–	–	7.1	3.3	1.2
Securinega virosa[4]	Nabutwe	–	2.3	–	–	–	0.6
Celtis zenkeri[1]	Papao	–	–	4.2	–	–	0.6
Cassia siamea[2]	Kasiatso	–	–	–	–	3.3	0.6
Trichilia prieuriana[1]	Okumnadue	2.0	–	–	–	–	0.6
Spathodea campanulata[1]	Votso	–	2.3	–	–	–	0.6
Napoleonaea vogelii[1]	Kpakutso	2.0	–	–	–	–	0.6
Sample size		51	43	24	14	30	162

1 = forest tree; 2 = exotic tree; 3 = tree associated with savanna orchard bush; 4 = forest shrub.

particular *Garcinia* species (*sokodua*) and willingness to spend money on this item.

Medicines and the Conservation of Genetic Resources

The potential uses of plants in healing forms one of the areas which has aroused growing interest in the conservation of tropical rainforests and in the knowledge of forest dwellers about herbal medicines. With increasing disappearance of forest species and biodiversity, the conservation of forests and plants with potential medicinal value has becomes an important issue in the pharmaceutical field.

A large number of common present-day drugs are produced from plants rather than laboratory synthesis (Abbiw, 1990). Where it is cheaper to produce drugs through synthesis, however, pharmaceutical companies will replace these natural products. In Ghana a few plants such as *Griffonia simplicifolia*, *Paullinia pinnata*, *Voacanga africana*, *Heliotropium indicum*, *Catharanthus roseus*, *Rauvolfia vomitoria*, *Physostigma venenosum*, and *Corynanthe pachyceras* have been exported as raw materials for the pharmaceutical industry in recent times (Abbiw, 1990). But these products have not found stable markets since the alkaloids are eventually produced in laboratories by synthesis, or other alternative and cheaper sources for the manufacture of the drugs are found.

Abbiw (1990) describes trips by European organic chemists to Africa to collect plants for screening for medicinal value. Many of these research efforts have utilized local knowledge systems and used methodological approaches based on compiling databases of folk remedies for subsequent screening. This approach often results in success. The works of Dalziel (1937) and Irvine (1930, 1961) bear testimony to the early interest of botanists in folk knowledge of herbal remedies on the Gold Coast.

Herbal medical practitioners form an important stratum of the health delivery system in Ghana, complementing institution-based medical services in areas with no health centres. It has been estimated that there are about 100,000 registered Traditional Medical Practitioners (TMPs) in Ghana, forming a ratio of one 'informal' medical practitioner to 140 people, compared with one scientifically trained medical practitioner to 20,000 people. TMPs provide health care for about 75 per cent of the population. In contrast, about 80 per cent of the 990 scientifically trained doctors are situated in urban areas (*People's Daily Graphic*, 12 October 1991). With the decline of government medical services, the removal of subsidies, and shortages of drugs, TMPs have assumed greater importance in the medical delivery system. A large percentage of the people use both formal and informal medical systems. TMPs have established reputations in such fields as bone-setting in which they successfully compete against formal medical institutions.

Local herbal knowledge has been recognized as important by the state, which has given official recognition and support to the Centre for Scientific Research into Plant Medicines, established in 1973 at Mampong, Akuapem. The organization and registration of herbal practitioners has been encouraged through such structures as the Traditional Medical Association. Current research at the University of Ghana, Legon also includes a project to investigate local remedies for malaria. Contemporary health policy issues being raised within state institutions include problems of integrating the informal medical sector with the scientific institutional framework, and the establishment of a national advisory committee on medicinal plants and natural products to assist the Ministry of Health in the formulation of a national policy on the utilization and conservation of medicinal plants.

Within the Krobo district three types of interrelated plant-based medical knowledge systems exist:

1 A practice closely associated with priestly cults (*wɔtsɛ*), fusing a rational approach, based on the medical utility of plants, with an expressionist approach which personifies natural forces and accords supernatural properties to plants, often based on aesthetic qualities. This system has important value as a repository in which genetic material is preserved and classified, an important focus for environmental conservation. Often plants, which are rare in farmers' fallows, are conserved in 'sacred groves';

2 A utilitarian rationalistic approach, which may draw from priestly knowledge, but which concentrates on the efficacy of the healer's knowledge of plants, and which presents this knowledge outside of a religio-metaphysical system. The practitioner obtains financial reward for medical services, and the ingredients of the most powerful herbal cures are secretly guarded;

3 A popular folk culture of medical plants, freely communicated and administered to sick friends, relatives and neighbours.

Research largely focused on the popular use of fallow plants. However in the process of searching for specimens of rare plants for identification, *wɔtsɛ* ('fetish priests') were found to be important curators of genetic material, preserving pristine forest species in the fallow and planting favoured species around their compounds. In some cases they could provide a cutting or seed of particular plants for a token fee, and showed remarkable patience and interest in roaming through fallows to locate particular species.

Table 5.6 lists the species which farmers in the five localities cited as popular medicinal plants they utilized. This by no means reflects the total number of species which are used within the Krobo area, or which farmers have knowledge about, but those most readily impressed in farmers' memories and which they can articulate under survey questionnaire conditions.

The most commonly cited species include *Azadirachta indica* (*sabolatso*), *Cassia siamea* (*kasiatso*), *Alstonia boonei* (*adawura*), *Parkia clappertoniana* (*dudue*), mango, *Hoslundia opposita* (*su*), *Newbouldia laevis* (*nyabatso*), *Jatropha curcas* (*kitibletso*), guava (*agowa*), *Chromolaena odorata* (*acheampong*), lime (*kpetetso*), papaw (*gɔtso*), cashew nut (*atia*) and *Anthocleista nobilis* (*frakpa*).

A wide range of plants were cited, including forest trees (*Khaya grandifoliola, Alstonia boonei, Cola gigantea var. glabrescens, Anthocleista nobilis, Trichilia prieuriana, Bombax buonopozense, Baphia pubescens, Trichilia monadelpha, Newbouldia laevis, Anogeissus leiocarpus, Spathodea campanulata, Albizia* species); fruit trees (guava, mango, lime, papaw, cocoa); understorey and shrub species (*Cassia alata, C. occidentalis, Mallotus oppositifolius, Paullinia pinnata, Securinega virosa, Spiropetalum heterophyllum, Ocimum* species, *Justicia flava, Momordica charantia*); and weeds associated with regeneration on food farms (*Solanum verbascifolium, Sida acuta, Mallotus oppositifolius, Chromolaena odorata, Mucuna pruriens, Panicum maximum, Boerhavia diffusa, Alternanthera pungens*). Few species associated with mature semi-deciduous dry forest were commonly cited. Many of the tree species are associated with secondary forest pioneer species, transgressors which survive on either side of the forest-savanna transition zone (*Newbouldia laevis, Dialium guineense, Blighia sapida*), introduced savanna species (*Parkia clappertoniana, Tamarindus indica, Panicum maximum, Digitaria ciliaris*) and introduced exotic species (*Azadirachta indica, Cassia siamea, Chromolaena odorata*).

Several species have been deliberately preserved and some carried into the forest specifically for their medicinal value (*Newbouldia laevis, Tamarindus indica, Parkia clappertoniana, Azadirachta indica, Kigelia africana*). The large number of savanna and transition zone species may reflect patterns of Krobo migration, and the fact that the historical roots of Krobo herbal knowledge developed in the outer zone of the forest ecotone. It was likely that farmers carried their prized medical species with them into dry semi-deciduous forest. Farmers also exhibit adaptability: the ability to find medical value for recently introduced plants, such as *Chromolaena odorata* (*acheampong*) and *Digitaria ciliaris* (*limann*).

The contemporary use of medicinal plants reflects changes in the environment. This is also revealed in the use of plants in different localities. *Azadirachta indica* and *Cassia siamea* were frequently cited at Awoweso and Akrusu Saisi, where they were dominant, but hardly gained a mention at Odometa.

In the sample 24 per cent of farmers were unable to name any plants they

TABLE 5.6. Popular medicinal plants (% of farmers using)

Scientific name	Krobo name	Odometa	Awoweso Kpeti	Awoweso Adome	Awoweso Sisi	Akrusu Saisi	Total
Trees:							
Azadirachta indica [1]	Sabolatso	3.9	48.8	50.0	57.1	73.3	40.1
Cassia siamea [1]	Kasiatso	9.8	39.5	50.0	7.1	40.0	29.0
Alstonia boonei	Adawura	15.7	32.6	20.8	14.3	13.3	20.4
Parkia clappertoniana [2]	Dudue	3.9	14.0	33.3	42.9	13.3	16.0
Mangifera indica [4]	Mango	9.8	23.3	12.5	14.3	16.7	15.4
Newbouldia laevis	Nyabatso	5.9	18.6	29.2	0.0	6.7	12.3
Psidium guajava [4]	Guava	2.0	2.3	16.7	28.6	13.3	8.6
Carica papaya [4]	Gɔtso	2.0	18.6	4.2	7.1	3.3	7.4
Citrus aurantiifolia [4]	Kpetetso	2.0	7.0	12.5	7.1	13.3	7.4
Anacardium occidentale [4]	Atia	3.9	11.6	12.5	7.1	0.0	6.8
Anthocleista nobilis	Frakpa	2.0	4.7	12.5	21.4	3.3	6.2
Spathodea campanulata	Votso	2.0	4.7	4.2	7.1	3.3	3.7
Khaya grandifoliola	Mahogany/Dipɔgo	3.9	4.7	4.2	7.1	3.3	4.3
Baphia pubescens	Tutso	5.9	0.0	4.2	0.0	6.7	3.7
Elaeis guineensis	Ta	2.0	2.3	4.2	0.0	3.3	2.5
Cocos nucifera	Agɔlengmɛ	0.0	7.0	0.0	0.0	3.3	2.5
Trichilia monadelpha	Gbagblabata	0.0	2.3	0.0	0.0	10.0	2.5
Dialium guineense	Mieletso	0.0	0.0	0.0	0.0	13.3	2.5
Tamarindus indica [1]	Odompo	0.0	0.0	0.0	21.4	0.0	1.9
Spondias mombin [1]	Akole	0.0	0.0	0.0	7.1	6.7	1.9
Theobroma cacao [4]	Koko	0.0	7.0	0.0	0.0	0.0	1.9
Blighia sapida	Kingatso	0.0	4.7	0.0	0.0	3.3	1.9
Antiaris toxicaria	Hatso	0.0	2.3	0.0	0.0	3.3	1.2

TABLE 5.6 CONT. Popular medicinal plants (% of farmers using)

Scientific name	Krobo name	Odometa	Awoweso Kpeti	Awoweso Adome	Awoweso Sisi	Akrusu Saisi	Total
Cola gigantea var. glabrescens	Ovuga	2.0	0.0	4.2	0.0	0.0	1.2
Albizia adianthifolia	Papa	2.0	0.0	0.0	0.0	3.3	1.2
Cola nitida	Tsle	0.0	0.0	4.2	0.0	3.3	1.2
Anogeissus leiocarpus[2]	Sakane	0.0	0.0	0.0	7.1	3.3	1.2
Trichilia prieuriana	Okumnadue	0.0	0.0	0.0	0.0	3.3	0.6
Persea americana[4]	Paya	2.0	0.0	0.0	0.0	0.0	0.6
Acacia zygia	Papaku	0.0	0.0	0.0	0.0	3.3	0.6
Ficus exasperata	Slabatso	2.0	0.0	0.0	0.0	0.0	0.6
Pycnanthus angolensis	Otie	2.0	0.0	0.0	0.0	0.0	0.6
Kigelia africana	Lile	0.0	2.3	0.0	0.0	0.0	0.6
Thevetia peruviana[1]	Mɔkɔtso	0.0	0.0	4.2	0.0	0.0	0.6
Bombax buonopozense	Mangosiedu	0.0	0.0	4.2	0.0	0.0	0.6
Markhamia lutea	Mɔmɔtso	2.0	0.0	0.0	0.0	0.0	0.6
Citrus sinensis[4]	Akutu	2.0	0.0	0.0	0.0	0.0	0.6
Rouvoltia vomitoria	Apɔtạtɔo	2.0	0.0	0.0	0.0	0.0	0.6
Shrubs, herbaceous plants, food crops and grasses:							
Hoslundia opposita	Su	9.8	14.0	4.2	21.4	20.0	13.0
Jatropha curcas[1]	Kitibletso	9.8	4.7	12.5	21.4	13.3	10.5
Chromolaena odorata[1]	Acheampong	9.8	7.0	8.3	0.0	10.0	8.0
Cassia alata[1]	Sinɔgbetso	5.9	0.0	8.3	0.0	10.0	4.9
Mallotus oppositifolius	Satwetso	2.0	9.3	8.3	0.0	3.3	4.9
Securinega virosa	Nabutwe	2.0	4.7	0.0	0.0	13.3	4.3
Gossypium arboreum	Dote	2.0	2.3	8.3	7.1	3.3	3.7
Momordica charantia	Nyanyela	5.9	0.0	0.0	0.0	3.3	2.5

TABLE 5.6 CONT. Popular medicinal plants (% of farmers using)

Scientific name	Krobo name	Odometa	Awoweso Kpeti	Awoweso Adome	Awoweso Sisi	Akrusu Saisi	Total
Manihot esculenta[4]	Agbili	0.0	4.7	4.2	0.0	3.3	2.5
Paullinia pinnata	Aklokingkpa	2.0	2.3	0.0	0.0	6.7	2.5
Justicia flava	Mu	3.9	0.0	0.0	0.0	3.3	1.9
Oxytenanthera abyssinica[1]	Pamploo	0.0	2.3	0.0	14.3	0.0	1.9
Ananas comosus[4]	Blɛfota	0.0	0.0	0.0	0.0	10.0	1.9
Alternanthera pungens	Klagba	2.0	2.3	0.0	0.0	3.3	1.9
Sida acuta[1]	Tɔgɛtɔgɛ	0.0	0.0	0.0	0.0	6.7	1.2
Hyptis suaveolens	Kadoki	2.0	0.0	0.0	0.0	3.3	1.2
Solanum verbascifolium[1]	Agbafro	2.0	0.0	0.0	0.0	3.3	1.2
Strophanthus hispida	Tsukpangwa	0.0	0.0	0.0	7.1	3.3	1.2
Calliandra portoricensis	Dedemotue	0.0	2.3	0.0	0.0	3.3	1.2
Portulaca oleracea	Nleyu	2.0	0.0	0.0	0.0	3.3	1.2
Pergularia daemia	Managbemanagbe	0.0	2.3	0.0	0.0	3.3	1.2
Paspalum orbiculare	Otikpɔku	0.0	0.0	0.0	0.0	3.3	0.6
Digitaria ciliaris[3]	Limann	0.0	0.0	0.0	0.0	3.3	0.6
Costus afer	Tsɔne	2.0	0.0	0.0	0.0	0.0	0.6
Mucuna pruriens var. pruriens	Tsakatsaka	0.0	0.0	0.0	0.0	3.3	0.6
Panicum maximum[3]	Go	2.0	0.0	0.0	0.0	0.0	0.6
?	Busamanklo	0.0	2.3	0.0	0.0	0.0	0.6
Heliotropium indicum	Kungɔkulamle	0.0	2.3	0.0	0.0	0.0	0.6
Musa paradisiaca[4]	Madaa	0.0	2.3	0.0	0.0	0.0	0.6
Clausena anisata	Kpadebatso	2.0	0.0	0.0	0.0	0.0	0.6
Alchornea cordifolia	Boblo	0.0	2.3	0.0	0.0	0.0	0.6

TABLE 5.6 CONT. Popular medicinal plants (% of farmers using)

Scientific name	Krobo name	Odometa	Awoweso Kpeti	Awoweso Adome	Awoweso Sisi	Akrusu Saisi	Total
Xanthosoma mafaffa [4]	Amakani	0.0	0.0	4.2	0.0	0.0	0.6
Musa paradisiaca var. sapientum [4]	Kɔdu	0.0	2.3	0.0	0.0	0.0	0.6
Ricinus communis	Kumelo	0.0	2.3	0.0	0.0	0.0	0.6
Grewia carpinifolia	Akpekpa	0.0	0.0	0.0	0.0	3.3	0.6
Leea guineensis	Nisiensientso	0.0	0.0	4.2	0.0	0.0	0.6
Cyclosorus afer	Tahite	2.0	0.0	0.0	0.0	0.0	0.6
Lecaniodiscus cupanioides	Nyumukulakpade	0.0	2.3	0.0	0.0	0.0	0.6
Cassia occidentalis	Sinɔgbetsowayo	0.0	0.0	0.0	0.0	3.3	0.6
Ocimum canum	Danue	0.0	0.0	0.0	0.0	3.3	0.6
Spiropetalum heterophyllum	Kpangwa	0.0	0.0	0.0	0.0	3.3	0.6
Boerhavia diffusa	Ababu	0.0	0.0	0.0	0.0	3.3	0.6
Bryophyllum pinnatum	Gbɔ	2.0	0.0	0.0	0.0	0.0	0.6
Pupalia lappacea	Metemetebi	0.0	0.0	0.0	0.0	3.3	0.6
Vernonia amygdalina	Agbatso	2.0	0.0	0.0	0.0	0.0	0.6
Ocimum gratissimum	Kungaba	0.0	0.0	0.0	0.0	3.3	0.6
No. of farmers		51	43	24	14	30	162

1 = exotic species; 2 = trees associated with savanna orchard bush; 3 = savanna grasses; 4 = fruits and food crops of exotic origin.

used for medicinal purposes, 21 per cent named 1–2 species, 33 per cent 2–5, and 17 per cent over 5 species. Some farmers could name over 30 species which had medicinal value.

No effort was made to collect information on the specific ailments plants were used to cure, since this lies beyond the scope of the present work and may have led to reluctance of farmers to disclose medicinal herbs. Nevertheless, a wide range of ailments are treated – fevers, skin complaints and eruptions, stomach complaints, dysentery, haemorrhoids, anthelmintic ailments, cuts, bruises and sprains, backache, bone fractures, and snake and scorpion bites.

Out of the total sample of 178 farmers, five earned a supplementary income from selling herbal preparations. They felt they could gain a good income from selling medicines. One farmer estimated that he could earn over ₵2,000 on a market day from selling herbal preparations. He also sold some medicines to a private health clinic at Asesewa. He had once tried to interest a pharmaceutical firm in Accra in some of his treatments. They had started testing his preparations, but the encounter was a bitter experience. Once he had revealed the ingredients of his medical preparations, the firm lost all interest and refused to have any more dealings with him. Medical practitioners are suspicious of formal and commercial institutions, and feel vulnerable – that their preparations will be stolen from them without any acknowledgement or reward.

PLANT GENETIC RESOURCES AND INTELLECTUAL PROPERTY RIGHTS

While issues arising from the incorporation of TMPs into the formal health structure have been addressed by the state, intellectual property rights for TMPs are not being addressed. At the international level protection of the world's tropical forest is being seen as important in conserving genetic material, as is the 'indigenous knowledge' of forest peoples. Yet the main material benefit of this preservation accrues to large pharmaceutical companies and commercial firms, who may take out patents on knowledge about genetic materials which may have originated with rural communities.

The incorporation of the Declaration of Farmers' Rights into the April 1989 Third Session of the Commission on Plant Genetic Resources' International Undertaking, which recognizes the rights arising from 'the past, present and future contributions of farmers in conserving, improving and making available plant genetic resources particularly in the centres of origin/diversity', may be a step in the right direction. Annex 3 of the International Undertaking advocates the establishment of an international fund to support plant conservation. The Madras Plenary Session of the International Keystone Dialogue on Plant Genetic Resources recognizes that farmers have greatly contributed to the creation, conservation, exchange and knowledge of genetic and species utilization. It acknowledges that neither the market place nor current intellectual property systems have a way of assigning a value to this material. It advocates the setting up of an international fund along the lines suggested by the FAO:

> which supports genetic conservation and utilization programmes particularly, but not exclusively, in the Third World. The fund would not be designed to reward or compensate individual farmers, farm communities, Third World Centres, or governments, nor to compensate anyone or anything based strictly on their contribution to germplasm (Keystone International Dialogue 1990: 9).

While this recognizes the importance of folk knowledge to genetic resources, it does little to modify the inequality of international and national structures. It does not consider the implications of the commoditization of genetic resources and the environment for the knowledge systems of farming communities which have interacted with genetic resources throughout the centuries. If the promotion of research on the conservation of genetic resources does not protect the independence of popular knowledge systems from commodity markets or the process of commoditization, eventually these traditions will be eroded. If research in collaboration with local communities provides new knowledge which can be utilized by the commercial establishment, market forces dictate that these new products will eventually compete against the utilization of local folk knowledge within localities. If particular genetic resources are found to be commercially viable and communities are involved in their production for commodity markets, it is likely that the diversity of resource utilization will be replaced by a movement towards a monocrop economy. This will significantly alter the diversity of interactions between producers and the environment, the very foundation on which systems of genetic resource conservation and development are based. This is a fundamental problem arising from the process of commoditization (of which the patenting system and intellectual property rights are an extreme form) which has not been addressed. Much of the debate on genetic resources has been carried out in relation to agricultural crops. The emergence of agricultural crops and the potential of new crops result, however, from the totality of human interaction with the environment. Folk knowledge of the utilization of plants has also been appropriated by the pharmaceutical industry, with little acknowledgement of the role of rural communities in finding medicinal values.

The claim in favour of intellectual property rights for folk medicines is fraught with difficulties, since by definition the dissemination of popular knowledge occurs through informal channels, through the exchange of information on use values rather than high-commodity exchange values underpinned by a patent value. The concept of intellectual property rights, commoditizing environmental knowledge, may have a negative impact on the generation and dissemination of knowledge in local communities.

In the interests of conservation of the diversity of medicinal plants, an approach which focuses on strengthening the activities of folk medicine practitioners may be appropriate. Herbal medical practitioners would benefit from a support infrastructure which focuses on improving methods of preserving and packaging herbal preparations, and provides them with further training in medical knowledge. Some herbal medical practitioners in the Krobo area identified lack of containers and means of preserving treatments as major bottlenecks they experience. Approaches which focus on building local capabilities to process and manufacture medical applications, rather than on the provision of genetic material for screening by pharmaceutical companies and institutions, may benefit local communities, expand national pharmaceutical capacities, and in the long term promote more equitable international relations in the control and use of genetic resources.

Problems of drug abuse and quality control exist in relation to the activities of herbal medical practitioners. However, this does not only apply to the herbal medical sector. It also concerns the whole culture of drug dumping in developing countries. These questions need to be addressed through health education, rather than by limiting the field of operation of herbal practitioners. Since herbal medical practitioners are likely to remain the backbone of the health delivery system for many rural communities for years to come, an upgrading of their skills and approaches will be of benefit to the communities.

The conservation and utilization of genetic materials can be supported by strengthening forms of local folk economy. These are often rooted in diversification of resource utilization within localities, districts and regions. Perhaps this is an option which would be more appropriate than strengthening international research in genetic resource conservation for the eventual benefit of international commodity markets.

Foods and Beverages

CONDIMENTS AND SPICES

Common spices and condiments growing in the fallow include a variety of chilli peppers, *Xylopia aethiopica* (*so*), leaves of *Ocimum gratissimum* (*kungɔba*) and *Carissa edulis* (*akɔkɔbɛsa*), and the leaves and bark of *Cinnamomum zeylanicum* (cinnamon) used to flavour soups. The leaves of *Trichilia monadelpha* (*gbablabata*) may be added to cassava to impart a flavour akin to cocoyams (*Xanthosoma mafaffa*).

WILD FOODS

Wild foods do not play a prominent role in Krobo cuisine, although in crisis years, such as during the hunger of 1983, they can become significant. Important wild foods include several species of mushrooms, some reaching over three feet tall. These usually sprout during the lean season when food is most scarce and thus play a significant role in supplementing the diet. Leaves of *Talinum triangulare* (*nmlɔnmlɔ*), may be used as a leaf vegetable, when cocoyam leaves are not available. Green papaws (*gɔ*) may also be used in the dry season when tomatoes are scarce to make stews. The fruits of *Solanum torvum* (*sesrebɛ*) are cooked with palm soup to form a high protein meal which is reputed to be good for the blood. This is also called *alitsega*, 'lazy person's garden egg'. Honey is occasionally harvested from wild bee hives and sold on the market.

GAME

In the Krobo area fish and not meat is the main source of protein. The Krobo have never relied on hunting as the main source of meat, and for centuries they have depended on exchange of agricultural staple products with fishermen to gain their protein. Game thus forms a supplement to fish in the diet. There is no large-scale trade in game, as there is in some Akan forest communities.

In the survey, only 28 per cent of farmers claimed to have killed any game in the last year. This ranged from 62 per cent of the sample at Awoweso Sisi, 30 per cent at Odometa, 29 per cent at Awoweso Adome, 22 per cent at Akrusu Saisi and 17 per cent at Awoweso Kpeti. While more farmers killed game at Awoweso Sisi, this was related to one species, the grasscutter or cane rat, which favours the habitat of *Panicum maximum*. In terms of diversity of game killed, Awoweso Sisi fared worse than the other settlements, with five species of game caught as compared with six at Awoweso Kpeti, seven at Akrusu Saisi, nine at Awoweso Adome, and thirteen at Odometa. The largest number of game were also killed at Odometa, with one farmer claiming to have killed over 100 animals in the last year (mostly small rodents). Twenty-one per cent of farmers managed to kill grasscutters, 10 per cent royal antelope (*adowa*), 8 per cent western ground squirrel (*ajiri*), 5 per cent double-spurred francolin (*hehe*), 4 per cent Gambian giant rat (*jesi*), and 3 per cent African civet (*tɔ*). The emphasis is on small game since most large game has disappeared from the area. Rats (*jesi*) and the giant forest snail (*ahua*) are not eaten by the Krobo, and if caught are sold to Akan people. Snails are often gathered by children for sale.

Most farmers attributed the low levels of game killed to lack of guns and capital to buy guns. Fewer farmers now own guns than in the past and cartridges are considered very expensive. Increasing concern with problems of farm yields and weeding, and greater weariness from working on the food plots, may also account for less interest in hunting than in the past.

LIVESTOCK AND FODDER

Livestock forms an important sector of the Krobo farming economy, which has not developed its potential. Livestock is unanimously recognized by farmers as an important income-generating activity, which realizes capital for times of need, for paying hospital bills and children's school fees, for meeting extraordinary expenses, and providing meat.

The main livestock kept by farmers are goats, sheep and fowls. In addition two farmers kept pigs, and a few reared guinea fowls and ducks. At Akrusu Saisi there were two herds of cows. One of the cattle herders, who was interviewed in the survey, had eight cows. The number of goats reared by farmers in the sample was in the range 0–35, with a mean of 2.6. The number of sheep was in the range 0–11 with a mean of 1.5. Fowl numbered 0–75, with a mean of 12.7. Table 5.7 shows the frequency distribution of small livestock. A large number of farmers have no goats or sheep, and there are very few medium-sized or large flocks. Most farmers also have few fowls.

Factors which inhibit the expansion of livestock include the risk of the enterprise. Livestock are highly susceptible to disease in the area, and this makes a potentially profitable investment risky. This reflects the poor development of livestock extension in the area, and the lack of any coherent livestock policy towards small-scale farmers.

TABLE 5.7. Percentage of farmers owning goats, sheep and fowl

No. of animals	Goats	Sheep	Fowl
0	35.3%	50.6%	16.4%
1-5	50.0%	43.5%	41.3%
5-10	13.5%	5.3%	21.9%
Over 10	1.2%	0.6%	20.4%
No. of farmers	165	165	165

With the development of veterinary support services oriented towards small-scale farmers, livestock rearing has the potential to expand and be an important income-generating activity on smallholder farms with insufficient land. This is recognized by some smallholder farmers who are attempting to develop their goat and sheep resources. Most goat and sheep are tethered, however, or roam around the household freely. Very few farmers build livestock pens. Livestock are also reputed to destroy crops.

Table 5.8 shows the mean number of livestock owned by farmers in the

TABLE 5.8. Average numbers of livestock owned by farmers

Settlement	Goat		Sheep		Fowl		No. of farmers
	Mean	Std	Mean	Std	Mean	Std	
Odometa	2.2	(2.86)	1.2	(1.80)	10.0	(12.62)	67
Awoweso Kpeti	1.8	(2.13)	0.95	(1.27)	4.9	(4.97)	43
Awoweso Adome	3.8	(3.00)	1.4	(1.79)	10.12	(13.5)	24
Awoweso Sisi	5.0	(9.2)	2.3	(2.56)	5.23	(5.79)	13
Akrusu Saisi	2.4	(15.25)	2.7	(3.3)	13.4	(20.81)	23
Total	2.6	(3.8)	1.5	(2.04)	8.8	(12.67)	170

different localities. Although there are considerable differences in the range and distribution of livestock in the different settlements, these figures suggest that goat and sheep rearing may be more important in the more degraded, grassy settlements, with highest means recorded for Awoweso Sisi and Akrusu Saisi. Farmers are also beginning to respond to degradation at Akrusu Saisi by investing in cows – an attempt to adapt to and gain economic advantage from the transformation of the vegetation into *Panicum maximum* grassland, and to diversify economic activities away from a total reliance on food crops. Despite the lack of development of livestock resources, small livestock are becoming more important in the farming system as land becomes scarcer and yields from food crops less reliable. In a survey of Awoweso, La Anyane (1956) found only five of 21 farmers kept sheep (the mean number of sheep was 0.6) and no farmers reared goats.

At Odometa Apirede, where land is particularly scarce, farmers are increasingly focusing on building their livestock resources, to the extent that other farmers are bringing them their livestock to tend, since they are considered to have established some expertise in animal rearing. Under these contracts the offspring of livestock are shared equally between the rearer and the owner. Such contracts are common for all livestock, including fowl. When farmers begin to build up numbers of animals, they usually hire them out to relatives and friends, to minimize mortalities in the eventuality of infectious disease. From the 1920s to the 1960s professional stockmen were common in Upper Manya Krobo. They originated from northern Ghana, Niger and Burkina Faso, and supplemented farm labouring and *abusa* tenancies with livestock rearing. With the decline of the rural economy, many have moved from the area. Farmers at Apirede are building on knowledge they have acquired from these migrant stockmen.

TABLE 5.9. Browse and fodder species utilized by farmers (% of farmers)

Scientific name	Krobo name	Odometa	Awoweso Kpeti	Awoweso Adome	Awoweso Sisi	Akrusu Saisi	Total
Panicum maximum[3]	Go	19.6	34.9	79.2	85.7	73.3	50.6
Griffonia simplicifolia[2]	Totolimo	23.5	69.8	79.2	71.4	–	43.8
Ficus exasperata[1]	Slabatso	60.8	32.6	29.2	–	10.0	35.2
Albizia adianthifolia[1]	Papa	27.5	9.3	16.7	7.1	–	14.8
Antiaris toxicaria[1]	Hatso	7.8	20.9	25.0	7.1	3.3	13.0
Manihot esculenta[4]	Agbili	23.5	9.3	8.3	–	6.7	12.3
Baphia pubescens[1]	Tutso	21.6	7.0	4.2	–	3.3	11.1
Trichilia monadelpha[1]	Gbagblabata	2.0	20.9	25.0	–	3.3	10.5
Newbouldia laevis[1]	Nyabatso	7.8	18.6	16.7	–	–	9.9
Hypselodelphis violacea[2]	Bebɛdua	17.6	7.0	12.5	–	–	9.3
Elaeis guineensis[1]	Kikle	11.8	4.7	–	–	–	6.2
Leucaena leucocephala (glauca)[5]	Tɛboni	–	7.0	20.8	–	–	4.9
Musa paradisiaca[4]	Madaa	7.8	–	–	–	–	2.5
Securinega virosa[2]	Nabutwe	–	–	–	–	10.0	1.9
Combretum combretaceae[2]	Laga	2.0	–	–	–	6.7	1.9
Synedrella nodiflora[2]	Nmlɔnmlɔ	–	2.3	–	7.1	3.3	1.9
Musa paradisiaca var. sapientum[4]	Kɔdu	5.9	–	–	–	–	1.9
Mallotus oppositifolius[2]	Satwetso	–	2.3	–	–	–	1.2
Paullinia pinnata[2]	Aklokingakpa	–	–	4.2	–	3.3	1.2
Dialium guineense[2]	Miɛletso	2.0	–	–	–	3.3	1.2
Digitaria ciliaris[3]	Limann	–	–	–	–	6.7	1.2
?[1]	Otikpɔku	–	2.3	–	–	–	0.6
Oxytenanthera abyssinica[5]	Pamploo	–	–	–	–	3.3	0.6
Grewia carpinifolia[2]	Akpekpa	–	–	–	–	3.3	0.6

TABLE 5.9 CONT. Browse and fodder species utilized by farmers (% of farmers)

Scientific name	Krobo name	Odometa	Awoweso Kpeti	Awoweso Adome	Awoweso Sisi	Akrusu Saisi	Total
Holarrhena floribunda [1]	Osese	2.0	–	–	–	–	0.6
Albizia zygia [1]	Papaku	2.0	–	–	–	–	0.6
Xanthosoma mafaffa [4]	Amakani	2.0	–	–	–	–	0.6
Cassia siamea [5]	Kasiatso	2.0	–	–	–	–	0.6
Alchornea cordifolia [2]	Boblo	–	2.3	–	–	–	0.6
Diospyros canaliculata [1]	Tetso	–	2.3	–	–	–	0.6
Psidium guajava [4]	Agowa	–	2.3	–	–	–	0.6
No. of farmers		51	43	24	30	14	162

1 = forest tree; 2 = forest shrub or herb; 3 = savanna grass; 4 = food crop or fruit; 5 = exotic tree or shrub.

Small livestock are usually fed on household wastes (cassava, plantain, and other tuber peels), browse and fodder plants. Fodder is cut from trees branches, shrubs and grass, bundled and taken back to the compound for livestock to feed on. Livestock are also taken out to graze on patches of browse. Table 5.9 shows the main browse and fodder plants utilized in the various sample localities. A total of 31 browse and fodder species were mentioned by farmers. *Centrosema pubescens* is also used as fodder but was not mentioned in the survey, perhaps because most farmers do not have a name for it. The most common fodder plants included the grass *Panicum maximum* (*go*), the shrub *Griffonia simplicifolia* (*totolimo*), and the tree *Ficus exasperata* (*slabatso*). Other important fodder crops include *Albizia adianthifolia* and *A. zygia* (*papa* and *papaku*), *Antiaris toxicaria* (*hatso*), cassava leaves (*agbili*), *Baphia pubescens* (*tutso*), *Trichilia monadelpha* (*gbagblabata*), *Newbouldia laevis* (*nyabatso*), *Hypselodelphis violacea* (*bebedua*) and oil palm fronds (*kikle*). Differences in the uses of these fodder plants between settlements reflect changes in environment. Grassy species (*Panicum maximum*) were more important in the more degraded settlements, and trees such as *Ficus exasperata* and *Baphia pubescens* and forest shrubs such as *Hypselodelphis violacea* assumed greater importance at Odometa. At Awoweso Adome *Leucaena leucocephala* (*glauca*) was also an important fodder plant.

Fodder shrub and tree species are generally higher in protein, phosphorous and vitamin A (McGinnies *et al.*, 1971), and grass species are superior in calorific content. Little research, however, has being carried out into the variety of fodder species used by farmers. Some of the species used may be richer fodder plants than others, and a variety of species may complement each other. Further research is needed into the quality of the species combinations which farmers use, and into the seasonal flushes of different varieties. Research into various species used by farmers in different localities may yield a database of various prime fodder species (not all of which may be utilized within the environments in which they grow) and various optimal combinations which can further the development of animal weights and dry season grazing. However, a large number of farmers probably use the optimal fodder species occurring in their locality, when considerations of plant availability are taken into account.

The diversity of fodder species is a valuable cultural resource which deserves to be strengthened and incorporated into small livestock programmes, as a means of fostering self-reliant development of livestock subsystems among farming communities. Preserving diversity of fodder and browse may be a better strategy than planting monocrop browse species, or promoting the use of feed concentrates.

ALCOHOL

The main source of alcohol is palm wine, processed from the toddy of the oil palm. The palm is felled and the palm rachis cut away. A rectangular slit is cut in the palm cabbage below the growing point and heated on a daily basis to encourage the fermentation of the tree sap. A thin hollow reed of *Clerodendrum capitatum* (*tabetso*) or *Olyra latifolia* (*adodobegye*) is inserted into the slot and the fermented toddy drips down into a pot or gourd under the felled tree. A thin slice is cut from the cabbage each day to maintain the cleanliness of the cut and prevent spread of infection. The collection of palm wine lasts from three to six weeks depending on the weather. The palm wine is rarely produced as an alcoholic beverage nowadays, since it can keep for only a day or two before it turns into vinegar. It is usually distilled on-farm to produce *akpeteshie* spirit.

Distillation of palm wine for the commercial market has developed as a response to the difficulties of producing palm oil competitively, and enables farmers to gain an income from the rearing of their favourite tree. The distillation of palm wine is now the most important product from the oil palm. Krobo farmers have built up considerable skills in both the tapping and distillation of palm wine. Asesewa is a major centre of *akpeteshie* production in Ghana. This industry generates the area's second most important source of revenue after maize. In recent years, with increasingly unreliable yields of maize, *akpeteshie* may have become the most important stable source of income in localities where the oil palm thrives.

In the major *akpeteshie*-producing settlements the scale of operations is relatively large: frequently more than one hundred trees on one farm are felled. Farmers do not usually produce their own palm wine and spirit but hire specialized palm-wine tappers (*tapotse*), who undertake the work with a number of skilled labourers. Alternatively, professional tappers purchase palm trees from farmers. The production of the alcohol requires a considerable array of equipment, including a still and many different types of containers and oil drums. This lies beyond the means of most farmers, resulting in the emergence of specialized tappers with sufficient capital to either buy or hire the equipment. During the slack season, from November to February, palm wine tapping reaches its peak. It is an important off-farm source of income, particularly for farmers with little land.

Felling a hundred palm trees for distillation can yield three to six barrels of *akpeteshie*, depending on weather conditions. Since each barrel sold at ₵50,000 in 1992, this yielded the equivalent of between 13 bags of maize per barrel at low harvest-season prices and five bags at high lean-season maize prices. From this the owner of the trees would receive 1.5–3 barrels from the total proceeds, the equivalent of 15–38 bags of maize. However, a large number of trees cannot be tapped on one piece of land each year without destroying the oil palm population. Thus felling of palm trees and distilling of palm wine is an activity usually reserved for raising a large amount of capital rapidly.

The felling of palm trees for palm wine is not as wasteful as is often assumed. Trees are usually felled when replacement saplings are beginning to mature, and when picking the fruits of old palm trees involves considerable labour in climbing the tall trees. Attempts to save oil palm fruits by tapping standing trees often leads to a reduction in palm fruit yields, and does not solve the problem of harvesting tall old trees, often past their peak bearing age. Felling of old trees may be a highly rational activity which maximizes capital, minimizes labour, and enables a maximization of turnover of oil palm trees and total palm products. The felling of trees is also necessary to produce lower densities which will enable food crops to be cultivated in association with oil palms.

Table 5.10 shows the number of palm trees farmers estimated they had felled for *akpeteshie* distillation in the last three years. The typical number of trees felled was 50–100. There are significant differences in the number of palm trees felled in the five localities. As degradation increases, oil palms fail to thrive. In recent years farmers at Awoweso and Akrusu Saisi have experienced difficulty in growing oil palms. At Odometa 32 per cent of farmers did not fell any palm trees in the last three years. At Akrusu Saisi this figure rose to 87 per cent, and at Awoweso Sisi, the most 'grassy' settlement, no farmers had felled any oil palms in this period. At Odometa 56 per cent of farmers had felled 50–199 trees, compared with 28 per cent at Awoweso Kpeti, 15 per cent at Awoweso Adome and 13 per cent at Akrusu Saisi. Failure of oil palm trees to mature and a loss of considerable income from the potential to tap palm wine is one of the effects of environmental degradation which most concerns farmers.

The distillation of *akpeteshie* by farmers is an important industry in Ghana, generating considerable revenue. Yet this industry has received minimum support from the state and research and development agencies. While there have been unsuccessful attempts to license tapping, no attempts have been

Table 5.10. Percentage of farmers felling palm trees in the last three years

No of palm trees felled	Odometa	Awoweso Kpeti	Awoweso Adome	Awoweso Sisi	Akrusu Saisi	Total
0	32.4	50.0	75.0	100.0	86.7	57.9
1–49	13.5	21.9	5.0	–	–	11.4
50–99	24.3	28.1	10.0	–	13.3	19.3
100–199	21.6	–	5.0	–	–	7.9
Over 199	8.1	–	5.0	–	–	3.5
No. of farmers	37	32	20	10	15	114

made to provide an alcoholic distilling infrastructure of equipment and training for farmers. The equipment used by palm tappers is often rough and ready, an improvised collection of odd containers, copper and reed tubes, and various building materials. Knives specifically for tapping are fashioned by blacksmiths from old cutlasses. The ways in which palm-wine tappers have assembled their equipment and mastered the distilling art exhibit their ingenuity.

In addition to the consumption of pure *akpeteshie*, the alcohol is often blended with roots and barks of various trees to create bitters. Perhaps the most reputed bitters is that made from mahogany, which is reported to be a blood tonic, aphrodisiac, stomachic and treatment for malaria. There is great potential to further develop and refine the oil palm distilling industry. All the wild fruits, herbs, condiments, bark and other flavours of the fallow bush provide a wide assortment of resources which can be used to create new and exciting alcoholic drinks.

COOKING OILS AND VEGETABLE FATS

The oil palm (*Elaeis guineensis*) is the main source of cooking oil, which yields both palm and kernel oil. Oil palms fruit twice in the year, between March and June and from November to December. Palm oil is produced by boiling the fruits in water, pounding the nuts in a pestle and mortar, and then boiling the pounded pericarp in water until the oil separates and is strained off. The methods used in the Krobo area are simple, laborious and time-consuming as compared with the array of large-scale and intermediate machinery used in the new palm belt (Gyasi, 1992). Kernel oil is produced by cracking the kernel husks with stones and then frying the kernels until oil is extracted. The flesh of the pericarp is also boiled to provide palm nut soup (*ywie honyu*). While palm oil production used to be the main economic activity of the Krobo area, palm oil is now largely produced for home consumption. Nevertheless palm oil occupies a central place in the Krobo diet. The decline of oil palm trees in the more degraded settlements has had a profound effect on the Krobo diet and many farmers at Awoweso and Akrusu Saisi bemoan the loss of palm nut soup.

Table 5.11 shows the numerical distribution of oil palms throughout the different localities. The greater preponderance of oil palms at Odometa is revealed, as is the declining number of trees as one moves towards the Volta Lake. The figures do not reflect, however, the extent of the decline of the oil palm in more degraded settlements. While only mature trees of fruit-bearing age are being counted as oil palms at Odometa, small saplings which frequently fail to mature are being included at Awoweso and Akrusu. The decline of the oil palm in the more degraded settlements is more accurately reflected by figures on the numbers of trees felled for palm wine tapping

TABLE 5.11. Farmer estimates of number of oil palms on their farms (% of farmers)

No of palm trees	Odometa	Awoweso Kpeti	Awoweso Adome	Awoweso Sisi	Akrusu Saisi	Total
0	–	–	–	–	33.3	4.2
1–10	–	9.4	5.0	40.0	26.7	10.2
11–20	2.4	–	5.0	10.0	13.3	4.2
21–50	22.0	28.1	30.0	10.0	3.3	22.9
51–150	51.2	59.4	45.0	40.0	6.7	45.8
Over 150	24.4	3.1	15.0	–	6.7	12.7
No. of farmers	42	32	20	10	15	118

(Table 5.10). This reckoning of saplings as trees reflects the importance of the oil palm to the Krobo, and the fact that farmers in the more degraded settlements continue to attempt to grow and tend oil palms despite their failure to mature. A more accurate assessment of the impact of degradation on the production of oil palms would have measured the number of oil palms of fruit-bearing age or the number of fruit bunches harvested in the preceding year.

Table 5.12 shows the number of farmers marketing palm nuts and palm oil in 1990–1. This illustrates the decline in market sale of palm fruits and oil. Less than 10 per cent of farmers sold palm oil and only 13 per cent sold palm nuts. Kernel oil is rarely sold by farmers. Often the kernels are heaped up in a corner of the compound, waiting for anyone with the time to process them. Traditionally, the processing of kernel oil was the preserve of the old women.

During the 1950s a number of Department of Agriculture surveys were carried out into the Krobo oil palm industries. These revealed an average density of 102 trees per acre in the Asesewa area (Gold Coast Department of

TABLE 5.12. Percentage of farmers selling oil palm fruit products in 1990–1

Product marketed	Odometa	Awoweso Kpeti	Awoweso Adome	Awoweso Sisi	Akrusu Saisi	Total
Palm fruits	23.4	7.0	16.7	–	–	13.1
Palm oil	17.2	4.7	16.7	–	–	10.1
Kernel oil	–	2.3	–	–	–	0.6
No. of farmers	64	43	24	14	23	168

Agriculture, 1952), 89 trees per acre in Akrusu (La Anyane, 1954) and 68 in Awoweso Kpeti (La Anyane, 1956). Since then densities of oil palms have declined considerably within Akrusu and Awoweso. In 1955 La Anyane recorded that one farmer produced six drums of palm oil worth £54 and that between eight and 15 women were engaged in production at a time (La Anyane, 1956). Palm oil production is now confined to households, usually involving two to three people. The total amount produced in one harvest season would not reach a drum on most farms at Odometa.

FRUITS

Fruit trees are important in the farming system of the Krobo. They constitute a source of income without involving high annual labour expenditures. Fruit trees form a supplement to food crops rather than the major farm activity. They are not usually grown as a plantation or orchard crop but are integrated into the farm and fallow or grown around the household compound. They form an important supplement to food crops rather than the major farm activity. They provide a significant source of income without taking up much space. In the past, export fruit crops (oil palm and cocoa) have been the most important crops defining the farming system. The Krobo farmers have considerable experience in integrating trees into a bush-fallowing system, although their technique of management has been disrupted by the decline of the frontier and increasing land shortage. Trees are occasionally weeded around their roots and tended when young.

Fruit trees grown in the survey localities are shown in Table 5.13. In addition other cultivated fruit trees include *Spondias mombin* (*akole*), and *Tamarindus indica* (*odompo*). A number of wild forest trees are also exploited for their fruits including *Dialium guineense* (*mieletso*), *Blighia sapida* (*kingatso*), *Vitex doniana* (*punyu*), *Napoleonaea vogelii* (*kpakutso*), *Carpolobia lutea* (*opiongo*) and *Synsepalum dulcificum* (*atamami*). These plants are sometimes deliberately cultivated and tended. *Dialium guineense*, *Blighia sapida*, and *Vitex doniana* are occasionally sold on the market.

A large number of cultivated fruit trees are not mainstream commercial fruits. They are of peripheral and exotic value and include *Parkia clappertoniana* (West African locust bean or *dudue*), custard apple (*habuɛ*), papaw (*gɔtso*), sour sop (*alugutugu*), guava (*agowa*), star apple (*latsa*) and miraculous berry (*atamami*). Commercial fruit trees are mainly of foreign origin and indigenous fruit crops of minor commercial importance. In recent years, however, growing interest has developed in local minor fruit, and the Kade Agricultural Research Station is now producing *Synsepalum dulcificum* seedlings.

Differences in the fruits cultivated in the localities reflect environmental degradation. The patterns of cultivation at Odometa reflect a more

TABLE 5.13. Percentage of farmers cultivating species of fruit trees

Scientific name	Krobo name	Odometa	Awoweso Kpeti	Awoweso Adome	Awoweso Sisi	Akrusu Saisi	Total
Mangifera indica (Mango)	Mango	92.7	100	100	80	86.7	94.1
Annona reticulata (Custard apple)	Habuɛ	53.7	71.9	85	80	80	69.5
Musa paradisiaca var. sapientum (Banana)	Kɔdu	63.4	60.6	53	40	6.7	53.4
Parkia clappertoniana (Indian tamarind)	Dudue	34.1	65.6	60	100	40	53.4
Carica papaya (Papaw)	Gɔ	48.8	40.6	55	40	73.3	50.0
Musa paradisiaca (Plantain)	Madaa	85.5	31.3	40	40	20	49.2
Psidium guajava (Guava)	Agowa	43.9	56.3	70	10	33.3	47.5
Citrus species (Citrus)	Akutu	80.5	18.8	20	0	0	36.4
Cocos nucifera (Coconut)	Agɔlenmɛ	58.5	25	30	10	6.7	33.9

TABLE 5.13 CONT. Percentage of farmers cultivating species of fruit trees

Scientific name	Krobo name	Odometa	Awoweso Kpeti	Awoweso Adome	Awoweso Sisi	Akrusu Saisi	Total
Anacardium occidentale (Cashew nut)	Atia	31.7	25	45	10	0	26.3
Annona muricata (Sour sop)	Alugutugu	19.5	21.9	50	10	20	24.6
Persea americana (Avocado)	Paya	44.7	0	10	0	6.7	17.4
Synsepalum dulcificum (Miraculous berry)	Atamami	9.8	18.8	20	10	6.7	13.6
Theobroma cacao (Cocoa)	Koko	26.8	6.3	5	0	0	11.9
Cola nitida (Cola)	Tsle	12.0	6.3	5.3	0	0	6.7
Chrysophyllum albidum (Star apple)	Latsa	14.6	0	5	0	0	5.9
Artocarpus incisa (Breadnut)	Blefo akate	7.3	3.1	0	0	0	3.4
No. of farmers		41	32	20	10	15	118

favourable commercial status of fruit trees, with citrus, plantain, avocado, mango and coconut forming the main grown and marketed fruits. Avocado, however, has difficulty in surviving at Odometa as a result of less reliable rainfall and longer dry seasons. At Awoweso and Akrusu Saisi increasing desiccation results in the failure of orange, avocado, cola and plantain to survive and bear fruits. The loss of fruit trees, particularly citrus, is keenly felt by the farmers in these settlements, and they continually attempt to grow them without much success. In the case of citrus varieties, failure is also a reflection of management techniques. Most farmers plant commercial orange varieties from seeds, rather than grafting them onto root stocks of drought-resistant rough lemon varieties. While they are able to survive in the wetter settlements, in the forest border areas they are highly susceptible to water stress. At Odometa oranges are now giving poor yields. In drier areas mango and custard apple (popular on the Accra market) are the main market-oriented fruit crops. Custard apple has been developed by farmers at Awoweso Adome as a market crop.

The outlets for Krobo fruits lie in the south-eastern regional and urban markets. Marketing of fruits constitutes a problem for farmers. Marketing outlets for oranges and mangoes are generally well organized, with traders prepared to purchase from farms. Some orange traders make arrangements to pick the fruits themselves from the farmers' trees. In the case of mangoes, lorries ply feeder routes and drop off wooden crates at the farm gate to be filled with mangoes by farmers for later carriage.

Farmers feel that the prices they are offered are poor. The high perishability of fruit prevents them holding out for better prices. At Odometa the district assembly representative was thinking of organizing a citrus growers' association. He was interested in starting a small craft-based juice bottling plant and the production of preserves as means of getting better prices.

Marketing outlets and prices for minor fruit products such as custard apple and *Parkia clappertoniana* are even more of a problem. *Dialium guineense*, *Vitex doniana* and *Blighia sapida* lie on the fringe of commercial viability. Despite official interest in *Synsepalum dulcificum* from government agencies, no market outlets exist for this crop. One farmer narrated how he had decided to cultivate *Synsepalum dulcificum* following a visit from staff and students of the University of Ghana who were interested in promoting its cultivation. There had been no subsequent follow-up to this visit and he had found no market for the fruit. Surprisingly, coffee suffers a similar fate. While it is being promoted by the Cocoa Marketing Board as part of an attempt to diversify export crops, farmers were not well informed of marketing outlets. Only one farmer was found to grow coffee in the survey, and she had a basket of coffee beans which she did not know what to do with. She had started cutting her coffee trees for firewood, since she felt it was a useless product. Cashew nuts are also being encouraged by government agricultural services. Despite the fact they are being widely cultivated by farmers, no market outlets exist in the Krobo area for the nuts. The trees are mainly cultivated for their fruits, which are consumed by the household rather than sold at market.

Marketing outlets for fruits are largely the result of the initiative of private traders. Although the state is now interested in developing the export of a variety of fruits as part of the expansion of non-traditional exports, it has left the development of this sector to private traders. The provision of services and training in the management of fruit trees for farmers is very poorly developed. The Agroforestry Department and the extension service have focused on providing seedlings to farmers rather than training them in the production and maintenance of fruit trees.

The state has largely oriented itself towards the marketing of cocoa in forest areas, even in areas where cocoa has been devastated. Local traders have played the dominant role in developing the infrastructure for a domestic-based urban market for fruits. They tend to take advantage of the poor marketing infrastructure and high perishability of fruit to gain a market monopoly. The poor transport infrastructure and lack of development of storage facilities may also result in high costs from losses of perishable fruit for traders.

Table 5.14 shows the percentage of farmers selling fruit in the 1990 farming year in various localities. Although 1990 was a bad year in which many fruits failed to thrive as a result of lack of rain, the number of fruits marketed compares very unfavourably with the extent of cultivation of fruit trees. Farmers at Awoweso Sisi and Akrusu Saisi failed to sell any fruit on the market.

Farmers tend to cultivate a variety of fruit, many of which do not have a market. Fruits are often grown for intellectual curiosity and for household use. They form an important part of the diet of children. This intellectual curiosity is exemplified by *Synsepalum dulcificum*. This fruit has hardly any flesh, but is extremely sweet owing to a glycoprotein it contains. After consuming a few berries all subsequent foods ingested taste exceptionally sweet, including such things as a sour lemon. Eating this berry constitutes a gastronomic game, particularly for children who then go on to consume all manner of foods and fruits to experience the change in flavour. As well as its curiosity value, it has potential commercial value as a sweetener (Abbiw, 1990; Enti, 1979).

Even with commercial exotic fruits, farmers' interest in diversity is apparent. Seven different varieties of citrus fruit were cultivated, including sweet orange, tangerine, jerusalem, mandarin, satsuma, lemon and grapefruit. Fruits such as grapefruit have a very limited market demand.

TABLE 5.14. Percentage of farmers selling fruits in 1990–1

Common name	Krobo name	Odometa	Awoweso Kpeti	Awoweso Adome	Awoweso Sisi	Akrusu Saisi	Total
Mango	Mango	32.8	55.8	70.8	–	–	2.4
Citrus	Akutu	29.7	–	–	–	–	11.3
Plantain	Amadaa	14.0	–	–	–	–	5.4
Custard apple	Habuɛ	4.8	–	25.0	–	–	4.8
Coconut	Agolengmɛ	4.7	–	4.2	–	–	2.4
Banana	Kɔdu	6.3	–	–	–	–	2.4
Cocoa	Koko	4.7	–	–	–	–	1.8
Locust bean	Dudue	1.6	–	4.7	–	–	1.8
Avocado	Paya	3.1	–	–	–	–	1.2
Cola	Tsle	1.6	–	–	–	–	0.6
Papaw	Gɔ	1.6	–	–	–	–	0.6
No. of farmers		c 64	43	24	14	23	168

Table 5.15 shows the numerical distribution of fruit trees cultivated by farmers. Few farmers cultivate large numbers of single fruit species. This suggests that farmers tend to diversify among fruits rather than focus on

TABLE 5.15. Numbers of fruit trees cultivated by farmers

Fruit	Farmers cultivating different numbers of trees (as % of farmers cultivating the fruit)			No. of farmers cultivating fruit
	1–10 trees	11–20 trees	over 20 trees	
Mango	76.6	13.5	9.9	111
Citrus	81.4	11.6	7.0	43
Plantain	51.7	8.6	39.7	58
Banana	66.7	9.5	23.8	63
Custard apple	74.5	13.4	12.1	82
Coconut	95.0	5.0	–	40
Avocado	85.0	10.0	5.0	20
Cocoa	71.4	7.2	21.4	14
Papaw	89.8	3.4	6.9	59
Locust bean	96.8	1.6	1.6	63
Guava	96.4	3.6	–	56
Sour sop	100	–	–	29
Cola	100	–	–	8
Cashew	100	–	–	31
Miraculous berry	100	–	–	16
Star apple	100	–	–	7
Breadnut	100	–	–	4

monocultural cultivation of fruits with maximum commercial potential. While this may not augur well from a commercial viewpoint, it shows a potential to build on ecological diversity.

FOOD CROPS

The range of food crops grown and the yield patterns reflect adaptations to a changing environment. Table 5.16 shows the range of food crops cultivated by farmers in the survey localities. Thirteen different food crops were grown. In the Krobo area there have been considerable changes in patterns of crops grown over the last 100 years, which have been described in previous chapters. Maize and cassava remain important staple crops. In recent years there has been a transformation of cropping systems. Plantain and cocoyam have declined as they fail to grow or provide good yields. Yams are also in decline, although a large number still cultivate them. Some species of white and yellow yams (*bale* and *kane*) are hardly grown now. The main yam cultivated is wateryam (*alamoa*). Early maturing cassava varieties are now replacing long-duration varieties. Farmers largely cultivate local cultivars and have not become dependent upon modern varieties.

The most significant recent introduction is cowpea. This crop has spread rapidly in the last eight years as migrant Ada and Ewe fishermen from savanna areas have moved into the vicinity of the Volta Lake and started cultivating the surrounding land. The adaptation of this crop is a response to increasing

TABLE 5.16. Percentage of farmers growing particular food crops

Scientific name	Krobo name	Odometa	Awoweso Kpeti	Awoweso Adome	Awoweso Sisi	Akrusu Saisi	Total
Maize	Blɛfo	100.0	100.0	95.8	92.9	82.6	96.5
Cassava	Agbili	100.0	100.0	95.8	92.9	91.3	97.6
Yams	Hyiɛ	67.2	88.1	91.7	85.7	52.2	75.3
Cowpea	Yɔ	38.8	69.0	91.7	92.9	47.8	59.4
Cocoyam	Amakani	61.2	69.0	29.2	–	–	45.3
Pepper	Kwadaa	17.9	14.3	29.2	28.6	47.8	23.5
Sweet potato[1]	Anago	–	–	4.2	7.1	69.6	10.6
Tomato	Tomatosi	7.5	4.8	8.3	7.1	52.2	12.9
Eggplant	Ga	17.6	–	–	7.1	4.3	5.8
Okro	Muɔmi	3.0	2.4	–	14.3	13.0	4.7
Plantain	Amadaa	6.0	2.4	4.3	–	–	3.6
Lima bean/ butter bean	Akɔtrɔmɔ	–	2.4	8.3	–	–	1.8
Groundnut	Akate	–	–	–	–	4.3	0.6
No. of farmers		67	42	24	14	23	170

1. All sweet potato is produced on the Volta lakeshore. Farmers at other localities producing sweet potato are also farming at Akrusu Saisi.

desiccation, the search for a minor crop which will survive declining rainfall in the minor season. It is replacing maize as the main minor season crop. It is also a response to declining soil fertility, since the crop is a legume. It also has a good market price. Cowpea has largely replaced lima bean (*Akɔtrɔmɔ*) as a pulse eaten in soups, since it grows quicker and yields better.

Sweet potato has recently become important at Akrusu Saisi and in other settlements along the Volta Lake. The crop is grown on the lakeshore with tomato and cassava, using floodwater retreat techniques. Farmers utilize the rise and fall of the lake to gain the maximum benefit from the moisture of the soils on the banks. When the lake begins to recede in October tomato is planted, followed by cassava and sweet potato lower down the banks. The sweet potato is harvested before April, when the water begins to rise. The cassava is harvested by June, when the water rises to its location.

There are other notable changes in cropping systems in the more degraded environments. Tomato and pepper are more important at Awoweso Sisi and Akrusu Saisi. In the past vegetables have been important cash crops for women. In the more degraded settlements they are increasingly featuring in male cropping systems. While only 2 per cent of males at Odometa cultivate tomatoes as compared to 18 per cent of women, 50 per cent of males at Akrusu Saisi and 57 per cent of females cultivate this crop. Nine per cent of males and 36 per cent of females at Odometa grow pepper as compared to 36 per cent males and 71 per cent of females at Akrusu Saisi. Garden egg is another cash crop which has featured in women's farm plots, but its cultivation is declining as a result of diminishing soil fertility and poor yields without the use of chemical inputs.

As forest-based crops (plantain and cocoyam) suffer increasingly from the degradation of the forest-fallow environment, cropping strategies have tended to diversify in recent years, and have incorporated crops and techniques borrowed from the neighbouring savanna areas.

The ability to incorporate new cash crops into cropping systems and to adapt cropping systems to environmental conditions is also determined by market outlets for particular crops.

Table 5.17 records the crops which farmers marketed in the 1990–1 season. There are significant differences in marketing patterns between the settlements, reflecting environmental change and degradation. Percentages of farmers marketing maize and cassava decline in relation to increasing environmental degradation and savannization. Cocoyam production for the market is limited to Odometa, where only 20 per cent of farmers now have surplus cocoyam for sale. Yams, an important crop from the 1930s to 1950s, is now only produced in small quantities to add occasional variety to domestic consumption.

At Akrusu Saisi, a different cash crop economy is coming into being in

TABLE 5.17. Percentage of farmers selling various crops in 1990–1

Scientific name	Krobo name	Odometa name	Awoweso Kpeti	Awoweso Adome	Awoweso Sisi	Akrusu Saisi	Total
Maize	Blefo	85.9	69.8	70.8	64.3	30.4	70.2
Cowpea	Yɔɔ	25.0	62.8	87.5	85.7	26.1	48.2
Cassava	Agbili	51.6	18.6	33.3	28.6	26.1	35.1
Palm nut	Ywie	23.4	7.0	16.7	–	–	13.1
Palm oil	Nutsu	23.4	7.0	16.7	–	–	10.1
Pepper	Kwadaa	15.6	7.0	8.3	7.1	21.7	12.5
Tomato	Tomatosi	10.9	–	–	7.1	43.5	10.7
Sweet potato[1]	Anago	–	–	4.2	–	78.3	11.4
Charcoal	Ha	–	18.6	16.7	14.3	21.7	11.3
Firewood	Lɛ	1.6	14.0	25.0	–	17.4	10.1
Cocoyams	Amakani	20.3	–	–	–	–	7.7
Egg plant	Ga	10.9	–	–	–	4.3	4.8
Okro	Muɔmi	3.1	–	–	7.1	8.7	3.0
No. of farmers		64	43	24	14	23	168

1. All sweet potato is produced on the Volta lakeshore. Farmers at other localities producing sweet potato are also farming at Akrusu Saisi.

which maize is increasingly being replaced by sweet potato and vegetables (tomato, pepper, okro, garden egg). The lakeshore water has been incorporated into cropping strategies and farmers are experimenting with incorporating new crop species and developing new cropping systems. The emergence of sweet potato has not been without problems. Apart from mastering the technical aspects of lakeshore sweet potato cultivation, farmers have also had to create and find marketing outlets for the crop. While Akrusu Saisi has the advantage of hosting a Tuesday fish market, finding a sufficiently large market outlet for the crop has involved farmers in hiring lorries to take their crop to Agomanya market, a distance of 40 km. Success in creating market outlets has led to the expansion of sweet potato cultivation within Akrusu Saisi, and the hiring of lakeshore land specifically for this activity. A saturation point has now been reached: market prices are beginning to drop, while the cost of production is rising as a result of the large local demand for hired lakeshore land. Farmers are faced with the problem of finding new outlets for sweet potato, or attempting to find alternative and viable avenues for further cash crop diversification.

Data were collected on farmers' estimates of the actual amount of maize and cowpea (the main cash crops) they had marketed in the last year. Data are much harder to collect for cassava, vegetables, and other tubers, since there are few standard measures for marketing these crops, and since they are marketed in small amounts over a long period of time. Farmers are frequently unaware of the total amount of such crops they have marketed.

Table 5.18 provides summary statistics on quantities of cowpea and maize marketed by producers in the 1990–1 season. Overall yields were highly depressed, particularly for maize, the major cash earner, with producers marketing a mean of 1.8 bags (1 bag = 100 kg) of dried maize in the year. Forty-nine per cent of farmers failed to sell more than one bag and only 16 per cent of producers marketed four or more bags of maize. Twenty-eight per cent of maize cultivators failed to produce sufficient yield to market any output. The largest market output was 10 bags. The mean quantity of cowpea sold was 0.9 bags (1 bag = 109 kg). Over 80 per cent of farmers failed to market more than one bag of cowpea and 25 per cent of cowpea cultivators failed to produce sufficient output for sale. The largest quantity sold on the market was eight bags – by the same farmer who had the largest maize output.

Given that a bag of cowpea was between 2.7 to 4.7 times dearer than an equivalent bag of maize between December 1990 and December 1991, cowpea is overall as important a cash crop as maize. Cowpea is more important in the localities dominated by grassland and increasing desiccation, and maize more important at Odometa.

Generally an inverse relation can be seen between maize and cowpea sales, with farmers in the more desiccated environments selling less maize and more cowpea, and those in the more forested areas less cowpea. Some farmers at Awoweso Adome, however, seem to have achieved the best adaptation, getting highest cowpea yields and rivalling Odometa in quantities of maize marketed. In the case of maize, the high mean sale at Awoweso Adome was achieved by a few farmers who managed to gain the highest yields in the survey. But a significantly greater number of Awoweso Adome farmers than at Odometa failed to sell more than one bag of maize.

Not all crops are produced for the market. Crops other than maize, cowpea and sweet potato play important subsistence roles, particularly cassava which is the major staple during the lean season.

Another important reflection on the decline of crop yields is the variety of food crops which farmers purchase on the market. However, purchase of foodstuffs cannot be regarded as a direct reflection of cropping failure. Large profits realized from crop sales may be spent on foods not produced on the farm, indicating increasing commercialization and wealth. Krobo farmers do not attempt to be completely sufficient in food crops, and several foods are purchased at market with the profits which the farmers realize from specialization in other cash crops. Krobo farmers traditionally purchase shallot and onion throughout the year, and tomato, okro, egg plant and pepper during the dry season. Rice is an exotic staple which in the past was purchased occasionally, and generally regarded as a Christmas speciality. It is now being increasingly bought as a regular staple.

Growing market expenditure on staple foods which have historically been

TABLE 5.18. Summary statistics on maize and cowpea marketed by producers in the 1990–1 season

Crop	Odometa	Awoweso Kpeti	Awoweso Adome	Awoweso Sisi	Akrusu Saisi	Total
Maize:						
Mean (bags)	2.1	1.4	2.2	1.2	1.7	1.8
Lowest no. of bags	0.0	0.0	0.0	0.0	0.0	0.0
Highest no. of bags	5.0	6.0	10.0	3.0	5.0	10.0
Producers (%)[1] selling none	15.8	28.6	26.1	30.8	63.2	27.9
Producers (%) selling 1 or less bags	31.6	62.8	39.1	84.7	63.2	49.2
Producers (%) selling 4 or more bags	22.8	9.6	21.6	–	21.1	16.2
No. of producers	57	42	23	13	19	154
Cowpea:						
Mean (bags)	0.5	0.5	1.5	1.2	1.0	0.9
Lowest no. of bags	0.0	0.0	0.0	0.0	0.0	0.0
Highest no. of bags	2.0	2.0	8.0	2.0	3.0	8.0
Producers (%) selling none	38.5	20.7	9.1	7.7	45.5	24.7
Producers (%) selling 1 or less bags	95.5	96.3	77.3	53.9	54.6	81.2
Producers (%) selling 2 or more bags	4.5	3.4	13.5	30.8	27.3	11.2
No. of producers	22	29	22	13	11	97

1. Percentages refer to the proportion of farmers planting the crop and not the total number of farmers in the sample.

TABLE 5.19. Percentage of farmers regularly purchasing staple foods on the market in 1990–1

Crop	Odometa	Awoweso Kpeti	Awoweso Adome	Awoweso Sisi	Akrusu Saisi	Total
Plantain	27.4	78.6	91.7	64.3	73.9	59.4
Rice	50.8	71.4	75.0	35.7	26.1	54.8
Yams	22.2	73.8	70.8	35.7	60.9	48.8
Cassava	7.9	61.9	54.2	28.6	56.5	36.7
Cocoyam	–	38.1	75.0	50.0	52.2	31.9
Maize	1.6	9.5	12.5	14.3	43.5	12.0
No. of farmers	63	42	24	14	23	166

produced within the Krobo district is a fair indication of crop failures and changing crop patterns. Table 5.19 shows staples which were purchased by farmers in the 1990–1 season. This indicates serious decline in crop production, particularly in Awoweso and Akrusu Saisi, where large amounts of cassava, plantain, yams and cocoyams were purchased by farmers. At Odometa, farmers managed to remain self-sufficient in cocoyam and cassava to a greater extent, but relied on purchases of plantain and yams to supplement domestic production.

Purchases of cassava, plantain and cocoyam constitute the most serious sign of increasing crop failures, since *fufu*, the basic staple, is produced from cassava, or combinations of cocoyam or plantain with cassava to improve its nutritional status. While 1990 was regarded as a poor year in which yields suffered from unreliable rainfall, farmers pointed out that the purchase of staple foods is a trend which has grown in the last three years, and is not confined to 1990–1. This suggests a trend arising from increasing environmental degradation and desiccation.

The cropping systems of farmers in the Asesewa district are characterized by diversity and adaptation to changing environmental conditions. Some crops are falling out of production as a result of degradation and new crops are being introduced. This process of adaptation takes place as a response to crisis and crop failures, and occurs within the context of increasing economic and environmental decline.

Conclusion

Within Upper Manya Krobo the nature of degradation varies between localities as do responses. New innovations based on diversifying cropping systems seem to develop in the more degraded areas and then spread to other areas. Degradation is complex and involves both qualitative and quantitative changes. It cannot be assumed that degradation results in declining quantities of all commodities. In some localities increasing degradation has resulted in the replacement of a few large forest trees with numerous, small, fast-growing, introduced exotic species. This results in better fuelwood resources in the worst degraded settlements.

Increasing diversity of production may also be a response to degradation. In the most degraded areas diverse production systems are being experimented with in an attempt to find a viable economic base. This may promote a more diverse use and preservation of the environment than in the heavily monocultural new cocoa-growing areas and the new oil palm belt, where the forest ecology is being replaced by a uniform plantation economy of high-yielding varieties. New technologies have allowed these monocultures to be developed to a degree which the early pioneer cocoa farmers of the Eastern Region were never able to practise.

Increasing economic diversity takes place alongside the loss of other species, particularly mature forest trees and forest food crops in the more degraded settlements. The present diversity of the economy is based on a combination of forest and savanna species, which one would expect to characterize the transitional forest zone. Pioneer forest species are particularly important and constitute multi-purpose trees, for which farmers have developed a variety of uses. At present seed banks exist for species from both forest and savanna ecological systems, although the forest seed bank is declining and the savanna seed bank rising. There is the potential to create a dynamic economy, based on utilizing the diversity produced by the conjunction of both systems.

Farmers in the Asesewa district have a keen environmental awareness which is reflected in the wide diversity of plants they use. They are concerned with the totality of the environment and not only with the agricultural subsystem. However, the wide diversity of uses which they have found for fallow products is not reflected in the market, which focuses on a few commodities. Many commonly cultivated fruits, which are being promoted by the state in an effort to diversify exports, suffer from poor market linkages. This inhibits more extensive and diversified cultivation by farmers. Problems in the development of sweet potato cultivation at Akrusu Saisi clearly illustrate this problem: the farmers have had to develop the initiative in finding market outlets, despite the fact that they have no control over transport. Market constraints have important implications for development approaches concerned with promoting biodiversity and minor forest products. If the market cannot provide security and outlets for mainstream products there is little chance of developing new crops which utilize local biodiversity. Attention needs to be focused on improving market outlets and transport infrastructure to serve the farmers' needs and realize the potential of their systems of environmental resource utilization. The evidence suggests that farmers experiment with new crops and favour strategies based on diversifying production, but are hampered by poor, unsympathetic and unresponsive marketing infrastructures.

Increasing degradation has also been associated with attempts to increase the diversity of products used in the locality. Farmers have responded to scarcity of traditionally used plant products by developing new substitutes based on more diverse use of the environment. Earlier patterns of resource use suggest an over-exploitation of prime species, without attempts to manage their utilization on a sustainable basis. As these become scarce, farmers replace them with a diversity of less optimal species, as reflected in chewing stick and fuelwood utilization. But these are largely developed for home consumption and rarely enter the market, which conservatively holds to its desire for established species. With the decline of traditional commodities in the old areas of cultivation, traders search for new areas in which to continue processes of forest resource depletion.

Farmers' strategies reflect similar patterns of resource use to those developed in formal research and development programmes. For instance, the timber industry in Ghana has traditionally concentrated on a few merchantable timbers, of which eight species constitute 84 per cent of exports and only 23 species are classified as commercial timbers. Faced with increasing depletion of these prime forest timber species, the Utilization Branch of the Department of Forestry and the Forest Products Research Institute of the Centre for Scientific and Industrial Research (CSIR) have conducted research on the suitability of other timbers for furniture construction. A decade ago only 15–20 species were considered marketable: now 40–60 species are considered potentially marketable (Tuffuor, 1992). Despite these promising results, domestic and export market utilization of these timbers remains undeveloped (Abbiw, 1990).

An alternative strategy developed by farmers in response to diminishing fuelwood resources has been to plant fast-growing exotic species such as *Azadirachta indica* and *Cassia siamea*. This pattern of resource use has also been developed by the Forestry Department, which has responded to diminishing forests by establishing plantations of fast-growing exotic species such as teak, *gmelina* and *cedrela*. While farmers have often been blamed for the degradation of the forests, the strategies they develop in response to degradation are strikingly similar to those of the formal scientific establishment.

In the Asesewa district increasing degradation has also led to the diversification of production, with farmers searching for new commodities to supplement old ones which are failing to produce sustainable yields. Growing land pressures also result in attempts to diversify the resource base. Several developments exemplify this approach:

1 The creation of the oil palm distilling industry, which seeks to find new palm products as new areas of production displace the Krobo area. Work in the distilling industry also provides an alternative source of income for farmers with land shortage.

2 The introduction of cowpea – a new crop which can survive lower rainfall and, because it is leguminous, can be integrated into more intensive fallow cycles and combat declining soil fertility.

3 Increasing diversification into livestock – a source of income for those with insufficient land, which makes use of the browse and fodder potential of the fallow.

These developments are based completely on the self-reliant initiatives of the people, and receive little support or encouragement from the state. Thus the oil palm distilling industry has developed in the most difficult circumstances, conjuring up an array of equipment from a variety of scrap materials. Little research exists into the industry and no support services for farmers. Yet it makes a significant contribution to national GDP. Cowpea cultivation has spread from savanna farmers, and the Krobo farmers are still in the process of working out optimum cultivation methods for the crops, without the assistance of agricultural extension officers whose focus is on-line planting of high-yielding maize varieties, and on fertilizer and pesticide use. Livestock farming is risky and no extension service exists in the area to cater for the needs of the small farmer.

Many fallow products are unlikely to find commercial export or national markets in their present state. Biodiversity has become a fashionable concept, and changing consumer tastes in the West open up avenues for new tropical products. However, approaches to biodiversity are frequently based on the perspectives of world commodity markets, rather than on the needs of forest peoples or the necessity of creating market mechanisms which promote biodiversity. As Sattour (1991: 18–19) comments on the potential of developing new marginal crops:

> wild or marginally domestic plants have evolved to thrive and reproduce in often restricted environments where characteristics undesirable to people may have given them the edge. . . . To succeed economically such plants must be bred to expand most of their energy producing substances, i.e. what we want them to produce, in environments chosen by humans and in such a way as to make harvesting convenient. Before breeders invest the time and cash required to develop such strains, they want some assurance of an essential return on the investment. The danger, of course, is of slipping into a vicious circle: as long as an underutilized crop stays confined to a small patch, it will remain obscure to potential consumers,

and thus promote little popular demand. Lack of demand, will make it hard to find the venture capital needed to fund the research necessary to grow the crop on a large enough scale to promote its worth.

In a similar vein Meadley (1989: 25) remarks:

> futures in maize and soya are being traded by people who drive a Porsche rather than a Massey Ferguson, and they can do that because the grades are clearly defined and consistent. Thus if you introduce small amounts of an unknown commodity of inconsistent quality into the market you will find little interest. The development of new crops must be market led and developed to meet specific needs more cheaply and effectively, fitting into the market and industry, without requiring any major changes in the market grades and industrial equipment.

The recognition of the importance of preserving diversity, of promoting economic diversification into new commodities, and of commoditizing or valorizing natural resources which previously had limited commodity values on domestic markets are not necessarily strategies, in themselves, which contain solutions to environmental degradation. In Ghana, in recent years *Ceiba pentandra* has been developed as a new timber resource with a market in South East Asia. But its recent commoditization does not reflect a more balanced exploitation of the forest. On the contrary, it reflects the extent of degradation of the forest. In many parts of the forest area *Ceiba pentandra* is the only large tree remaining. Its extraction sounds the death bell for the remaining members of the high forest canopy. Its extraction has become so controversial that legislation has been proposed to halt its exportation. This is resulting in intensive exploitation before legislation comes into being. These developments are taking place in a policy environment in which the state agencies, commercial timber operators and donors are concerned with promoting an image of sustainable forest management.

Increasing interest in genetic resources and diversity has been accompanied by a growing awareness of the potential commercial value of natural resources and forests outside of existing industrial development in the present age of biotechnology. Yet this is not the first time that genetic resources have achieved such importance. The colonial mode of international trade over the last 400 years, which has fostered the present unbalanced exploitation of natural resources and environmental degradation, developed under the impetus of heightened awareness of the economic value of genetic resources (Juma, 1989; Brockway, 1979; Kloppenburg, 1990). If this awareness of the new potential of genetic resources is not accompanied by a critical analysis of the impact of commoditization on the environment, the lessons from the past will not be learned and the new knowledge of genetic resources may in the end further exacerbate environmental degradation.

The central problem in present systems of valuation is the estimation of natural resources as exchange values, without examining the interaction of various use values within particular localities. The valuation of a natural resource as an exchange value results in its abstraction from its environment as an autonomous commodity, bereft of interactions with humans and other species. Its value becomes defined by industry and research in metropolitan centres, and its interactions with elements outside its environment. However, if the value of a commodity lies in its interaction with other elements within its environment, in which value is estimated by the processing and transformation of a number of elements within a locality, a more balanced development within the locality may be possible in which value is determined by the total development of resource utilization within a locality rather than the extraction of larger quantities of particular commodities.

Balanced exploitation of natural resources can only be achieved by starting from the needs of localities. Economic development must aim to build stable and dynamic rural economies which start with the potential of economic diversification within the locality rather than the ephemeral demands and desires of export markets and metropolitan industries.

One possible but modest avenue for promoting a biodiverse and stable economic base is to develop the potentials of craft-based and cottage industries. What is needed, here, is an infrastructure of craft tools and containers, training and assistance. Methods of preparing and preserving conserves could be taken up by the farming population, utilizing the wide varieties of fruits, condiments and other flavours in the fallow. Uniform quality of fallow produce would not be a major stumbling block, since the skill would lie in the combination of elements which might not capture a market in their own right. The development of an economic craft base would also create an incentive for the local cultivation and breeding of marginal produce. The initial market for craft produce would be the home market, but as skills and commodities improve in quality they may compete on international markets. A nascent cottage industry is reflected in such local industries as palm wine distilling, where farmers have developed initiatives to find local markets. Local markets for semi-cultivated minor fruits in urban areas also suggest the potential of the home market to respond to new forest produce. In recent years there has been an expansion of the craft sector in such fields as cloth weaving, basket weaving, leather goods, and cane furniture which reveals a future potential. There are, however, major constraints on the development of cottage industries: these include the depressed incomes of the majority of the urban population, limiting the consumption of non-staple products on the domestic market, and a poor rural service infrastructure.

6
Dynamics of Farm and Fallow Ecology

The nature of farmer management of the environment is revealed in the system of bush-fallowing, the methods through which the environment is harnessed for production. The Krobo system of bush-fallowing has gone through considerable transformation in the last two hundred years. While there is evidence of severe land degradation within the district in the present period, there is also evidence that farmers are attempting to adapt their farming strategies to changing conditions and to solve some of the environmental problems which have emerged. These problems have given the Krobo insights into the processes of degradation within particular localities. This knowledge may constitute a valuable cultural resource base for the creation of new forms of stable resource management.

This chapter aims to identify the main causes of degradation within the farmers' system of land management, and examines farmer perceptions of the pressures on the bush-fallowing system and their attempts to develop new forms of land management to address these problems. Farmer environmental perceptions are important since the success of environmental programmes will in the final analysis be determined by their willingness to implement systems of local resource management. An analysis of farmer perceptions of the changing local environment also reveals the extent to which a local environmental consciousness is developing.

Ecological Perspective on Agriculture

In recent years 'sustainable agriculture' has become a prime concern in international development agendas. This quest is by no means simple. The practice of agriculture involves people in a relationship with the natural environment which has intimations of contradiction.

By definition, agriculture involves the selection and breeding of a few high-energy yielding plants and their cultivation to the exclusion of all other competing plants. The diversity of the total range of agricultural crops in the world encompasses about 70 species, which is low when compared with the total number of plant species in the world. In the Malaysian forests 7,900 plant species have been identified in 132,000 square kilometres. In the Ghana forests, constituting an area of 82,000 square kilometres, 2,100 plant species have been identified and new ones are still coming to light. In contrast, vast areas of the world are under monocultural cultivation of food crops.

Natural ecosystems are characterized by diversity, in which the cohabitation of low numbers of a wide variety of species with different needs and qualities ensures self-sustained nutrient cycling and low entropy. The maximization of diversity of species occurring in low abundance extracts the minimum energy requirements from the soil resulting in low rates of disturbance within the system. Removal of the diverse flora and replacement by agricultural crops destroys this low entropy, and introduces a narrow range of nutrient-hungry plants in high densities (Turnbull, 1969). This results in increasing energy requirements and disruption of the ecosystem. Pest populations thrive on the nutritious crops and multiply rapidly. Nutrients are extracted from the soil by heavy feeding crops and enter food chains outside the farm locality, resulting in declining soil fertility. Weed populations multiply. They are able to compete with the crops as a result of the removal of forest shade and to replace the natural vegetation which suffers from the stress they encounter in farming systems. Since many food crops are related to grass and shrub species, cultivation creates favourable conditions for these weeds. In response to this crisis agriculturalists may invent a series of high-energy strategies to protect their much loved food crops. This includes manual tillage methods, mechanization, utilization of organic and inorganic fertilizers, and chemical weed and pest control. This may result in an escalating series of energy interventions, as increasing applications of labour, petroleum products and chemicals are needed to maintain the same levels of production, which in the long term may lead to the pollution of the land and of the crops humans consume.

Within tropical forests these high-energy technological solutions may lead to rapid degradation of the land. Tropical rainforest ecosystems are highly fragile. Trees play an important role in ameliorating the climate and protecting the soil from the natural elements. A large percentage of the nutrients in these natural systems are preserved in woody biomass, where they are more securely stored than in the soil. Trees also play important roles in shading the soil and preserving its structure through the influence of their rooting systems which create a root mat (Richards, 1952). High-energy tilling techniques frequently destroy the root mat of the forest floor. The nutrient bank of woody biomass is removed. The desiccating effect of the sun and leaching by heavy rains can rapidly destroy the soil. No system of continuous arable mechanization has yet being created which is sustainable in the conditions characteristic of West African tropical forests (Ahn, 1970).

BUSH-FALLOWING AND SHIFTING AGRICULTURE

For the small-scale farmer in tropical countries high-technology solutions to agricultural problems are not available. Faced with declining yields, increasing labour requirements and pest attacks, the farmers give in to the disorder they have created, return the plot to nature, and carry on cultivation on another portion of land. This constitutes the essence of the system of bush-fallowing or shifting cultivation, of which there are numerous systems (Allan, 1965; Ruthenberg, 1980; de Schlippe, 1956).

The dynamics of bush-fallowing in West Africa have been described by Ahn (1970), Nye and Greenland (1960) and Hopkins (1974). The general practice involves the clearing of the bush prior to the rainy season, burning of the woody biomass to release nutrients into the soil and to clear the farm, and the planting of crops during the rains. The farm plot is cultivated for a short period of one to four years and then allowed to fallow for a period to recover its fertility before subsequent clearing for another period of cultivation. Systems of bush-fallowing have been subdivided into shifting cultivation in which the cultivator ranges over fairly large areas of forest, cultivating small plots and allowing them to regenerate into secondary forest; and fallow systems, in which cultivation takes place in clearly defined holdings with short rest periods, and in which the vegetation is characterized by forest-bush rather than secondary forest (Ruthenberg, 1980).

In the past, shifting agriculture has been regarded as a senseless form of land robbery. Recent approaches have discovered sound ecological principles in its methods, when population densities are low and fallow intervals long. Shifting agriculturalists have been seen to have a rich fund of ecological knowledge of the various successional stages of forest regeneration, which they use to determine the fertility of the land for cropping and the various cropping strategies to be employed on the plot (Allan, 1965; Conklin, 1957; Ruthenberg, 1980). Shifting agriculture has also been interpreted as a rational form of transitional land management, which opens up new forests for subsequent, more intensive cultivation. It maximizes the advantage of low populations of pioneer frontier areas (Grandstaff, 1981; Ruthenberg, 1980; Richards, 1985).

Pioneering forms of shifting agriculture require few energy inputs in the way of capital and labour requirements. Some systems of shifting cultivation have been practised without tools or the need for weeding (Ruthenberg, 1980). Studies have shown that the energy dynamics of shifting agriculture are highly efficient and return greater yields for calorific value than other agricultural systems (Uhl and Murphy, 1981; Ellen, 1982; Rappaport, 1971; Norman, 1978).

As population pressures increase and land shortage becomes a problem, shorter fallows may prevail. Under this constraint, insufficient fallowing may result in a continuous fall in soil productivity over a number of years. This problem has been addressed by a large number of studies (Nye and Greenland, 1960; Ahn, 1970; Sanchez, 1976; Young 1976). Concern over soil fertility under shifting cultivation and declining fallow intervals has led researchers into trying to devise new systems of land management which intensify production and adapt to higher population densities (Greenland, 1975). To date, the most important solutions which are being disseminated to farmers in Africa to cater for declining soil fertility in systems of short fallow regeneration are based on alley-cropping. This involves the planting of rows of nitrogen-fixing leguminous trees interspersed with rows of food crops, and has the potential to rapidly increase the nutrient status of the soil, paving the way for a system of permanent cultivation.

Other studies have recognized that the soil nutrient status is not the only constraint in fallowing systems. Cultivated plots are often abandoned long before soils have become exhausted (Nye and Greenland, 1960). Other factors such as increasing competition from weeds, greater expenditure of time on weeding for declining yields, and pest invasions are important in determining the decision of bush-fallow cultivators to abandon a plot of land. A matrix of factors, in which declining soil fertility is only one among many, usually informs the decision to abandon a plot. Degradation of food plots and fallow land is usually experienced as an increase in the energy dynamics of the system.

Conversely, labour requirements may also determine maximum fallow intervals. Farmers sometimes use short fallows to minimize on labour inputs. Conversion of forest into secondary bush results in a reduced labour requirement to clear the land and allows larger areas to be cleared for cultivation. Farmers often maintain fallow as secondary forest, preventing its full regeneration into mature forest where the clearing of trees becomes a major task involving considerable outlays in labour. Shorter fallows may result in lower yields per area of land but this may be compensated for by higher total yields from the larger plots farmers are able to clear (Ruthenberg, 1980).

Drawing on data from the Congo, Nye and Greenland have suggested that the leafing part of vegetation is as great after five years of fallow as after 18 years, and that over half the mobilized nutrients, with the exception of phosphorus, found in an 18-year fallow have accumulated after the first five years (Nye and Greenland, 1960). The utilization of shorter fallows may be more cost-effective than long fallows, when rates of nutrients mobilized are assessed in relation to returns to labour in clearing biomass.

While alley-cropping may increase the nutrient status of the soil, it also requires large labour inputs in managing the tree component, which may be beyond the means of the farmer. This increase in the labour requirement may also offset the gain to soil fertility.

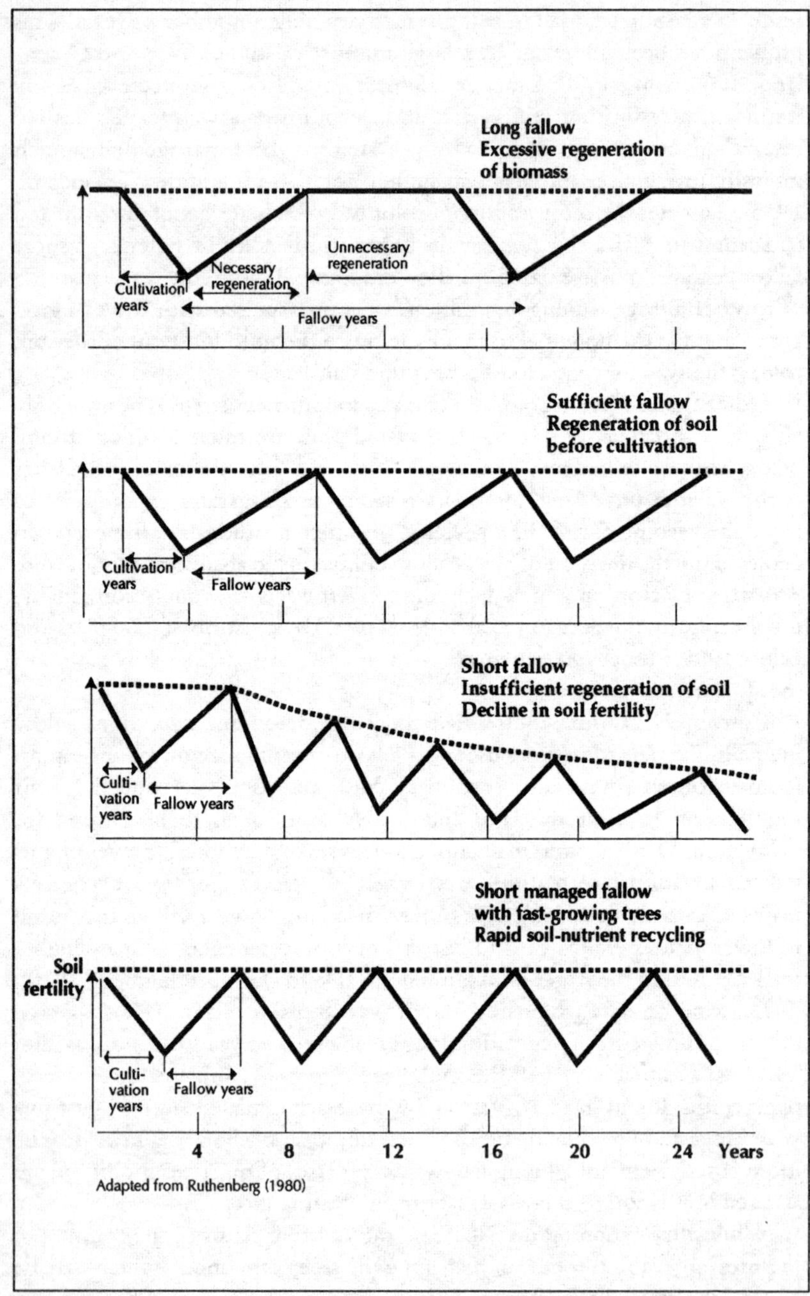

FIGURE 6.1. Hypothetical model of the relationship between soil recuperation and fallowing systems

Other solutions devised by farmers include multi-storey tree gardens, in which an assortment of tree and herbaceous crops are grown together densely. This is achieved by utilizing the different aerial and soil depth requirements of different species. These systems mimic the diversity of the forest and create stable systems which produce an all-year-round dense leaf litter and maintain soil fertility without additions of fertilizer. Multi-storey tree gardens often require minimal labour for weeding (Nair, 1989).

Some studies have also shown that the quality of fallow regeneration is not solely determined by the duration of fallowing, but that management techniques may also promote differing rates of soil-nutrient recycling. In the Minandao area of Indonesia, Kellman (1969) found that rates of soil restoration under fallow were not exponential: the dominance of fast-growing secondary forest species could lead to rapid early soil recuperation, after which there were few benefits to be achieved through continued fallowing, unless for an extended period. Rates of soil and fallow regeneration may vary in response to different micro-environments, colonization by different plant associations, and various farming techniques (Unruh, 1988; Uhl *et al.*, 1981). In the light of research carried out in the Peruvian Amazon, Unruh (1988) has suggested that careful management of fallow species in favour of rapidly growing softwood can promote rapid nutrient cycling and more pronounced soil-nutrient recovery.

Land degradation may also lead to slower rates of fallow regeneration and poorer nutrient cycling if particular weeds dominate the fallow. These weeds may be exotic species (Tuffuor, 1992) imported into the farming system or species encroaching from neighbouring savanna areas.

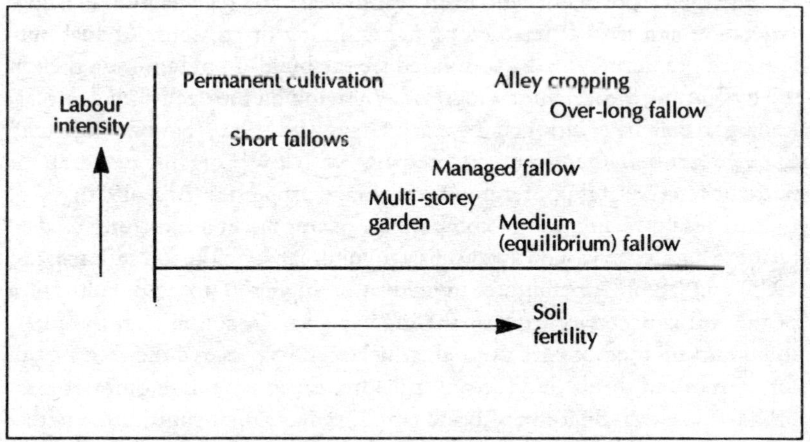

FIGURE 6.2. Labour intensity and soil recuperation under different systems of land management

Patterns of degradation are complex in bush-fallowing systems and cannot be singularly attributed to the practices of the cultivator. No theory has been able to relate particular patterns of degradation to different systems of fallow management (Grandstaff, 1981).

In recent years, as interest in agroforestry has grown, a wide spectrum of agroforestry systems devised by farmers have been found. Cultivators have developed innovatory responses to increasing land shortage. In the Agroforestry Systems Inventory developed by ICRAF, a bewildering array of agroforestry systems worldwide have been documented, in which over 2,000 trees are being managed. Some of these agroforestry systems are highly complex, containing over 50 species, and have evolved stable systems of land management under high population densities, based on permanent cultivation (Nair, 1989). While scientists have been attempting to develop solutions for shifting cultivation, the cultivator has not stood still but has experimented in finding solutions for changing conditions. This suggests that shifting cultivation is not a static form of agriculture, but a rational adaptation to specific conditions with the capacity to evolve in response to changing social and ecological conditions.

FOREST AND SAVANNA FALLOWS

Since the Krobo area is situated in the transition zone, and intrusion of the savanna forms a major source of degradation, it is important to understand the impact of these two ecological systems on fallow regeneration and nutrient cycling.

The patterns of savanna fallow regeneration differ from those described above for forests. In contrast with forests, savanna grasses do not continue to increase their store of nutrients from year to year. The regeneration of fallow vegetation and trees is retarded by fire and long dry seasons. Annual outbreaks of fire during the dry season reduce the build-up of humus in the top soil by burning the leaf litter. Grasses may also inhibit nitrogen-fixing *rhizobia* leading to deficits of nitrogen (Nye and Greenland, 1960). Savanna soils tend to be poorer than their forest counterparts, with lower organic matter, poor nutrient reserves and poorer moisture-storage properties (Ahn, 1970).

As a result, techniques of composting, manuring, and mulching tend to be more highly developed in savanna agriculture than in the forest (Richards, 1985) and labour expenditures in cultivation higher. Thorough cultivation of the soil is necessary to clear the grass species. In contrast, in the forest minimum till methods are utilized, which seek to preserve the root mat of forest trees and shrubs and the soil structure. Excessive tillage of forest areas has adverse effects on forest soils and rapidly reduces their constitution to that of a savanna soil (Nye and Greenland, 1960).

Within the transitional zone, invasion of fallows by encroaching savanna grasses may create conditions for the degradation of the environment into derived savanna. As farmers develop more rigorous methods of weeding to counteract invading species, the structure of the soil is disturbed and its nutrient status declines. Forest regeneration becomes slower and savanna grasses are further able to establish themselves, intensifying the encroachment of savanna.

General Principles of Bush-Fallowing in Krobo

The early patterns of Krobo land colonization have been described in preceding chapters. From the nineteenth century to the early twentieth, Krobo agriculture was characterized by a phase of pioneer frontier settlement. The objectives of the system were to take advantage of the availability of land, the expanding markets in the colonial trading system and regional markets. The new virgin land was cleared by burning the large forest trees, and planted with a combination of tree crops and food crops. The first cropping cycle was based on maize and yams. Cocoyams, plantains, bananas, and cassava were intercropped in this cycle. Apart from providing food and cash, these crops were integrated ecologically into the farm as shade-bearing plants, which protected the soil from the heat of the sun and from the kinetic impact of raindrops. Some of these plants (cassava and banana) were not important food crops in the frontier days, but were largely incorporated into cropping systems for their shade-bearing characteristics. Oil palms and cocoa were planted under these shade-bearing crops. Cropping continued on the land until the fruit trees began to mature, outgrew the shade crops, and created a canopy of orchard crops protecting the soil. The farmer moved onto new land to begin the processes of colonization with food crops. This system did not entail a significant bush-fallowing component.

By the 1940s the devastation of cocoa by swollen shoot disease and the decline of the frontier resulted in the adoption of a bush-fallowing system based on food crop production. As will become evident in this chapter, Krobo bush-fallowing techniques are undergoing transformation and variations are emerging. Here the general principles which characterize the evolution of this system from the 1940s to the present are elucidated.

CROPPING SYSTEMS

The context of the contemporary Krobo farming cycle is a bimodal rainfall regime. A long, heavy rain season between March and early July (*gbo*) is followed by a short, light rain season in September and October (*gbiɛ*). Krobo farmers take advantage of this to make two farms in a year (see Figure 6.4).

The farm cycle begins with the clearing of the major season farm from December to January in the harmattan season (*hlabata*). The shrub layer is cut and some larger trees are pollarded. The leaf litter is left to cover the soil until the first early showers, at the beginning of the rains, when it is burnt. Burning patterns vary in relation to vegetation type, timing of clearing and interpretation of the weather. The preferred method is a controlled light burn in which the litter is burnt in small heaps. This enables small standing trees in the farm to survive. Their singed leaves contribute to the leaf fall and this enables light to penetrate the farm during the early period of crop growth. The trees recover rapidly, putting out new coppice regrowth and root shoots, which provide the basis for rapid regeneration of the fallow.

The burn is recognized as playing several important roles in the farm cycle. The ashes are important in raising the fertility of the soil and improving its friability. Burning also destroys small weeds and insect pests. A significant proportion of the sample gave equivocal answers, however, noting some problems. These included clauses which suggest the burn only has good effects if the land is well regenerated, and if rainfall is good ('burning can dry the land and without rainfall the ashes don't get washed into the soil'). The majority of farmers, however, felt that the burn was necessary, since without it they would be unable to organize and clear the plot for planting, and crops would not do well. While the government has introduced a national campaign against burning, it has not addressed the issue of how forest farmers are to convert the biomass on their farm plots to benefit their crops. If the biomass is left to rot, decomposition will take years. The biomass will also be an obstacle to food crops if it is left on the plot. If it is removed from the plot, the cycle of nutrient recycling is disrupted.

The major farm (*hlabata nmɔmi*) is usually planted in March after the first heavy rain. The first crop planted is yams in mounds under small trees. The trees act as stakes on which the yam tendrils wind. Fires lit under the trees result in a leaf fall which enables the yam to gain sunlight and also raises soil fertility. With the coming of heavy rains, maize is planted. Two weeks after the sowing of maize cassava sticks are planted out between the maize. Cocoyam corms preserved in the fallow soil sprout. As the food crops grow, a dense intercrop of an upper storey of maize, and a lower storey of shade-bearing cassava and cocoyam plants develop, protecting the soil from the sun and the impact of rain drops. After the maize is harvested in October, cassava and cocoyam remain on the plot, shading out weed growth and protecting the soil. Cassava can remain for up to three years after which time the tubers are unpalatable and the farm plot covered by a dense regeneration of shrubs which dominate the farm. The farm is now left to fallow and the processes of bush regeneration are already well established.

Weeding techniques are characterized by minimum tillage. The only implement used is the cutlass. An important principle of weed control is based on the ability of the shade crops to suppress weed growth. Coppice growth and small trees are encouraged to regenerate and never weeded. This enables rapid fallow regeneration once the plot is abandoned.

Vegetables may also be planted from June, at the peak of the rain season, based on intercrops of eggplants, tomatoes and peppers. Peppers act as the long-term crop in these farms, shading out weeds and competing with the regenerating bush. Peppers may continue to be harvested in regenerated bush. Plantain suckers may also be planted in the food plot, adding another shade component which can survive in regenerating bush. They may also be planted out into regenerating bush. In the past, in addition to the newly cleared farm plot (*hwɛ he*), the Krobo had a concept of a regenerating bush farm (*tsokɔkwe*) in which crops (cocoyam, plantain, pepper) were harvested from non-weeded regenerating bush.

Minor season farms (*mawule nmɔmi*) are cleared at the end of August and in early September in lightly regenerating bush. Crops grown often consist of pure stands of maize or intercrops of maize and cassava. Where only maize is planted, the farm is immediately abandoned after the harvest. Cowpeas are planted in July and August. Minor season farms are only lightly cleared to encourage rapid regeneration of the bush after planting. The lower rainfall prevents the rapid regeneration of weeds which occurs on the major season farm.

Multiple cropping forms an important aspect of the Krobo farming system, and it embodies sound ecological principles of protecting the soil from sun and rain and suppressing the regeneration of weeds. This minimizes labour expended in weeding and tillage techniques which disturb the soil and open it to the elements. Although a food plot may remain in existence for three years, it is usually only cleared once during this period. The food crops which remain in the soil for the second and third year are selected for their ability to withstand competition from the regenerating bush. Since they are gradually harvested over a period of time, over the second and third years increasing proportions of the fallow gradually revert to bush. By the time the food plots have been completely harvested processes of fallow recovery are well established.

THE FALLOW

Krobo farmers utilize medium-duration fallowing systems. Fallow strategies aim at rapid regeneration of lightly wooded bush, which is relatively easy to clear. Optimal fallow intervals are generally considered to lie between three and six years. Three years is regarded as the minimum which allows for good vegetational regeneration. On large holdings where surplus land was in evidence farmers still generally cited three to six years as ideal fallow intervals, and preferred to use land which had regenerated within this period as opposed to more mature regenerating secondary forest.

TABLE 6.1. Trees preserved by farmers for soil enhancement (% of farmers preserving species).

Scientific name	Krobo name	Odometa	Awoweso Kpeti	Awoweso Adome	Awoweso Sisi	Akrusu Saisi	Total
Newbouldia laevis	Nyabatso	56.3	54.8	85.0	38.5	57.1	58.3
Baphia pubescens	Tutso	52.1	23.8	40.0	46.2	35.7	39.1
Nesogordonia papaverifera	Bano	8.3	16.7	40.0	30.8	39.3	22.5
Ficus exasperata	Slabatso	22.9	21.4	30.0	15.4	17.9	21.9
Milicia excelsa	Odum	6.3	31.0	20.0	7.7	35.7	20.5
Dialium guineense	Mieletso	12.5	7.1	30.0	23.1	35.7	18.5
Trichilia monadelpha	Gbagblabata	14.6	26.2	35.0	23.1	10.7	20.5
Ceiba pentandra	Leno	6.3	33.3	15.0	7.7	17.9	17.2
Albizia adianthifolia /A.zygia	Papa	22.9	14.3	5.0	7.7	7.1	13.9
Holarrhena floribunda	Osese	14.6	14.3	5.0	15.4	7.1	11.9
Ricinodendron heudelotii	Awama	6.3	16.7	10.0	7.7	14.3	11.3
Triplochiton scleroxylon	Otra	6.3	9.5	25.0	0.0	17.9	11.3
Cola gigantea var. glabrescens	Ovuga	10.4	21.4	10.0	7.7	0.0	11.3
Mangifera indica	Mango	6.3	16.7	20.0	0.0	3.6	9.9
Antiaris toxicaria	Hatso	10.4	2.4	10.0	0.0	10.7	7.3
Celtis zenkeri	Papao	6.3	11.9	30.0	0.0	7.2	10.6
Trema orientalis	Ayisia	2.1	4.8	25.0	7.7	0.0	6.0
Carica papaya	Gɔtso	8.3	4.8	5.0	0.0	3.6	5.3
Khaya grandifoliola	Mahogany	4.2	4.8	20.0	0.0	0.0	5.3
Sterculia tragacantha	Tɔgɔjɔ	0.0	4.8	10.0	0.0	10.7	4.6
Terminalia superba	Afram	2.1	4.8	5.0	7.7	7.1	4.6
Alstonia boonei	Adawura	2.1	11.9	0.0	0.0	0.0	4.0
Anogeissus leiocarpus	Sakane	0.0	4.8	0.0	23.1	3.6	4.0
No. of farmers		48	42	20	13	28	151

Farmers also practise some form of fallow management, deliberately preserving small, fast-regenerating, pioneer secondary forest species. These species are purported to have soil-enhancing qualities. Table 6.1 presents the most important species which farmers preserve for their soil-enhancing and nutrient-cycling properties. Important species include *Newbouldia laevis* (*nyabatso*), *Baphia pubescens* (*tutso*), *Nesogordonia papaverifera* (*bano*), *Ficus asperifolia* (*slabatso*), *Dialium guineense* (*mieletso*), *Trichilia monadelpha* (*gbagblabata*), *Albizia adianthifolia* (*papa*), and *A. zygia* (*papaku/papa*). *Baphia pubescens*, *Dialium guineense* and *Albizia* species are legumes. *Newbouldia laevis* is reputed among farmers to have special soil-enhancing properties and is the favoured tree around which yams are cultivated. Aubreville (1936) notes the widespread distribution of *Newbouldia laevis* in Senegal, Gambia, Guinea, and Côte d'Ivoire, and attributes this to preservation by local people. It is an important medicinal plant.

Fruit trees, such as mangoes, may also contribute to soil fertility by supporting a rich fauna in the branches whose droppings raise soil fertility, and a rich soil animal and microbial population feasting on the scores of rotten mangoes which collect under the tree.

Ceiba pentandra and *Antiaris toxicaria* represent emergent forest species which tower above the closed forest upper canopy, and play important roles in development of secondary forests. *Milicia excelsa* is the dominant dry, semi-deciduous forest species. These three species represent the main forest species which were preserved in the cocoa era.

Forest trees are rarely planted, but mainly preserved from suckers which generate in the food farm, coppice regrowth and young seedlings. Farmers rely on the natural successional mechanisms of forest regeneration to reproduce the modified fallow environment. Minimal-till cultivation methods aim to prevent the disruption of natural regenerative mechanisms and maintain the fallow seed bank and root stock. Fallow management is essentially based on the removal of unwanted species and preservation of desirable species.

A number of shrubs and herbs are also recognized as having good effects on soil fertility (Amanor, 1991). These include *Solanum verbascifolium* (*agbafro*), *Ricinus communis* (*kumelo*: castor oil plant), *Hypselodelphis violacea* (*bɛbɛdua*), *Griffonia simplicifolia* (*totolimo*), *Talinum triangulare* (*nmlɔnmlɔ*), *Synedrella nodiflora* (*klongɔ*), *Aspilia africana* (*ngasaku*), *Momordica charantia* (*nyanyela*), *Physalis angulata* (*nanimamusa*), and *Alchornea cardifolia* (*boblo*). More controversial species listed included well-regenerated *Chromolaena odorata* (*acheampong*), *Mucuna pruriens* (*tsakatsaka*), *Mallotus oppositifolius* (*satwetso*) and *Combretum* species (*laga*). These all have problems in weeding, resulting from vigorous growth (*Chromolaena odorata, Mallotus oppositifolius*), thorns (*Combretum* species) or irritant compounds. *Mucuna pruriens*, a legume, is recognized as having good soil-enhancing properties, but its pods contain an irritant which considerably slows down weeding. Land on which it is dominant is generally avoided if an alternative location is available. Most soil-enhancing herbs and shrubs are not preserved on the food farm. Exceptions include *Ricinus communis* and *Solanum verbascifolium*.

Declining Agricultural Productivity

While the organization of the fallowing cycle is based on sound ecological principles, the farming system is presently in crisis. This is reflected in yield data.

Table 6.2 provides summary information on farmer estimates of yield patterns for major and minor season corn and cowpea per *kpa ngwa* of land in the 1990–1 season. This shows highly depressed yields in general, with farmers getting on average less than two bags (1 bag = 100 kg) of maize in the major season from one *kpa ngwa* (0.4 – 0.8 ha). Minor season corn yields average only 0.7 bags per *kpa ngwa*. Cowpea yields averaged 1.2 bags (1 bag = 109 kg) per *kpa ngwa*.

There are significant variations in yields between the localities, with those situated towards the edge of the forest zone boundary receiving poorer yields of maize, particularly in the minor season. The localities with the worst overall maize yields, Awoweso Sisi and Akrusu Saisi, rank higher in cowpea production. These yield patterns for various settlements do not correspond completely to position in relation to the edge of the forest zone (or Volta Lake), since Awoweso Kpeti (the most forested locality but one) ranks as one of the settlements with the most depressed overall yields.

TABLE 6.2. Yield patterns for maize and cowpea in 1990–1 (per *kpa ngwa*)

Crop	Odometa	Awoweso Kpeti	Awoweso Adome	Awoweso Sisi	Akrusu Saisi	Total
Major season corn	2.5	1.4	1.9	1.5	1.3	1.9
(Std)	(1.42)	(0.77)	(1.02)	(0.92)	(1.27)	(1.29)
No. of cultivators	64	41	23	13	18	159
Minor season corn	1.5	1.1	1.8	0.8	0.7	1.4
(Std)	(1.06)	(1.16)	(0.85)	(1.01)	(0.35)	0.70
No. of cultivators	28	8	8	2	8	54
Cowpea	1.4	0.9	1.2	1.9	1.3	1.2
(Std)	(0.88)	(0.54)	(0.69)	(0.42)	(0.92)	(0.76)
No. of cultivators	25	31	22	12	10	100

Since 1990–1 was marked by poorer rains than usual and may have been an exceptional year, farmers were asked to assess major season maize yields they had experienced in the last three or four years and compare them with yields they received in the more distant past. Seventy-two per cent of the sample estimated that in recent years they had maize yields of 0–2 bags, 25 per cent had 2–4 bags and 4 per cent 4–6 bags. Table 6.3 shows the breakdown for the various localities. Again this shows most favourable yields at Odometa. At Awoweso, the Adome locality achieves significantly higher yields than the other areas.

TABLE 6.3. Average maize yields for the last 3-4 years (% of farmers)

No. of bags maize harvested per *kpa ngwa*	Odometa	Awoweso Kpeti	Awoweso Adome	Awoweso Sisi	Akrusu Saisi	Total
0-2	54.2	89.7	66.7	100	75	71.4
2-4	37.3	10.3	33.3	–	20	24.7
4-6	8.5	–	–	–	5	3.0
Sample size	60	36	24	13	23	156

In relation to changing patterns of maize yields, 31 per cent of farmers receiving yields of 2–4 bags of maize about five years ago claimed that present yields had declined to 0–2 bags in the last three years. Twenty-three per cent of farmers receiving 4–6 bags five to ten years ago now received 0–2 bags and 21 per cent claimed 2–4 bags.

The prevailing patterns suggest that yields have declined markedly. In general, farmers estimated that they received 6–10 bags of maize per *kpa ngwa* 10–15 years ago. This dropped from between 6–8 and 4–6 bags in the last 5–10 years to 0–4 bags at present. In the last 5–10 years dominant yields were 6–8 bags at Odometa, 4–8 bags at Awoweso Adome, 4–6 at Awoweso Kpeti and Akrusu Saisi and 2–4 at Awoweso Sisi.

Yields of cassava were difficult to assess since cassava is mainly grown for domestic consumption and harvested as needed. It is stored in the soil rather than uprooted at a specific harvest season and stored in barns. Nevertheless, many farmers complained of a decline by about half in sizes of tubers over the last five to ten years, and rapid consumption of cassava farms. While cassava farms lasted three years in the past, many were now being consumed in a period of between six months and one year.

Additional data were collected on crops which used to be staples, but which farmers were now experiencing difficulty in cultivating. Only 20 per cent of farmers felt that all the crops they attempted to cultivate could still grow successfully. There were significant differences between the localities. While 41 per cent of farmers at Odometa were confident that all the crops they tried cultivating would thrive, this fell to 12 per cent of farmers at Awoweso Kpeti, 4 per cent at Awoweso Adome, 7 per cent at Awoweso Sisi and nobody at Akrusu Saisi. Twenty-one per cent of respondents specifically attributed setbacks with crops to erratic rainfall ('if it rains well all crops will grow'). This ranged from 8 per cent at Odometa to 52 per cent at Akrusu Saisi.

At Odometa, the main crops which farmers were experiencing difficulty in cultivating were garden egg, pepper and tomato. These crops now require the use of inorganic fertilizers and pesticides for good yields. At Awoweso and Akrusu Saisi plantain and cocoyam also failed to thrive. At Akrusu Saisi plantains and cocoyams were virtually absent. Yams were a difficult crop for about 50 per cent of farmers in all the settlements. While farmers at Akrusu Saisi were marketing more vegetables than those in other localities, success in these crops was dependent upon cultivation in select sites along water-courses and on the banks of the lake, and on the use of chemical fertilizer.

Land Degradation

Since farmers largely rely on the manipulation of ecological factors through the crop-fallowing system, the causes of declining yields are liable to be related to processes of environmental degradation. Causes are likely to include:

- historical patterns of land usage;
- population pressures leading to land shortage and declining fallow intervals;
- unreliable rainfall;
- declining soil fertility;
- destruction of processes of vegetational regeneration;
- invasion of the fallow by exotic and savanna weeds;
- invasion of the fallow by pest populations.

There need not, however, be any directly causal relationship between any of these factors and degradation. Degradation may result from a complex interplay between factors intrinsic and external to the locality. A degradational cycle may originate in conflicts, contradictions and unforeseen linkages and consequences between a series of rational responses and adaptations to changing environmental and social-economic situations (Nyerges, 1989).

HISTORICAL PATTERNS OF LAND USE: THE COCOA ERA

This has been examined in detail in earlier chapters. Here it need only be pointed out that while the same ecological principles of shade control and protection of the soil from sun and rain and bush regeneration were used to establish cocoa plantations, the replacement of secondary bush regeneration by a cocoa canopy had severe effects on the regeneration of the forest understorey and young forest upper-storey species. By the 1930s cocoa had produced serious degradation in the Asesewa district. The decimation of cocoa by swollen shoot also exposed the soil to the detrimental effects of sun and rain, before the bush-fallowing system became established. This partly accounts for the greater rates of degradation in Upper Manya Krobo, the major Krobo cocoa-growing area, as compared to the old oil palm districts of Lower Manya Krobo.

The subsequent reliance on maize as the principal cash crop also created environmental pressures which would not have existed in a more mixed economy with greater emphasis on oil palm production. Since maize is an essentially sun-loving grass species, its increasing cultivation may have resulted in the removal of more secondary forest species than in a mixed economy. Farmers cited cultivation of maize as the major factor influencing the cutting of forest trees. Through encouraging maize cultivation, market pressures may have influenced rates of degradation.

DECLINING FALLOW INTERVALS

Increasing population is widely held to be a principal factor creating instability in systems of bush-fallowing, resulting in substantially reduced fallow periods as population densities increase (Greenland, 1975). Earlier chapters have shown, however, that within the Krobo locality population has declined in relation to the farming crisis. This suggests that population growth may not, in itself, be a determinant cause of degradation, but that a dynamic interaction exists between population and other factors within the farming system. Migration may act to stabilize carrying capacities until such time as new innovations create conditions in which agriculture again becomes economically viable under higher population densities.

Within the Asesewa district farmers are well aware of the detrimental effects of overcropping land. Farmers with small areas of land frequently hire or sharecrop land when they lack land of their own which has sufficiently regenerated to support cropping. The economic returns for this outlay in capital (or loss of crop in sharecropping arrangements) are often greater than diminishing returns from overcropping and allow for better future yields from their own rested plots.

Two different sets of data were collected on fallow intervals:

1 farmer perceptions of the fallowing regimes they used in general, i.e. their

perception of the minimum number of years land needed to be left before it had regenerated to an adequate degree to support cropping (Table 6.4);

2 the number of years particular food plots were fallowed before their present cultivation occurred (Table 6.5).

TABLE 6.4. Fallow intervals utilized by farmers (% of farmers)

Fallow interval	Odometa	Awoweso Kpeti	Awoweso Adome	Awoweso Sisi	Akrusu Saisi	Total
Permanent cultivation	5.9	–	–	14.3	10.3	5.1
1 year	2.9	–	8.3	–	6.9	3.4
2 years	19.1	37.2	–	64.3	17.2	24.2
2–3 years	5.9	7.0	8.3	14.3	3.4	6.7
3 years	39.7	39.5	66.7	–	24.1	37.6
3–4 years	19.1	11.6	16.7	–	13.8	14.6
Over 4 years	7.4	4.6	–	7.1	24.1	8.4
No. of farmers	68	43	24	14	29	178

TABLE 6.5. Fallow intervals on specific food plots (% of farmers)

Fallow interval	Odometa	Awoweso Kpeti	Awoweso Adome	Awoweso Sisi	Akrusu Saisi	Total
Permanent cultivation	10.8	–	–	–	30.6	9.8
1 year	13.5	2.0	–	–	–	3.1
2 years	16.2	14.2	28.1	–	4.1	12.4
3 years	21.6	28.6	31.3	7.1	8.2	19.7
4 years	18.9	22.4	6.3	14.3	16.3	16.6
5 years	8.1	8.1	18.8	14.3	8.2	10.9
6 years	5.4	14.3	15.6	17.4	16.3	14.0
Over 6 years	5.4	10.2	–	39.3	16.3	13.5
No. of farms	37	49	32	28	49	193

The main problem with collecting data on ideal representations of fallowing regimes is that they do not reflect the various fallowing regimes and strategies which develop in different micro-environments on the farm. The main problem with collecting data on particular fallow regimes on specific plots is that they do not reflect the overall fallowing patterns which occur over a number of years, merely the chance outcome in one year, which may be an extreme value.

Both sets of data concur in representing three years as the modal fallow interval. Data for Odometa, Awoweso Kpeti and Awoweso Adome are fairly consistent. Greater land pressures are reflected at Odometa. Data for Akrusu Saisi and Awoweso Sisi in the two tables are inconsistent. Short fallow intervals are suggested for Awoweso Sisi in Table 6.4 and long fallow intervals in Table 6.5. Table 6.5 suggests greater recourse to permanent cultivation at Akrusu Saisi than Table 6.4. Some of the fallow intervals collected in Table 6.5 for Akrusu Saisi and Awoweso Sisi were extremely high, with intervals of 10, 12, 15 and 20 (recorded three times), which clearly cannot form the basis for contemporary fallowing strategies.

These differences are explained by the changes which have been occurring in these two localities in recent years and the development of new farming strategies.

At Akrusu Saisi farmers are exploiting three different micro-environments for agricultural purposes:

1 the lakeshore, resulting in permanent cultivation of sweet potato, tomato and cassava, utilising floodwater and annual deposits of silt;
2 grassland for cowpea cultivation, resulting in short to medium fallows, in which the legume is an important crop in maintaining soil fertility, on land in which the annual burning of vegetation by bushfires prevents the build-up of nutrients and efficient nutrient cycling;
3 regenerating degraded forest bush, in which medium-term fallows are used for maize-cassava-yam intercrops.

At Awoweso Sisi, farmers had difficulty in quantifying their fallow strategies, since a process of change was occurring. Originally, farmers had avoided farming grassland, and concentrated their efforts on farming 'islands' of remaining bush, hoping that the grassland would eventually regenerate into forest bush. This resulted in increasing land pressure on these remaining 'islands'. As these lands eventually became degraded into grassland, farmers were forced to confront grass. They now had large areas of grassland which had lain fallow for many years. Nutrient recycling on these grasslands is not as efficient as in forests and there is no significant transformation of the nutrient status of the soil under grass. On the other hand, grassland can withstand longer periods of cultivation without the rapid decline of its nutrient store, unlike forest land (Nye and Greenland, 1960). The clearing of grassland, however, is labour-intensive and difficult. Given these constraints, farmers may strive to establish short fallow cycles with extended cultivation involving crop rotations. The grasslands are frequently recultivated for three years (three annual cropping cycles) before being abandoned to fallow. Crop rotations with cowpea are important in extending the period of cultivation and may raise the fertility of the soil.

Long-term fallows in Akrusu Saisi and Awoweso Sisi are symptomatic of degradation, reflecting the abandonment of poorly regenerated land which fails to produce good crops, or poor rates of regeneration resulting in extended fallow recuperation. At Akrusu Saisi examples were found of farmers who had followed a deliberate strategy of leaving their own land to rest over many years while hiring land from other farmers or farming elsewhere. Several farmers had recently returned to their lands at Akrusu Saisi. The development of the Akrusu fish market and legends about the money to be made from lakeshore sweet potato cultivation may be leading to a return of population to Akrusu and a new expansion of agriculture.

The most pronounced movement towards permanent cultivation takes place along watercourses as a result of unreliable rainfall. While this was most evident at Akrusu Saisi, with the development of lakeshore cultivation, other examples were found in other localities, where farmers were engaging in permanent cultivation on the lower slopes and banks of streams, because upper slopes were not productive.

The evidence suggests that there is no direct correlation between demographic pressures and declining fallow intervals, nor a distinct exponential decline in fallow intervals. There are complex mechanisms and relations between the environment and the economies of agriculture which continually modify farming strategies and fallowing systems. Processes of vegetational regeneration and succession, rainfall patterns, outmigration, land hiring and agricultural innovation all play important roles in redefining the fallow system.

SOIL

During the 1950s, La Anyane (1956) described the soils of Awoweso as poor. But in a study of Mensah Dawa *huza* in Upper Manya Krobo, Benneh (1970) noted that, despite the shortness of the fallow periods, crops appeared to be in 'remarkably good condition'. He ascribed this to the fact that the cultivation-fallow cycle had only been repeated three or four times since the cocoa era. In the present survey of the Asesewa district, 23 per cent of farmers reported declining soil conditions or unfertile soil, 39 per cent experienced variable fertility between different locations on the farm and about 30 per cent affirmed that their soils were good and that lack of rain and desiccation by the sun were the main problems they experienced in farming.

There is a poverty of data on the conditions of the soil under management by small-scale cultivators in Ghana, despite pioneering work carried out by Nye and Greenland in the early 1960s. To gain a general overview of the condition of the soil under small-scale farmer cultivation, the effects of degradation and land use patterns on the soil, and the extent to which the present crisis in agricultural production could be attributed to declining soil conditions, 100 top soil samples (60 mm deep) were taken from various sites. These included 63 new farms, 31 old cassava farms, and six samples from

TABLE 6.6. Characteristics of topsoils recorded in fallow vegetation

Site	pH	%C	%N	C/N	%OM	P	K	CEC
						(PPM)	Cmol/kg	
Nye and Greenland (1960):								
Savanna								
I. Long fallow under *Andropogoneae* grass	6.0	0.59	0.04	14.5	1.01	–	–	–
II. Short fallow under *Andropogoneae* grass	6.0	0.44	0.03	12.9	0.75	–	–	–
III. *Andropogoneae* Grassland almost continual cropping	6.5	0.34	0.04	10.0	0.58	–	–	–
Semi-deciduous forest								
IV. Kade: moist semi-deciduous forest	5.21	2.22	0.21	10.57	3.81	9.8	–	10.1
V. Kade (as above), cleared and burnt, but not cultivated	7.9	2.26	0.20	11.41	3.89	30.0	–	9.9
VI. Semi-deciduous virgin and old secondary forest	6.3	1.85	0.17	10.9	3.18	–	–	–
Asesewa district survey								
VII. Odometa, relict old secondary semi-deciduous forest	5.96	2.39	0.20	11.95	4.11	7.88	0.64	7.41
VIII. Odometa, 8-year fallow, cleared but not burnt	6.18	1.31	0.11	11.91	2.25	4.13	0.32	5.02
IX. Akrusu Saisi, woodland, 25–30 year fallow	7.08	1.42	0.10	14.2	2.44	7.88	0.38	12.34
X. Awoweso Adome, 5-6 year farmer-managed fallow in former *Panicum* grassland	6.28	1.90	0.13	14.62	3.27	5.25	0.90	12.11
XI. Awoweso Sisi, 3-year farmer-managed fallow, abandoned 3 months ago	7.11	1.51	0.09	16.78	2.60	4.05	0.38	7.63
XII. Awoweso Adome, farmer-managed fallow with *Newbouldia laevis*, 3-year fallow	5.25	1.07	0.07	15.29	1.84	1.10	0.15	5.11

regenerating fallow land, long-term fallow and conditions approximating mature secondary forest. Chemical fertilizers had not been used on these farms in the recent past. However, no soil profiles were taken and the inherent characteristics of the soil remain unknown.

The soils of the Asesewa district are tropical ochrosols formed over Voltaic sandstones. They lie on undulating slopes with gradients of up to 10 per cent. The soil catennas of the upper slopes are red, merging into brown loamy soils on the middle slopes and pale grey alluviums along stream courses. Soils along the Volta Lake are sandy and have been transformed by the annual inundation (Ametekpor, 1987). Topsoils are generally crumbly, sandy loams which are light and easy to work, with favourable pH values but low levels of phosphorus.

At Odometa a single sample was collected from a small relic of old secondary forest. The characteristics of this topsoil were similar to those recorded by Nye and Greenland for a moist semi-deciduous forest soil in mature secondary forest, although available phosphorus levels and cation exchange capacity (CEC) were lower (Table 6.6). A few samples were also collected from medium- to long-term fallow vegetation, including data from degraded land in which farmers had attempted to develop techniques to encourage rapid fallow regeneration.

Ahn (1970) suggests that organic matter (% OM) content for virgin West African forest topsoils may lie between 5 and 12 per cent, declining to between 2 and 4 per cent in cultivated plots, 3–5 per cent after three years' fallow and 3–7 per cent after 10 years' fallow. The values for cultivated plots are under optimum conditions and will be lower for degraded agricultural land. In contrast, organic matter content in savanna soils may lie between 1.0 and 1.5 per cent in cultivated plots and 1.0–3.0 per cent in fallow land. Organic matter is important in maintaining the soil structure, improving circulation of water and air, and plays an important role in preserving the CEC and water storage capacities of the soil. Deterioration in organic matter can lead to a rapid reduction in the productivity of soil. It is difficult to build up organic matter once it is seriously depleted.

The first rows in Table 6.6 contrast the conditions under savanna soils and semi-deciduous forest topsoils, using data from Nye and Greenland (1960). Forest topsoils contain a much higher nutrient pool, although this is susceptible to more rapid depletion than savanna soils. Data provided by Nye and Greenland also show the beneficial effect of the burn in raising soil pH, and available phosphorus (Table 6.6, IV and V). While other nutrients contained in the vegetation are lost through oxidization, the burn does not lead to a decline in the nutrient pool.

Insufficient data were collected to examine the relationship between fallow regeneration and fallowing regimes and strategies. Such an analysis would require comprehensive data on the history of cropping systems and vegetational successions, levels of degradation, the inherent fertility of the subsoil, and changes in nutrient cycling over time.

Nevertheless, the data in Table 6.6 suggest that the interventions of farmers in encouraging fallow regeneration (farmer-managed fallows) can influence the rapid build-up of soil organic matter. There was no direct relationship between duration of the fallowing periods utilized and nutrient cycling. In areas where farmers have deliberately attempted to promote coppice regrowth and regeneration of young pioneer forest trees, and introduced techniques aimed at suppressing grasses, rapid gains in organic matter have been achieved, reaching levels of 3.27 per cent in five to six years and over 2.5 per cent in three years in grassland. In contrast rates of nutrient recovery on land left to regenerate by itself may be quite slow. The existence of long-term fallow land may be symptomatic of poor rates of regeneration. Farmers may hold the land under fallow, hoping for changes in vegetational succession. The long fallow sample from Akrusu Saisi may reflect such processes. Despite the length of fallow, the land did not resemble maturing secondary forest, but consisted of a few pioneer species intermixed with many neem trees, a curious mixture of forest and scrubland plants. All fallow sites were characterized by slow rates of phosphorus replenishment.

Table 6.7 provides summary statistics for the soil samples on the farm plots in general. This suggests that in general the soils under small-scale farmer cultivation in the Asesewa district have established an equilibrium of about 50–60 per cent of stable conditions under well-established secondary forest with closed nutrient cycling. CEC and pH values remain stable under cultivation and may improve. Phosphorus levels may be a constraint on improved yields on many farms.

The data show considerable variation in values for soil fertility. The top 25 per cent of soils reflect good build-up of organic matter and CEC, favourable pH values and moderate percentages of nitrogen. The bottom 25 per cent of soils show the effects of severe degradation with acidic pHs, poor

TABLE 6.7. Fertility of topsoils in the Asesewa district

	pH	%C[1]	%N[2]	C/N	%OM	Av. P[3] (PPM)	K[4]	CEC[5]
							cmol/kg	
Maximum	7.92	3.28	0.24	23.43	5.64	20.78	1.83	14.35
25% highest	7.19	1.72	0.11	15.94	2.96	10.80	0.87	9.66
Mean	6.82	1.42	0.10	14.48	2.43	7.69	0.67	8.32
Median	6.80	1.38	0.10	14.22	2.37	6.35	0.58	8.15
25% lowest soil	6.36	1.11	0.75	12.80	1.90	4.44	0.40	6.64
Minimum	5.23	0.20	0.03	6.58	0.34	2.25	0.19	3.84

Methods of determination:
1 Walkley Black wet-oxidation method.
2 Kjeldahl method.
3 $NaHCO_3$ method.
4 NH_4OAc method at pH7.
5 NH_4OAc method at pH7.

CECs, and low levels of organic matter and nitrogen. These are characteristics of leached soils with poor physical structures.

Table 6.8 provides data on the mean levels of fertility for topsoils of the different catenary sequences on lower, middle and upper slopes and on the Volta lakeshore. The data suggest that the fertility of topsoils on the lower slopes and lakeshore is much lower. These differences may be related to cropping patterns, however, and do not necessarily reflect the inherent fertility of the various soil catennas. While 100 per cent of the Volta lakeshore and 24 per cent of lower slopes were under permanent cultivation, only 14 per cent of middle slopes and 7 per cent of upper slopes were constantly cultivated. On the Volta lakeshore the physical processes of the seasonal rise and fall of the lake have an adverse effect on soil structures and the soils of this area have been transformed into sand (Ametekpor, 1987).

TABLE 6.8. Average fertility of topsoils in different catennas

Slope	pH	% C	% N	C/N	%OM	Av.P (PPM)	K cmol/kg	CEC cmol/kg
Upper	6.78	1.51	0.10	14.64	2.58	7.08	0.63	8.36
Middle	6.94	1.52	0.10	15.23	2.61	7.53	0.69	8.49
Lower	6.80	1.13	0.09	12.42	1.94	9.11	0.72	8.46
Volta lakeshore	6.02	0.63	0.05	12.89	1.09	5.94	0.45	5.04

Table 6.9 provides data on the mean fertility of new and old farms in the various localities in the sample area. The data suggest that the topsoils at Odometa, Awoweso Kpeti and Awoweso Adome are more fertile than those at Awoweso Sisi and Akrusu Saisi, with fairly stable organic matter contents, CECs and pHs, and fair levels of nitrogen. These soils are not badly degraded and fall within the normal averages of small-scale farmer cultivation of forest lands when chemical fertilizers are not utilized. Highest levels of soil fertility are found at Awoweso Adome. Topsoils at Awoweso Sisi and Akrusu Saisi suffer from higher levels of depletion, which is particularly marked in the declining organic matter composition (below 2 per cent) and percentage of nitrogen. On old cassava farms, however, the data suggest that conditions of the topsoil level out, with an improvement of organic level matter at Awoweso Sisi and a slower decline in organic matter depletion at Akrusu Saisi than at Odometa, Awoweso Kpeti and Awoweso Adome.

These differences can be explained by two factors:

1 The replacement of a forest bush environment at Awoweso Sisi and Akrusu Saisi by grassland in which *Panicum maximum* is dominant. The

TABLE 6.9. Mean fertility of old and new farms in different localities

Farm type & settlement	pH	%C	%N	C/N	%OM	Av.P (PPM)	K	CEC	(No. of samples)
							cmol/kg		
New farms									
Odometa	6.68	1.47	0.10	14.66	2.52	6.55	0.51	8.26	(16)
Awoweso Kpeti	6.65	1.59	0.11	14.34	2.74	8.96	0.77	9.6	(13)
Awoweso Adome	7.04	1.83	0.11	15.84	3.14	10.10	1.02	8.70	(15)
Awoweso Sisi	6.41	0.94	0.07	13.34	1.62	5.60	0.53	8.16	(5)
Akrusu Saisi	6.79	1.01	0.09	13.34	1.74	9.46	0.57	7.65	(13)
Mean	6.76	1.44	0.10	11.91	8.45	0.70	0.70	8.32	(62)
Old farms									
Odometa	6.97	1.35	0.09	14.9	2.33	5.75	0.55	7.87	(13)
Awoweso Kpeti	6.44	1.34	0.09	14.8	2.30	7.17	0.66	8.69	(8)
Awoweso Adome	–	–	–	–	–	–	–	–	(0)
Awoweso Sisi	7.01	1.45	0.09	16.8	2.50	7.47	0.82	8.83	(5)
Akrusu Saisi	7.56	1.32	0.10	13.4	2.28	4.37	0.51	8.36	(5)
Mean	6.94	1.36	0.90	14.96	2.34	6.18	0.61	8.31	(31)

grassland is less efficient at building up nutrients, may inhibit development of soil nitrogen, and is prone to annual burning by bushfires which destroy the store of nutrients and organic matter. Under these conditions soil levels may be built up under skilful cultivation and the incorporation of cowpea into crop rotations. Food plots are also protected from bushfires.

2 The increasing recourse to permanent cultivation along the Volta Lake at Akrusu, as a response to unreliable rainfall. While these soils rapidly become depleted of nutrients, they are not by definition represented in statistics for old farms at Akrusu Saisi, which are limited to maize–cassava intercrops in scrubland and cowpea rotations in grassland. Thus comparisons between new and old farms at Akrusu Saisi distort the data.

Analysis of organic matter content revealed that the lowest 25 per cent of samples were dominated by farms under permanent cultivation or under grassland vegetation. Of these poorest soils, 45 per cent consisted of those farmed under permanent cultivation, and 25 per cent consisted of those dominated by grassland, despite the fact that these types of condition were less prevalent in the sample.

An attempt was made to analyse the nutrient build-up of topsoils during fallowing by comparing their nutrient status on new farms with the duration they lay under fallow before being cleared and cultivated. Table 6.10 presents

TABLE 6.10. Build up of organic matter in relation to years of fallow preceding cultivation on new farms (mean)

	No. of years fallow							
Settlement	0	1	2	3	4	5	6	>6
Odometa	2.27	–	3.40	2.18	2.83	2.26	2.00	2.91
Awoweso Kpeti	–	–	3.03	2.79	3.07	2.12	2.37	2.92
Awoweso Adome	–	–	3.16	2.93	3.20	2.60	4.27	.
Awoweso Sisi	2.0	–	–	1.75	–	–	–	1.46
Akrusu Saisi	1.44	–	2.72	–	1.64	3.04	–	1.66
Mean	1.83	2.35	2.67	2.46	2.59	2.57	2.85	2.28

Note: Total number of farms = 62.

data for organic matter and Figure 6.3 plots the distributions for organic matter, CEC and nitrogen. The evidence suggests that there is no linear association between the fertility of topsoils and number of years fallowed. Soil fertility improved considerably with fallows of between two and four years, but levelled off with longer fallow periods.

The erratic fertility of soils fallowed for over four years may possibly be related to poor rates of initial vegetational regeneration. Farmers may have left them to recuperate for longer periods waiting for better recovery of fallow while they selected shorter fallow sites with better floral regeneration for cultivation. Patterns of cycles of cultivation in the long term on particular sites may be important in determining their present fertility, rather than the last cycle of fallow restoration. Factors associated with the interruption of vegetational succession by introduced weeds and tree species may also affect patterns of regeneration, causing rapid gains in initial fertility but preventing further build-up as forest vegetation successional patterns are inhibited and the flora and soil-nutrient cycle stabilize at sub-optimum levels. This may be the case where *Chromolaena odorata* dominates the vegetation. It promotes rapid early nutrient recycling, but it achieves its maximum growth early. As a result, rates of soil nutrient restoration fall off. Since it inhibits the regeneration of other species, it prevents the growth of secondary forest bush, which would gradually achieve a higher level of nutrient recycling. Farmer interventions in preserving forms of vegetation and coppice growth may also promote rapid early nutrient recovery. Higher rates of gain in organic matter in Awoweso Adome soils may reflect such practices.

The data suggest that in general the soils of the Asesewa district are not severely degraded or impoverished, when short- to medium-term fallows of two to four years are used within the conventional minimal-till inter-cropping systems, and when coppice growth and woody and herbaceous

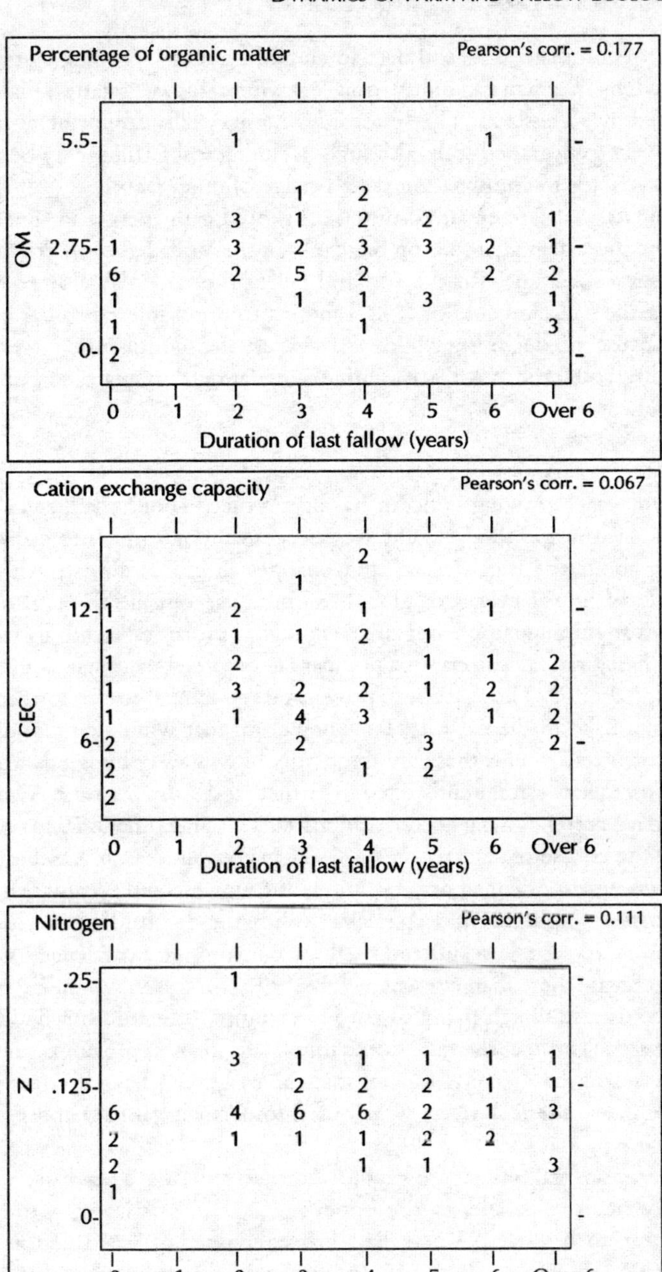

FIGURE 6.3. Organic matter, CEC and nitrogen in relation to length of last fallow on new farm plots

weeds predominate. The soil deteriorates when these cropping systems are replaced by permanent cultivation or where the vegetation has been degraded into grassland. The serious decline in yields cannot be attributed exclusively to degraded soils, although declining soil fertility may be a contributing factor in combination with a range of other factors.

The fact that farmers at Akrusu Saisi should gain their main livelihood from the most degraded soils on the banks of the Volta Lake, where physical processes associated with the rise and fall of the lake play a large part in eroding the soil (Ametekpor, 1987), points to unreliable rainfall as being a major cause of declining yields. At Akrusu Saisi moisture retention is overriding soil fertility as a factor influencing farmers' strategies to gain stable yields.

RAINFALL

In recent years growing concern has been voiced about changes in global climatic factors and the 'greenhouse effect'. Although much remains to be known about the mechanisms and changes in global climate, this is an example of how patterns of global resource use outside the control of a locality can impinge upon and affect ecological processes within its vicinity.

Changing rainfall patterns is a popular factor cited by farmers as a cause of agricultural crisis. They attribute present erratic rainfall to the formation of the Volta Lake in the early 1960s. They claim that while rain clouds form above their settlements these are frequently blown away by winds from the lake. This theory is frequently cited by farmers at Akrusu Saisi and Awoweso, but also has currency as far away as Odometa. This phenomenon was observed during the course of research in the 1991 major rain season. On numerous occasions we experienced dry conditions at Awoweso and Akrusu Saisi, only to return at night to find Asesewa wallowing in mud from torrential rainstorms. Akrusu Saisi suffered the least rain and we experienced a hotter micro-climate there than elsewhere. The 1991 rain season was an exceptionally wet year, in which many parts of the country suffered from flooding.

Farmers claim that the rains come much later than in previous times, that the dry season has become longer, that the early rains have become erratic and the intermittent showers which used to occur in January and February are becoming rare.

Meteorological records are kept for Asesewa and Bisa, a nearby settlement roughly running parallel to the upper reaches of Awoweso, with similar vegetation to Awoweso Kpeti. Bisa was established as a rain station in the late 1930s and Asesewa in the 1960s. Unfortunately comprehensive records for Bisa only date from 1957 and since 1981 have not been recorded consistently. Asesewa rainfall data have only been recorded consistently from the 1970s. This prevents a rigorous analysis of rainfall trends. Nevertheless,

Bisa rainfall data were examined for the period 1958–81 and Asesewa for 1970–90, dividing data into three periods for both stations (see Figure 6.4). Since rainfall is essentially variable, patterns are analysed for different percentiles. The 0.25 percentile reveals the years with the poorest rainfall – in 25 per cent of cases rainfall is lower than this figure. The 0.50 percentile reveals the median rain pattern. The 0.75 percentile reveals the wet years – in 75 per cent of cases rainfall is below this figure.

Significant changes in the patterns of rain are revealed. There has been a decline in rain from November to May. The dry season is much more parched than before. The first rain season comes much later. Late rains are consistent, but they extend into the short dry season of late July and August. The second dry season is consistent, with more rain than in the past in many years. But the prolongation of the first rain season and the contraction of the short dry season may create difficulties for farmers in the timing of farm operations, including the ripening of the major season crops they plant. Within a double cropping system these changes in climate are difficult to adjust to, since the delay in the commencement of the major rains is not followed by a delay in the minor rains. There is thus a contracting of the cropping season. A strategy of late planting in the major season could result in labour bottlenecks and delay in preparing the minor season farm, and crop failure as the ripening season coincides with the second rains. The increased desiccation during the harmattan season and prolongation of the dry season may lead to increasing evapotranspiration, producing water stress in forest trees and perennial crops such as plantain, and creating conditions which encourage the outbreak of bushfires.

These patterns are not only characteristic of the Krobo area, but occur throughout the transition zone, including the north-west transition zone, which is far from the Volta Lake (see Figure 6.5). The changing patterns reflect a trend towards a rainfall regime more in line with that of the savanna area, which is characterized by a single late rain season peaking around September and a long dry season. It is the length of the dry season rather than the total rainfall which accounts for the transition from forest to savanna vegetation. This trend is more pronounced in the north-west forest transition zone, where minor season rainfall is now more stable than the major season.

The data cannot confirm any relationship between the formation of the Volta Lake and declining rainfall, and suggest that changes in rainfall are occurring at a wider regional level. Nevertheless, it does substantiate farmer claims of changes in rainfall patterns from the late 1950s and early 1960s to the early 1980s. The location of rainfall stations does not allow micro-climatic data to be collected and analysed, or permit attempts to monitor the impact of economic development activities on the weather.

The historical climatology of Africa suggests that there are long-term cycles of dry and wet periods, with drier periods (in which major droughts occur) unfolding during 1738–56, 1800–30, 1900–20 and in the 1970s (Nicholson, 1981). In the last century, a dry period during 1900–1920 was followed by a wet period peaking between 1940 and 1960, and a dry cycle in the 1970s and 1980s. In the twentieth century these cycles have occurred within a more pronounced overall desiccation in which, for instance, the levels of lakes and discharges of rivers have fallen below eighteenth- and nineteenth-century values.

These cycles may have a significant impact on agriculture, with farmers taking full advantage of rainfall potential in wet periods and adapting to erratic rainfall in dry periods. Developments within African agriculture at present may reflect this process of adaptation from wet to dry rainfall cycles. They are probably more complex than this, involving both adaptations to climatic cycles and incorporation into the world economy.

Within the Manya Krobo district, increased desiccation was noticed in the Bisa area during the late 1920s allied to a process of savannization, which

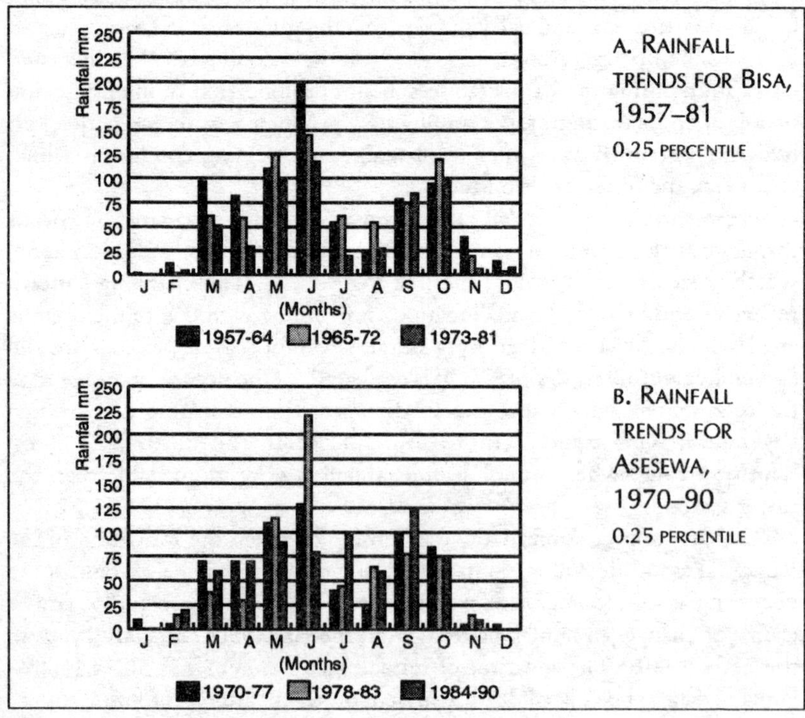

FIGURE 6.4. Rainfall patterns in Upper Manya Krobo

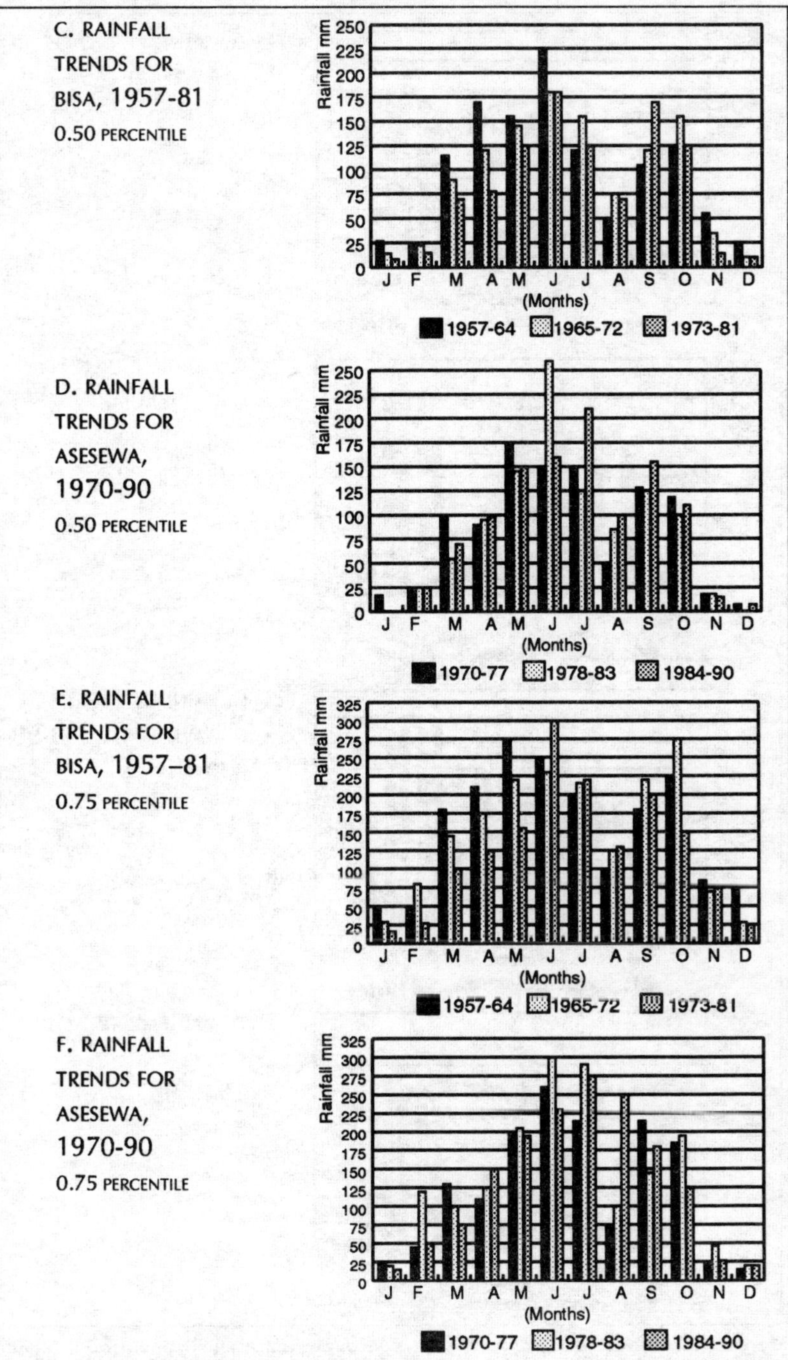
C. RAINFALL TRENDS FOR BISA, 1957-81
0.50 PERCENTILE
Rainfall mm
250
225
200
175
150
125
100
75
50
25
0
J F M A M J J A S O N D
(Months)
1957-64
1965-72
1973-81
D. RAINFALL TRENDS FOR ASESEWA, 1970-90
0.50 PERCENTILE
Rainfall mm
250
225
200
175
150
125
100
75
50
25
0
J F M A M J J A S O N D
(Months)
1970-77
1978-83
1984-90
E. RAINFALL TRENDS FOR BISA, 1957–81
0.75 PERCENTILE
Rainfall mm
325
300
275
250
225
200
175
150
125
100
75
50
25
0
J F M A M J J A S O N D
(Months)
1957-64
1965-72
1973-81
F. RAINFALL TRENDS FOR ASESEWA, 1970-90
0.75 PERCENTILE
Rainfall mm
325
300
275
250
225
200
175
150
125
100
75
50
25
0
J F M A M J J A S O N D
(Months)
1970-77
1978-83
1984-90

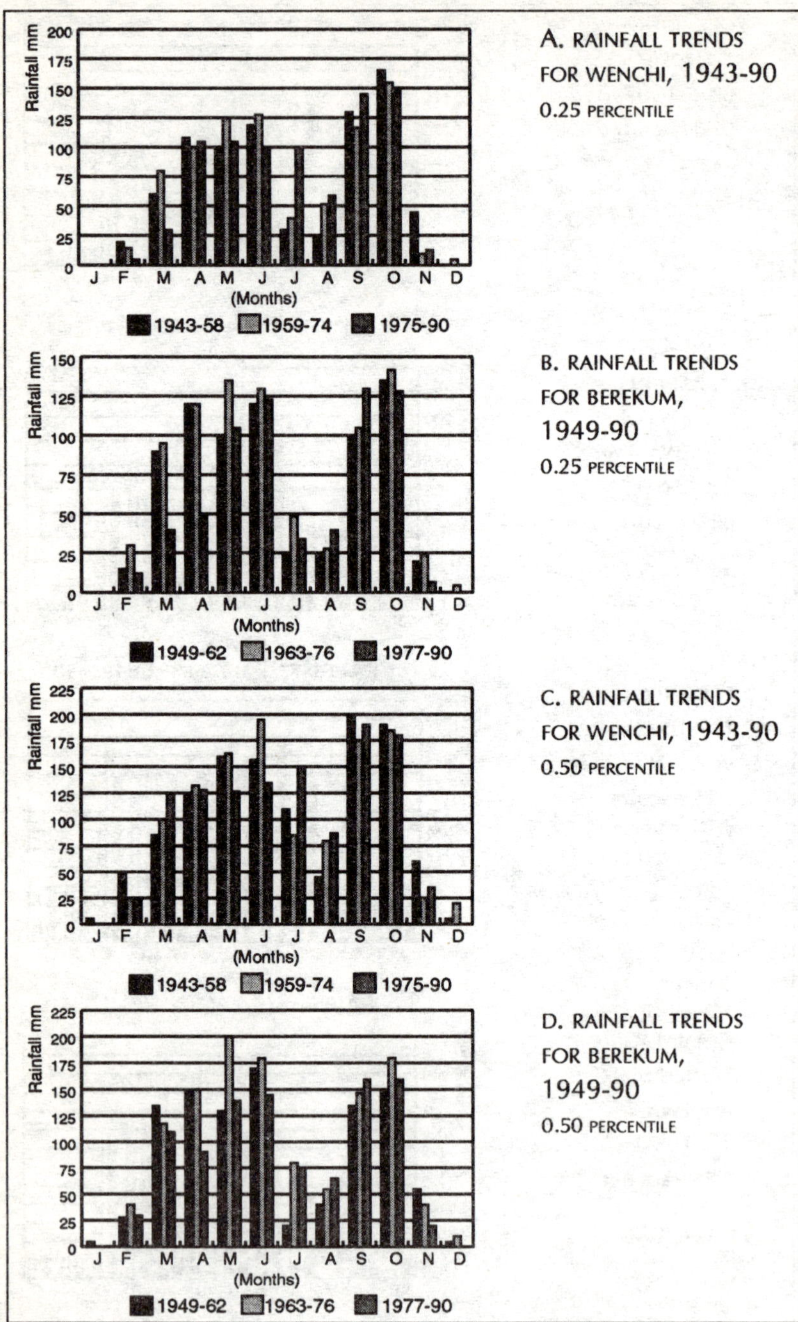

Figure 6.5. Rainfall patterns for the north-western transitional zone: Brong Ahafo

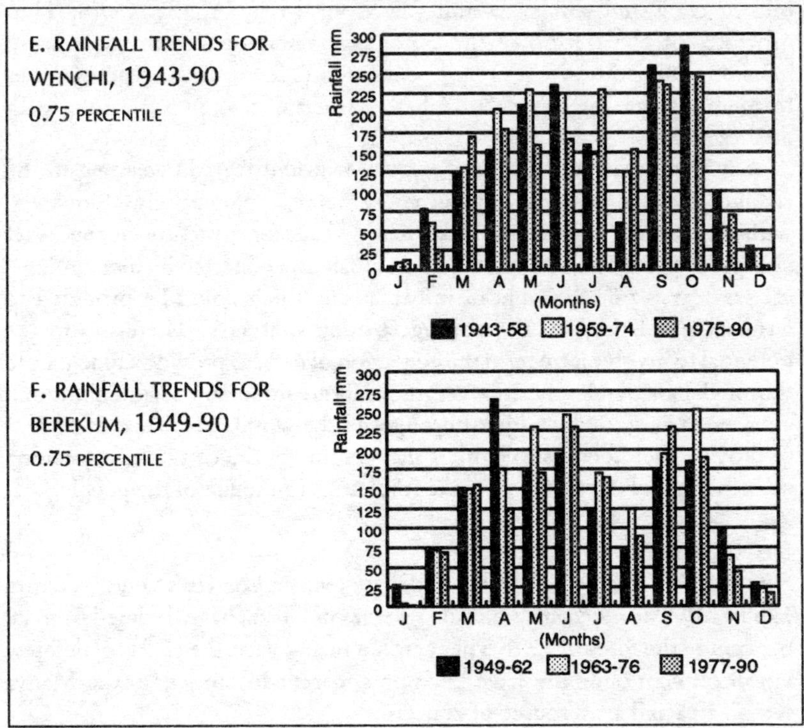

caused water stress in cocoa (Moor, 1930). La Anyane (1956) noted that during the 1950s the stream in Awoweso was dry during the harmattan season. To combat the effects of desiccating harmattan winds a policy was introduced by the colonial authorities of creating barrier forest reserves or shelter belts in the 1930s (Benneh and Agyepong, 1990). In the Krobo area a shelter belt of six forest and savanna reserves was established in the northern forest ecotone zone of the Afram River. These reserves were destroyed in the formation of the lake together with a large area of forest-zone farmland. The northern perimeter of the forest thus retreated southwards. This is likely to have exposed areas further into the forest to the desiccating effects of the harmattan, and led to increasing water stress for trees in this area and susceptibility to bushfires.

Forests play an important role in influencing local climates. Water vapour from the transpiration of plants maintains high levels of relative humidity in tropical forest, which does not fall below 80 per cent. In contrast, within open savanna country relative humidity may fall to 15 per cent or less in the harmattan season. Winds blowing over forests may also collect moisture from the transpiration of the leaves of trees. When the air is forced upwards over hills, it cools and condenses and falls as local rain (Abbiw, 1990). Thus processes of contraction of the outer perimeters of forests may lead to increasing desiccation within adjacent interior forest areas. Many farmers throughout the forest area in Ghana associate changing weather with deforestation.

It is likely that over the years farmers will find ways of adapting to the changing weather patterns and will adjust their cropping patterns. However, without climatic data it may take many years for a picture of the exact changes in the weather to crystallize. Rainfall data collected by meteorological services is one example of information which could be provided to farmers to aid them in developing farming strategies. There is also the potential to involve farmers in the collection of data, to provide a much more thorough base of relevant data. Weather data are important in agriculture and are used extensively by farmers throughout the world. In Ghana, the failure to provide such services to farmers shows some of the constraints operating on science, and the failure to make it relevant to the life of the people.

DEGRADATION OF THE FOREST

Deforestation has proceeded at high rates throughout this century. From 1950 to 1972 forested areas outside reserves in Ghana have declined from 20 per cent of the forest zone to 5 per cent. In recent years the effects of deforestation on economic life have become apparent to farmers in the Manya Krobo area and are a source of concern.

Forests play important roles in ameliorating local environments and protecting them from the hostile effects of the elements. They conserve soils and water catchment areas, retain moisture and have a cooling effect on local micro-climates. They also provide a whole series of use values which may be commercialized. For the bush-fallow cultivator the processes of forest regeneration and its various successional stages perform a central role in maintaining productivity and low energy dynamics in farming. When these successional stages are disrupted, an escalating series of contradictions emerge in the system, which result in increasing weed problems and replacement of the diversity of the fallow by large populations of gregarious species.

In the Upper Manya Krobo area, virgin and mature secondary forest rapidly disappeared during the cocoa era. It has been replaced by forest bush, scrubland and grassland, in which very few species of mature forest are preserved, and coexist with a dominant tree population of hardy pioneer species and introduced exotic species. A further influence in Upper Manya Krobo is the encroachment of the savanna into fallows.

The main trees characteristic of mature forest which still remain in fallows include *Ceiba pentandra* (*leno*), *Antiaris toxicaria* (*hatso*), *Bombax buonopozense* (*mangosiedu*), *Milicia excelsa* (*odum*), *Triplochiton scleroxylon* (*otra*), *Cola gigantea var. glabrescens* (*ovuga*) and *Alstonia boonei* (*adawura*). They are sparsely distributed, but between one and five trees remain on about 50 per cent of farms in Odometa, Awoweso Kpeti and Awoweso Adome. At Awoweso Sisi and Akrusu Saisi they occur on about 30 per cent of farms, usually in stunted forms, and their numbers are decreasing through mounting destruction by bushfires and water stress. Other mature forest trees which occur in low densities on not more than 20 per cent of farms include *Morus mesozygia* (*odongma*), *Cola millenii* (*asokonabea*), *Terminalia superba* (*afram*), *T. ivorensis* (*amle*), *Trema orientalis* (*ayisia*), *Ricinodendron heudelotii* (*awama*), *Diospyros canaliculata* (*tɛtso*), *Hildegardia barteri* (*okpɔtso*), *Anthocleista nobilis* (*frakpa*), *Spathodea campanulata* (*votso*) and *Markhamia lutea* (*mɔmɔtso*). *Celtis zenkeri* (*papao*), *Trichilia prieuriana* (*okumnadue*), *Ritchiea reflexa* (*ayiribi*), *Napoleonaea vogelii* (*kpakutso*) are rare. *Piptadeniastrum africana* (*odahuma*) has disappeared from the area. A variety of small forest trees still exist interspersed with the shrub layer.

Musanga cecropioides (*ojima*), the most characteristic species of early secondary forest regeneration (in lands not constantly under agricultural cultivation), occurs on about 10 per cent of farms. The main forest pioneer species present in fallow regrowth include *Newbouldia laevis (nyabatso), Baphia pubescens (tutso), Albizia adianthifolia (papa), A. zygia (papaku), Nesogordonia papaverifera (bano), Trichilia monadelpha (gbagblabata), Ficus exasperata (slabatso), Holarrhena floribunda (osɛsɛ), Sterculia tragacantha (tɔgɔjɔ)* and *Alchornea cordifolia (boblo)*. These are hardy fast-growing species which are able to regenerate from coppice regrowth or from root suckers. They form the main forest resource on which farmers rely for regeneration of fallow and preserving the root mat under cultivation. They occur on 80–90 per cent of farms in the area. On the grasslands of Awoweso Sisi and Akrusu Saisi, *Anogeissus leiocarpus* (*sakane*), a fire-resistant tree characteristic of the outer zone of dry semi-deciduous forest, is also a prominent but slow-growing species.

The above species represent the trees which farmers have selected from the original forest for incorporation into their agricultural environment, or those which have been able to survive farmer transformation of the environment. Despite marked differences in appearance of the environment in the different localities, seed and root stocks from these trees are distributed throughout the survey localities, although to different degrees. At Odometa a more balanced distribution of these species occurs, while in the other settlements it is more exaggerated as a result of farmer intervention and increasing environmental stress.

In addition to deforestation, degradation can also be created by farmer additions to the environment. The introduction of three trees, *Cassia siamea* (*kasiatso*), *Azadirachta indica* (*sabolatso*) and *Leucaena leucocephala* (*glauca*) (*teboni*) has had a profound effect in modifying the environment in the various localities. These species are fast-growing, and this has led to their introduction for firewood and fencing. But since they grow easily, they have been able to compete aggressively with forest species, and they can occupy large areas of fallow land as monocultural species. These species play a prominent role in determining the outward appearance of the vegetation of different settlements. While Awoweso Kpeti appears to be distinctly more savanna-like than Odometa, the composition of the degraded forest root stock and seed bank are not that different, and forest trees can be found there which have disappeared at Odometa. The main difference, however, lies in the total domination of the upper storey of Awoweso Kpeti by *Cassia siamea,* which has been able to prevent a widespread and balanced regeneration of the forest shrub layer and tree seedlings. There are more trees at Awoweso Kpeti than at Odometa, but less diversity and a lower quality of biomass, resulting in a drier and more savanna-like environment. In a similar fashion *Azadirachta indica* (neem) dominates the landscape of Akrusu Saisi, both as an upper storey of mature trees and as a lower storey of young saplings. At Awoweso Adome, *Leucaena leucocephala* (*glauca*) has established complete dominance over some areas, which farmers have abandoned from cultivation since clearing and weeding *Leucaena* has become a major problem. These are species which also characterize the derived savanna zone on the Accra Plains, where the original outlier forest tree root and seed bank has been largely replaced by savanna scrub and grass species. Paradoxically these three species figure prominently in formal agroforestry systems. *Cassia siamea* and *Leucaena leucocephala* are being promoted by the Ministry of Agriculture Agroforestry Unit.

Within the understorey two processes of degradation are at work: the colonization of cleared land by grass species originating from neighbouring areas, and invasion by exotic species. The Krobo forest zone districts are very prone to degradation through savannization, since there has historically been a constant movement of farmers from their home towns on the Accra Plains to their forest farms. Grass species have spread up the open roads and paths into clearances made for farms. One of the earliest grasses to spread into Krobo farms during the cocoa era, *Setaria barbata,* was known as *blɔgo,* which literally means the road grass. The creation of the Volta Lake and removal of shelter-belt forests have enabled a southward penetration of grass species from the Afram Plains. Increasing maize farming, which requires open sunlight conditions, and greater areas of land under food crop cultivation (as opposed to the sheltered canopy of cocoa and oil palms) have also encouraged the spread of grass species. The main grass species invading farm plots is *Panicum maximum.* In recent years *Digitaria ciliaris* has also encroached on farms. Under the worst conditions, usually associated with permanent cultivation, *Imperata cylindrica* (*henyu*) and *Cynodon dactylon* (*gli glas*) become the dominant weeds.

The main exotic dominating the undergrowth is *Chromolaena odorata* (*acheampong*). This plant was introduced into Ghana by the University of Ghana Botanical Gardens and has spread beyond its perimeters throughout the forest area of Ghana (Abbiw, 1990). It grows to a height of two metres and spreads vigorously throughout farm and fallow land, dominating the undergrowth and preventing germination of the forest seed bank. It is increasingly taking over the role of fallow vegetation in Odometa. *Chromolaena* has properties of promoting soil nutrient recovery, and some farmers suggest that after a three-year *acheampong* fallow land is very fertile. *Chromolaena odorata* is liked by some foresters who regard it as a good cover crop, and has been advocated by some researchers as a green manure for raising soil fertility (Litzenberger and Ho Tong Lip, 1961; van der Meulen 1977). On the other hand, many farmers have noticed that since the coming of *acheampong* many forest herbs and shrubs have disappeared. *Chromolaena odorata* is the dominant weed in Odometa. It occurs in mixtures with *Mallotus oppositifolius* (*satwetso*) and *Panicum maximum* in Awoweso Kpeti and Awoweso Adome, and only occurs in small patches in Awoweso Sisi and Akrusu Saisi, where *Panicum maximum* achieves dominance.

According to farmers, change in the composition of weeds since the 1930s has brought first an increase in population and number of species, then increasing domination by one species. In the early years of land colonization the main plants competing with food crops were forest herbaceous shrub and tree species. During this period the most serious weed was *Solanum verbascifolium* (*agbafro*), a small tree which now occurs in sparse densities on less than 50 per cent of farms with a reputation as a soil-enhancing plant. Other weeds characteristic of this period included *Hypselodelphis violacea* (*bebedua*), *Costus afer* (*tsɔne*), *Marantochloa leucantha* (*sibli*), *Synedrella nodiflora* (*klongɔ*), *Talinum triangulare* (*mlɔmlɔ*), *Momordica charantia* (*nyanyela*), *Paspalum orbiculare* (*fenigugusa*), *Physalis angulata* (*nanimamusa*) and *Mucuna pruriens* (*tsakatsaka*). The undergrowth was not dense, but characterized more by shrubs and herbaceous plants, which cast a shade on the forest floor and prevented exotic weeds from generating or thriving. These weeds were later replaced by a plethora of small herbaceous species and a denser undergrowth. As conditions further deteriorated highly aggressive species began to dominate, replacing the diverse undergrowth of herbaceous species and inhibiting the regeneration of other species. As the land became increasingly exposed to the desiccating effects of the sun, shrubs associated with early successional series gradually disappeared and are now frequently confined to valley bottom land.

WEEDING AND CLEARING

The transformation of the flora has a profound effect on the agricultural system, resulting in increasing labour expenditure in clearing and weeding. The new weeds are harder to clear efficiently and regenerate quickly. Farmers argue that the weeding requirements of making a farm have increased substantially. They estimate that while in the 1930s a farm only needed to be weeded once a year, they now usually weed three times. Some farmers have introduced fourth and fifth weedings. The total numbers of days spent in weeding one *kpa ngwa* of major season maize and cassava intercrop has risen from about four to six days in the 1930s to about 30 days at present. The number of days spent in clearing one *kpa ngwa* has risen from an average of four days in the 1940s and 1950s to sixteen days.

There are significant differences involved in the clearing and weeding of different types of land. Where thorns or *Mucuna pruriens* are abundant, more labour-time is expended. Grassland also involves considerably higher labour expenditure in clearing than land dominated by shrubs. This is reflected in costs of hiring labour to carry out clearing, which varies from ₵4,000 for land dominated by *Chromolaena odorata* to ₵10,000 for land dominated by *Panicum maximum*. However, if clearing is carried out efficiently on grassland, weeding requirements may be minimal. Table 6.11 presents data on the numbers of days farmers estimated they spent in weeding and clearing in the various localities, and Table 6.12 presents data on the number of times farmers weed a plot.

The data indicate that labour requirements are much higher on the grasslands of Awoweso Sisi than in the other areas. As the standard deviations indicate, however, there is considerable variation in the data. The age of a farmer also influences the time expended in weeding and clearing, with old farmers taking longer. Numbers of days spent in weeding and clearing do not necessarily reflect the energy dynamics of the system – only the labour input a farmer is willing or able to expend. Weeding is the decisive operation which differentiates degrees of success in farming. Different weeding

TABLE 6.11. Average number of days spent in weeding and clearing one *kpa ngwa*

	Odometa	Awoweso Kpeti	Awoweso Adome	Awoweso Sisi	Akrusu Saisi	Total
Clearing	12.5	14.3	13.3	49.1	12.8	16.3
(std)	(7.9)	(8.1)	(8.4)	(13.6)	(12.5)	(13.8)
Weeding	33.5	29.9	30.6	36.1	28.6	31.6
(std)	(16.5)	(11.6)	(12.5)	(13.1)	(15.7)	(15.4)
No. of farmers	61	42	24	14	26	167

TABLE 6.12. Number of times farmers weed a major season maize and cassava intercrop

No. of times weeded	Odometa	Awoweso Kpeti	Awoweso Adome	Awoweso Sisi	Akrusu Saisi	Total
2 *	7.5	2.3	–	28.6	36.7	11.8
3 *	80.6	97.7	75.0	50.0	53.3	77.0
4 *	10.4	–	12.5	21.4	10.0	9.0
5 *	1.5	–	12.5	–	–	2.2
No. of farmers	61	42	24	14	26	167

strategies exist. At Awoweso Sisi, farmers who were willing to expend considerable labour in clearing *Panicum maximum* (up to two months per *kpa ngwa*) found their expenditure paid off with considerably lower subsequent weeding requirements.

Weeding problems mean not only greater expenditure of time in weeding, but also greater intensity, stress and tediousness. The task of weeding out *Chromolaena* and *Panicum* with technologies adapted to minimal tillage results in greater exertion and problems of backache and exhaustion, which were never experienced in the past. Increasing degradation has led to a hotter micro-climate which makes weeding more stressful.

Weeding was identified by the majority of farmers as the main constraint in their farming system, with a major effect on yields. Significantly, by far the highest yield of maize and cowpea was achieved by three young brothers at Awoweso Adome who had decided to farm collectively, and were able to develop one of the most efficient weeding strategies. They weeded their farms five times. Most farmers working on an individual basis, or with the help of family labour (spouses who may have their own farms elsewhere and young children), would find such a weeding regime impossible to establish.

Weeding problems were very evident on cassava farms. This was particularly the case in areas dominated by *Chromolaena*. The rationale of the maize–cassava intercrop lies in its low weeding requirement. After the harvest of maize and third weeding, the cassava crop is able to shade out new weeds and hold its own in regenerating bush for a couple of years. From then on the farmer is able to extract a harvest without weeding and can focus his/her energies on the new farms. But *Chromolaena odorata* destroys this cycle. It rapidly overruns cassava plots. This results in declining yields of cassava and poor quality tubers which often spoil long before exhausting their potential lifespan. In contrast, on *Panicum maximum* grassland cassava is able to thrive and a good yield can be harvested. *Cassia siamea* and neem trees were also identified by farmers as having a negative impact on cassava yields.

Weeding problems create a series of escalating contradictions which erode the ecological basis of the system of minimum till, particularly on land dominated by grass species. Effective weeding is necessary to gain a yield, but efficient weeding of grass species results in increasing tillage, which disturbs the forest root mat and the physical structure of the soil, and allows desiccation by the sun. This inhibits rapid regeneration by forest shrub species and encourages further colonization by grasses, leading to a rapid process of savannization. While farmers are reluctant to change their weeding technologies, they are increasingly forced to do this to maintain weed control on their farm. Table 6.13 illustrates how, as grassland increasingly dominates food plots, farmers move from reliance on the cutlass as the sole weeding implement (still evident at Odometa) to a weeding technology increasingly centred on the hoe and tillage of the soil. Without implementation of other techniques to conserve the land, this development is likely to promote increasing degradation and destruction of the remnants of the forest seed bank and soil root mat.

TABLE 6.13. Weeding implements used by farmers (% of farmers)

	Odometa	Awoweso Kpeti	Awoweso Adome	Awoweso Sisi	Akrusu Saisi	Total
Cutlass only	89.0	44.0	12.5	7.0	17.0	49.5
Cutlass and hoe	11.0	56.0	87.5	93.0	83.0	50.5

BUSHFIRES

Bushfires are a major agent promoting degradation in Awoweso Sisi and Akrusu Saisi. The bushfires originate from pure grasslands around the Volta Lake and spread to the upper slopes, killing trees and creating conditions for further encroachment of grass. The processes of increasing desiccation, encroaching grass and annual bushfires work together to transform forest areas into savanna. Unless measures are taken to halt this advance the savanna is likely to make rapid inroads into the forest. In the 1982/3 dry season, bushfires extended over much of the forest area destroying many trees. Farmers at Odometa stated that the forest fallow has never recovered from the damage caused by the 1982/3 fire, and many trees have disappeared from the area since that year. The sources of bushfires are many. They do not usually originate with farmers' land-clearing activities. Intermittent bushfires are a natural phenomenon in the outer zone of semi-deciduous forest, and play important roles in defining the structure of this type of forest (Hall and Swaine, 1981).

PESTS

Degradation results in a greater incidence of pest attacks on crops. The decline of the forest fauna and disruption of food chains allows populations whose natural hosts include food crops to multiply. Other animals and organisms increasingly focus on food crops as their diverse natural food sources are increasingly depleted. Farmers report increasing crop losses to pests. The main predators on food crops include small rodents, mainly the western ground squirrel, the cane rat, the giant rat, mice, lizards, frogs and the double-spurred francolin. Main insect pests include termites, grasshoppers, aphids and thrips. Farmers probably underestimate damage from small pests, such as stem-borers, which are difficult to see and identify.

The main pest problems in the survey area occurred around Odometa and the upper reaches of Awoweso. Farmers at Odometa identified termites as a major cause of low crop yields, and grasshoppers as the main predators on cassava. These two pest problems are related to specific ecological processes. Studies carried out in Nigeria in the 1970s (Baker *et al.*, 1977) indicate that declining rainfall and the spread of *Chromolaena odorata* are two factors relevant to the growth and spread of grasshoppers (*Zonocerus variegatus*).

Increasing populations of termites (*macrotermes* species) are also a result of degradation. Termites are essentially a savanna species which colonize forest areas when they have been degraded by agricultural activities (Harris, 1961; Howse, 1970; Lee and Wood, 1971). When the forests begin to regenerate they abandon the land and their mounds form central areas of forest recolonization. They play important ecological roles in improving soils in degraded areas, increasing aeration, drainage and organic matter content (Lee and Wood, 1971). While they mainly feed on dry woody matter, they can become a major pest in agricultural lands, but usually attack crops which are 'temporarily embarrassed by drought' (Harris, 1961). The extent of the termite population in Odometa was quite exceptional: 80 large termite mounds were counted on a farm plot that covered a single hectare. There have been some indications that with heavy rainfalls in 1991 – leading to moister conditions, less dry biomass and improved regeneration – termites have begun to move out of Odometa.

CAUSES OF DEGRADATION

The causes of degradation involve a series of complex interactions. Degradation originates from two processes:

1 Deforestation, both outside and within the locality, has resulted from the creation of tree crop monocultures, expanded maize production, timber extraction and the formation of the Volta Lake.

2 Additions to the forests, or 'ecological pollutants' (Tuffuor, 1992), are a

largely overlooked factor, but one of great significance for present agroforestry strategies. The introduction of new plants to the forest may suppress the regeneration of forest plants and change the relationship between species which promote successional change. This includes the introduction of new plants for agriculture (cocoa), the spread of savanna plants through the creation of roads and paths (*Panicum maximum*), the introduction of fast-growing species for firewood and poles (*Cassia siamea, Azadirachta indica, Leucaena leucocephala* (*glauca*)), and the introduction of exotic plants by scientific institutions (*Chromolaena odorata*).

The interaction between these two processes undermines the dynamics of the bush-fallowing system. Desiccation from deforestation causes stress in forest plants and allows exotics which adapt well to low rainfall to dominate the fallow. They effectively compete with the forest vegetation, but reproduce conditions in which soil moisture retention is much lower, further repressing forest regeneration. Successful exotics will also be gregarious, leading to increasing weeding and clearing requirements in the agro-ecosystem.

Increased weeding leads to the destruction of the forest root mat, further promoting the domination by exotic weeds, poor regeneration, lower soil fertility and desiccation. The net effects are poor yields and higher expenditure of labour in weeding. As degradation becomes more pronounced, farmers may concentrate their farming activities on the small islands of land where forest plants still predominate, and where fallow regeneration is superior. They may leave areas dominated by poor weed regrowth for longer periods, hoping for improved regeneration. Domination of these areas by exotic and grass species may, however, prevent the development of serial stages of forest regeneration. Faced with increasing desiccation, farmers may also focus attention on the cultivation of moisture-retentive lower slopes. These responses lead to increasing intensity of cultivation on the less degraded lands and promote further degradation.

Farmer Experimentation with Regenerative Technologies

Farmers are becoming increasingly aware that their farming system is not working as it should, that the synergic principles on which the bush-fallowing system operate are being undermined. Trees are now been seen by farmers as playing crucial roles in maintaining the agro-ecosystem. With the decline of the forest tree population, natural processes of fallow regeneration and coppice regrowth cannot restore the agro-ecosystem to its previous balance. The forest tree stock has been depleted beyond the level which will promote balanced fallow regeneration.

In the survey 99 per cent of farmers expressed interest in planting trees which would enhance soil fertility. During interviews many farmers would ask me about the solution to their problems. One suggestion which was greeted enthusiastically was alley cropping. What interested farmers most about alley cropping, however, was not its soil-enhancing qualities, but its claim to provide fast-growing trees which can be cut during periods of cultivation to allow the sun to reach crops and which would then regenerate to provide a canopy during the dry season to protect the soil from the sun and shade out weeds (Fedden, 1988). In the course of the survey an agroforestry officer was called from the nearest FAO–UNDP–MoA Agroforestry Demonstration project at Huhunya to describe agroforestry techniques to farmers at Awoweso. This meeting was enthusiastically received by farmers and 25 signed up to establish agroforestry trials in the 1991 lean season. These still have not got under way due to logistic problems of support for extension programmes. Nevertheless, this illustrates farmers' growing interest in trees.

Major constraints identified by farmers as preventing them from developing their own tree-planting programmes include the lack of a tree-planting culture, lack of seeds, unfamiliarity with which species to plant, and shortage of land and labour. They argued that many forest tree species will not grow if one merely plants their seeds. These factors are more complex than they might appear on the surface.

A characteristic feature of tropical deciduous forest is a propensity to vegetative regeneration from suckers and coppice regrowth, since there is a higher probability of failure of regeneration from seeds, owing to conditions of stress during the dry season and other biotic factors (Janzen, 1975; Ewel, 1980; Nyerges, 1989).

While farmers do not have a culture of planting forest trees, they have developed techniques of managing vegetative reproduction, including coppice and root sucker regrowth and preserving seedlings which naturally regenerate. They have also begun to develop new innovatory regenerative technologies and approaches to combat increasing degradation in fallow land. These approaches focus either on transforming the cropping system or on introducing new techniques of fallow management.

TRANSFORMING THE CROPPING SYSTEM

The main innovation has been the introduction of cowpeas into the cropping system and the development of crop rotations. Two factors have influenced the adoption of cowpea:

1 increasing failure of minor season rains, resulting in the need for a drought-resistant crop;

2 increasing labour requirements in clearing grassland, and poor rates of

regeneration and nutrient cycling, resulting in a need to extend periods of cultivation on food plots and introduce crop rotations with leguminous plants which can restore soil fertility.

Cycles of three-year rotations have been introduced, based on maize–cassava intercrops followed by cowpea and a second maize–cassava cycle, or a twice-repeated cycle of maize followed by cowpea-cassava intercrops. Short, six-month maturing varieties of cassava have replaced the older long-maturing varieties to enable more intensive crop rotations to replace systems of intercropping. Cultivation of cowpea can improve soil fertility beyond the levels of nutrient cycling on grassland. It is also possible that the nutrients held in cassava leaves, which are eventually returned to the soil, may improve soil fertility beyond grassland which suffers from an annual burn, provided the farm is protected from bushfires. After a maximum of three years of cultivation the land is allowed to fallow. In areas in which *Chromolaena odorata* is the dominant vegetation, six-month cassava varieties are also becoming popular, since the rapid regrowth of *Chromolaena* leads to cassava farms being overrun. This means that in these areas shorter cultivation periods are being introduced, that more rapid early fallow regeneration is taking place and that the ratio of fallow resting to cultivation is increasing while cultivation cycles are being intensified.

Although cowpeas have been grown as minor crops for many years in Krobo, present systems based on cowpea as a major rotational crop have been introduced by fishing communities moving into the Volta Lake from savanna areas. Cowpea cultivation has spread from the pure grassland areas adjacent to the Volta Lake into the forest areas dominated by *Chromolaena odorata*. Experimentation with crop rotations are highly evolved in the savanna areas.

A second major innovation on the grassland of Awoweso Sisi involves new clearing techniques. After the occurrence of the first annual bushfires, partially burnt *Panicum maximum* is completely uprooted with a cutlass, cut from underneath its roots and then laid flat on the ground, creating a mulch which completely covers the soil. The soil is protected from the sun, soil moisture conserved and weed growth suppressed. The heavy mulch of charred grass rots during the rain season adds to soil nutrients. This is quite different from dominant savanna modes of cultivating which focus on ridging to make up for deficiencies in soil organic matter and preserve soil moisture (Ahn, 1970; Richards, 1985). This essentially involves the application of forest minimal till methods to grassland. The net gains from the efforts invested in clearing are easy weeding on the farm, estimated at about one week a year. Farmers practising this system appeared to be the most satisfied farmers and had an air of accomplishment, of finally coming to terms with mastering grassland. They were the only farmers who did not complain of declining yields. Their cassava farms appeared very green and flourishing, with hardly a weed in sight. This system is a recent innovation and few farmers are practising it. However, the labour inputs in clearing are extremely high, estimated at a minimum of thirty days of excruciating 'back-breaking work' for the strongest and fittest men to clear a single *kpa ngwa.* Even the most enthusiastic advocates of this system admitted that returns for labour in forest lands were much higher, and that they would prefer to cultivate forest land. Nevertheless this system works and is a monument to the hardiness and genius of the people.

FARMER-MANAGED FALLOWS

One technique used during the survey was to ask farmers to assess the numbers of different species of trees growing on farms. As we approached Awoweso Adome this exercise became increasingly perplexing: the more open the environment appeared, bereft of a canopy of forest trees, the more species of pioneer forest trees, climbing into hundreds, farmers claimed to have on their land. But as we carefully looked round farms we began to find innumerable quantities of small trees often less than a metre tall. In recent years farmers had begun to take increasing steps to preserve trees and young forest seedlings. From Awoweso Adome to Akrusu Saisi an environmental consciousness of the importance of trees is developing and farmers are taking steps to combat the savanna with its dreaded bushfires. This process is in an embryonic stage. It is likely that this will give rise to new systems of agroforestry in the future. During the survey we came across two systems of agroforestry which had been methodically created from this stock of pioneer forest species. The first is named the *managed pioneer fallow*, and the second the *nyabatso* agroforestry system.

Managed pioneer fallow

In this system farmers deliberately bring poorly regenerated fallow land dominated by *Panicum maximum* into cultivation and continue to crop the land for an extended period of three years. The rationale of extending cropping is to introduce a focused weeding regime in which grass species are rigorously weeded out and all regenerating shrub, tree seedlings and suckers actively preserved. By the third year the former grassland is covered with a rich flora of regenerating and established secondary forest regrowth, in which small, pioneer forest trees such as *Newbouldia laevis, Baphia pubescens, Albizia adianthifolia, Antiaris toxicaria, Holarrhena floribunda* and papaw (*Carica papaya*) are prominent. The vegetation is significantly different from the dominant *Panicum maximum* vegetation on land surrounding the managed fallow. Tekper Boboyoo, a farmer experimenting with this system at Awoweso Sisi, is developing a methodical strategy in which each year he will bring land surrounding the managed pioneer fallow into cultivation, gradually extending the qualitatively transformed fallow through his land. His main reason for introducing the system is to attempt to counter the effects of bushfires which promote the growth of grassland and destroy fallow regeneration. The managed fallow is also intended to serve as a fire break, and extension of cultivation around its perimeters is necessary to preserve it against bushfires. Soil analysis of the plot (Table 6.6, XI) revealed an improved organic matter content. A second example of the managed pioneer fallow was developed by Samuel Yermo at Awoweso Adome. The plot consisted of a dense foliage of small trees and shrubs, and was free of the intermixture of *Chromolaena odorata* and *Panicum maximum* which characterized surrounding land. The managed fallow had been created five years ago and was distinguished by secondary forest regeneration superior to other areas of the farm. The dominant trees were *Antiaris toxicaria, Albizia adianthifolia, Holarrhena floribunda*, and *Trichilia monadelpha*. Soil analysis (see Table 6.6, X) revealed a marked improvement in organic matter content and nutrient cycling compared with conventional fallows. Since these two examples were only discovered by chance, through visits to farm plots, other examples may exist.

Nyabatso *agroforestry system*

The *nyabatso* system is a fully fledged agroforestry scheme incorporating an integrated cropping component. *Newbouldia laevis* (*nyabatso*) grows to a height of about 15 metres. It has a slender, compact and elegant canopy, which makes it an attractive tree for integrating with crops since it does not compete for light with them. *Nyabatso* is easily propagated by seed or by cuttings. Root suckers, stem shoots and young seedlings are often deliberately preserved, and rapidly reproduce in a fairly even distribution between 3 and 6 metres apart. The plot is cleared for cultivation, but the land is not burned, since the density of the trees precludes this without causing damage. Crops are cultivated between the trees. Several variants of this system were observed. In the first, the *nyabatso* system was utilized for maize cropping at Akrusu Saisi. *Nyabatso* trees of up to 5 metres in height stood interspersed with the maize crop at distances of about 5 metres. The farmer, a woman, was highly suspicious of us and declined to be interviewed. However, she stated that she planted maize among the *nyabatso*, 'to see what would happen', indicating the experimental nature of the project. A second example of the *nyabatso* system was found in grassland at Awoweso Adome. The farmer, Osieko Teye, stated that he preserved *nyabatso* throughout his farm and had started doing this when he experienced shortage of trees for firewood and yam cultivation. He intended to plant cowpea among the *nyabatso* in the following minor season. In another variant of this system, very high densities of *nyabatso* are preserved, and pollarding techniques are developed to enable cultivation to take place. The cut branches and leaves are laid down on the ground to provide a deep mulch which protects the soil and adds to its humus layer. In the example seen oil palms and plantains were integrated into the system. The *nyabatso* trees were pollarded to a height of about one metre. The farmer, Tetteh Kwame, was preparing the plot for cassava cultivation. The land had been tended for four years under fallow, before being brought under cultivation. All the elements characteristic of alley cropping, with the exception of row planting, are present on his farm. The prevalence of young *nyabatso* trees in Awoweso Adome suggests there may be further experiments on these lines in the near future. It is not yet clear how this system will evolve should farmers continue to experiment.

Throughout the Krobo *huzas Newbouldia laevis* is a preserved tree, a favourite multipurpose tree with a reputation as a yam growing pole, a soil-enhancing species, fuelwood, and a medicinal plant. However great the density of plants preserved, the integration of *nyabatso* into general food crop production, and dispensing with the burn as in the above examples, results in a qualitatively new agroforestry system.

INNOVATION

The major centres of innovation in new agroforestry techniques appear to be the most degraded lands in which savanna is encroaching. No similar types of innovation were found at Odometa or Awoweso Kpeti. Factors which may account for this include:

- the necessity to transform production systems in the most degraded environments, as pre-existing cropping principles fail to work;
- a longer period of history of degradation, which has enabled farmers to observe in detail the interaction between savanna, forest and agro-ecosystems;
- the reduction of the forest stock to its hardiest, most robust species, enabling principles of forest regeneration to be grasped more readily and assisting farmers to harness the remaining energies of the forest in a framework of synergism;
- differential patterns of degradation. These forest regeneration techniques may not work in lands in which *Chromolaena odorata* is dominant, and the invasion of this exotic species may have carried out a more profound disruption of the dynamics of forest regeneration. In contrast there is a long history of environmental interaction between savanna and forest in which *Panicum maximum* can act as a successional stage in the rehabilitation of forest land. From the perspective of the savanna Rose Innes describes *Panicum maximum* as a 'primary nurse maid species in developing thicket and forest' (1977: 202).

Innovations in forest regenerative technologies appear to be a recent phenomenon which date from the 1980s. Present social and economic constraints related to the decline of the frontier create an environment in which innovation becomes imperative. The new frontier now lies in the application of the stock of ecological knowledge rural communities have built up over the centuries to the regeneration of degraded forest areas. However, more research is needed in other areas on patterns of innovation in farmer regenerative technologies to deduce underlying trends and potentials.

Implications for Research

In recent years many agroforestry projects have been implemented in Ghana by the state and NGOs. A national research capability has been established with adaptive research carried out at the Institute of Renewable Natural Resources and Forest Research Institute of Ghana at the University of Science and Technology. These research centres screen technologies devised by the International Institute of Tropical Agriculture (IITA) and the International Council for Research in Agroforestry (ICRAF). Adaptive trials are carried out by the FAO–UNDP–MoA Agroforestry Unit on demonstration sites which have been established in all the regions. Components developed on demonstration sites will be disseminated by the agricultural extension services to farmers. Agroforestry was first introduced into the country by NGOs and the most advanced agroforestry extension programmes are at present run by NGOs such as the Ghana Rural Reconstruction Movement in the Mampong Valley, which incorporates farmer-to-farmer extension of alley cropping techniques (Owusu, 1990).

A characteristic feature of all these institutions involved in agroforestry research and development is adherence to a 'central source' or 'transfer of technology' model of agricultural innovation (Röling, 1988; Biggs, 1989b). The main tenet of this approach is that a range of widely adaptable technology will be disseminated through a hierarchy of 'international centres of excellence' to national adaptive research centres and through extension and community organizations to the farmer. In Ghana the transfer of technology model finds expression in the view current among Agroforestry Unit officers and NGO staff that farmers' techniques of cultivation are backward, have a negative impact on the environment, and that alley cropping will place local farming systems on a scientific basis. In the light of the findings of this research, these views are questionable.

Furthermore, such views have been formulated in a research environment in which basic knowledge of fallowing regimes and problems faced by farmers are still relatively unknown, despite widespread articulation of the importance of principles of community participation. Although a country-wide diagnostic survey has been commissioned by the Agroforestry Unit on an agro-ecosystems basis, the findings of the report are rather general and broad and throw little light on the processes of degradation and responses of farmers (Otsinya, 1989).

A central source approach to technology diffusion is problematic in agroforestry research, particularly since it must address questions of environmental regeneration. Elements of agroforestry have been drawn from farming systems and fallows throughout the world and blended into new researcher-designed systems in experimental stations. These research programmes have been constrained by needs to develop a homogeneous technology with application to wide areas of the world. Several limitations on formal agroforestry research programmes have been outlined by Rocheleau *et al.* (1989). Research programmes are unable to test the wide range of potential agroforestry species and techniques which have developed throughout the world. They are unable to develop systems of formal testing on a scale which will incorporate the diversity of environments which exist. Formal experimentation is also limited by temporal constraints: trees take a long time to grow. Hence research programmes focus on rapid growing trees.

In contrast, farmers have experience of cultivating and managing trees which take time to mature. They are more likely to prefer trees which are robust and easy to maintain when established to rapid growing trees which need constant management. Farmers' innovations in local regenerative technologies address questions of local diversity and processes of environmental regeneration. They build upon the regenerative capabilities of pioneer species. Farmer techniques of managing pioneer forest species for fallow regenerative processes may be an important scientific innovation which could radically transform formal research approaches to fallow and soil regeneration.

The constraints on agroforestry research result in the commoditization of nature into abstract agro-ecosystems, in which components are unable to respond to central environmental concerns such as diversity of landscapes and promotion of biodiversity. A scenario in which farmers respond favourably to agroforestry extension and convert all the forests into woodlots and alley crops of *Leucaena*, *Glyricidia*, and *Cassia siamea* is not an environmentally attractive solution to degradation.

In the course of research, I visited the nearest agroforestry demonstration with my research partner, Michael Kwabla Odjidja, a retired nurseryman and smallholder farmer at Odometa. Our intention was to arrange an open day when we would bring farmers from the survey settlements to see alley cropping in operation. However, the site was disappointing: the maize and cassava was in poorer shape than on farmers' plots at Odometa. The rains. Odjidja was rather more impressed by a neighbouring farm with thriving plantains.

'That must have been an old refuse site,' he announced.

'Yes,' replied the agroforestry officer, surprised, 'but how did you know?'

'I can tell from the castor oil plant growing there,' Odjidja responded. 'Wherever you find it growing soils are always very rich. The farmer must also be getting good yields of yams.'

'How do you know?' asked the officer intrigued.

'The *nyabatso* tree looks very healthy,' responded Odjidja, authoritatively.

'*Nyabatso*, what is that?'

Odjidja went on to elaborate.

I looked towards the horizon, where tall forest trees graced the upper slopes.

'Would you encourage that farmer to plant a *Leucaena* alley crop?' I asked jauntily, pointing to the farm. The officer thought with his hand on chin, laughed and said no.

This pleasant exchange revealed that the agroforestry officer had been busy thinking in terms of the system dynamics of his commodity-oriented system, while the farmer, Odjidja, took in the total landscape. Odjidja strongly advised me against bringing the farmers to the agroforestry site, and told me that if we proceeded I would become the laughing stock of the farmers. In the end we agreed that the agroforestry officer would come to Awoweso and visit the farmers. The problems encountered on the demonstration farm may be teething problems. On the other hand, there may be lessons to be learnt. When the officer came to Awoweso, he remembered *nyabatso*. 'You farmers have trees which are good for yam cultivation, like *nyabatso*.' Everyone responded positively. 'But our trees are good for everything. That is why we call them multi-purpose trees,' he continued, and went on to list their miracle properties. However, having been warned by us of the prevalence of *Cassia siamea*, an alley-cropping species he much favoured with plantain cultivation, and *Leucaena* as unwanted weeds, he focused on *Glyricidia sepium*.

In *Woody Plants of Ghana*, Irvine (1961) noted the soil-restoring properties of *Leucaena*, but nevertheless classified it as a noxious weed. Studies of alley cropping in the Mampong Valley confirm that the labour demands in managing alley-cropping species is a major problem (Owusu, 1990; Gyasi, 1991).

Since these major alley-cropping species occur in abundance in the Asesewa district, it is unlikely that in themselves they will have a great impact on soil fertility. It therefore makes sense to encourage farmers to select and experiment with trees in their fallow which they consider to have soil-enhancing properties and which are easy to maintain.

Similarly, the dominant agroforestry species will make little impact as fuelwood species, since they were introduced for that purpose many years ago. In the areas where these trees are dominant there are no fuelwood problems. In areas where fuelwood shortages exist, many farmers took a conscious decision not to plant these fuelwood trees since they considered them a nuisance.

Other researchers have also been critical of the incorporation of technology transfer models into agroforestry and argue that new models are needed which take into account the fact that the main source of information on agroforestry is concentrated in local farming systems (Rocheleau *et al.*, 1989; Scherr, 1988).

A flexible approach to agroforestry is needed which seeks to build upon local regenerative technologies and adaptive skills. A workable framework could include the introduction of a variety of new technological elements (not packages), together with guidance and information which can assist farmers in experimenting within the adaptive technology systems they are developing. Input could include techniques developed by farmers in other areas and new methods of tree propagation (grafting, budding, layering, seeding and vegetative reproductive techniques) which farmers could test on forest trees and fruit trees in the locality. Research could also focus on the methods farmers use to manage trees, such as techniques of clearing which promote coppice regrowth and the use of fire to control and manage trees. It could aim to find out optimal ways of applying these technologies. Research could also examine the effects of establishing tree nurseries on fallow management. Can nurseries of pioneer species facilitate regenerative activities and complement the vegetative preservation of species, or do they carry implications (overloading the system) which interfere with existing regenerative mechanisms?

Information dissemination could also include exploring ways of making meteorological data relevant and accessible to farmers. Research into weeding technologies could also be valuable to farmers, provided it focuses both on finding simple labour-saving technologies adapted to the conditions of increased degradation on farms, and on techniques of environmental management which lessen the energy dynamics of farming. While new techniques based on minimum tillage have been introduced into West Africa, these largely focus on herbicides and have not been tailored to the needs of peasant farmers. Their long-term effects on the forest seed bank are relatively unknown. These technologies are expensive and beyond the means of small-scale farmers. The key is to develop technologies which are flexible, which reflect the concerns of cultivators and their styles of farming, and which are easily adapted and transformed by them to meet changing conditions and objectives.

To encourage farmer experimentation, support should be provided for the innovatory process to prevent farmers bearing all the risk costs involved. The experimenting traditions of farmers are often hampered by poverty. In some cases promising lines of research never get fully developed, as a result of the sheer weight of poverty and drudgery. They remain as bright but passing ideas. This is also the case with formal research, where researchers never fully develop their ideas because of other commitments and lack of funding. Poorly endowed research centres often produce poor research. The knowledge of farmers has also made and continues to make great contributions to formal agricultural research, providing varietal material and knowledge about varieties and methods of cultivation. This frequently rejuvenates formal sector agriculture. This knowledge has been appropriated for free, without a proper acknowledgement of the important roles farmers have played in crop research.

Meaningful support for farmers' informal experimentation must aim at building independent frameworks of enquiry and development which promote a confidence to face the future and build upon the positive features of popular culture. The aim must be to counter the negative features of a commodity-focused research tradition which creates levers to encourage farmers to take up externally generated technologies. These levers operate to create a monopoly over technology generation and adaptive research, and sap the initiative of the farmer.

Support for farmers' own independent research traditions in regenerative technology has the advantage of combining an investment in research with an investment in environmental regeneration. It creates a local climate conducive to an ongoing research agenda in forest regeneration. This will require new institutional arrangements and skills which do not exist at present within formal research institutions, with a focus on reciprocal learning and training and enquiry rather than dissemination of technology packages. A research agenda based on collaboration and exploration between researchers and farmers can provide the school in which new skills will emerge.

7

Regenerating Old Frontier Districts

Environments do not only exist in space but also in time. In time chance plays an important part in the history of environmental events, which includes the unleashing of destructive as well as life-sustaining forces. Variability is a part of nature and this can take the form of drought, cold spells or heat waves which can wreak great and terrible consequences on society. Nature sustains human society but lies beyond it. In the history of the earth the duration of human society stands like a speck of dust. Society can now unleash great forces from within the environment which may ultimately threaten the environment as we wish it to exist, but nature can also decide to take a course which threatens the very fabric of the modern world. In the past, some species have found themselves doomed to extinction by changes in climate and environment. Others have adapted to the changing conditions.

This element of chance is a fundamental problem in understanding environmental degradation. The presumption behind many conceptual frameworks is that the environment can be managed and regulated like a docile sheep; and that environmental management will enable humans or the privileged minority of world society to continue to live in the golden age they have known in the last 200–400 years. However, environments and society change through time. Many models of the environment and the interface between society and nature which are based on concepts of equilibrium, homeostasis and systems analysis are questionable in the light of the long-term history of environments and society. Concerns with strange weather, climatic variation and environmental change reflect the extent to which global society has been subjected to regulation and the desire to regulate that which cannot be regulated since its essence is variability and diversity. The environment is being constructed in the image of late twentieth-century capitalist society, and notions of social and ecological equilibrium reflect the desire to make this structure permanent for all time.

Paradoxically, concerns with the environment have been translated into an attempt to commoditize the whole of nature. Environmental economics strives to reckon commodity values for the whole of nature. But nature lies beyond commodities, since it is the mother of all products and commodities. The form and the value these natural resources take are transformed with new developments in society, technology and the interface between nature and culture. Thus, the commodity values of natural resources change with developments in society and are potentially unlimited.

A central contradiction in environmental managerial frameworks is the presumption that we can understand the environment for all time. Despite the wide array of highly technical machinery which has been concocted to calibrate the natural world, there are basic problems in interpreting the sophisticated global data which have been assembled. These data only exist for an insignificant, albeit dramatic, moment in world time. While the ozone hole over Antarctica can be measured, the extent to which this is a human-induced or a natural phenomenon is by no means certain. Given this uncertainty about the environment and the problems of its management, many proclamations on the environment reflect political and socio-economic interests in society. They are essentially concerned with debates about managing people.

Just as the soothsayers of tribal society used an array of magical equipment to make pronouncements on the natural world often rooted in socio-political world interests (Evans Pritchard, 1937), so the environmentalists of the late twentieth century exhibit a wide array of technical wizardry to make proclamations equally rooted in the political order of late twentieth-century capitalist society. In pre-industrial and pre-scientific society climatic calamities were often interpreted as punishments from God for sin, in order to restore the order of the cosmos. In present-day global society, a confidence in the ability of society to control nature has given way to increasing anxiety and a view of impending danger and doom from the social desire of the consumer society for unbridled instant gratification.

Which members of human society are responsible for sin against the environment is a matter which lies in the realm of political debate. Since the administrators, regulators and law-givers often represent the powerful and rich, environmental degradation is often interpreted in terms of the sins of the people. In fifteenth century Castile Alvar García de Santa Maria interpreted famine and plague:

> And all these things have afflicted and troubled Spain because of the sins of the people, and because of the bad way of life of those in Spain. Frequently they are bold enough to be drawn to tyranny, which is great sin, in a way which does not happen in other lands, because in other lands each person puts himself in his proper station and accepts what God gives

> him. But it is the opposite in Castile where each man who takes the tonsure wants to be pope, and the man who obtains wealth wants to be of royal lineage, even though his lineage is lowly, so that there is no contentment from the lowest to the highest, and there is a great deal of discontentment in all estates of society.... And, therefore, God in his justice against Spain sends these plagues, starvation, and the loss of people, as a punishment (quoted in MacKay, 1981, from García de Santa Maria, 1972).

In modern times policy makers are smelling out the sin of environmental degradation in the desire of developing countries to pursue high rates of growth, in the livelihood strategies of the poor, in population growth, and in the mismanagement of the commons. Atonement for this sin involves the regulation of the activities of the poor through legislation, through expropriation of common lands and creation of individual property rights, and through the control exerted by development projects. The effects of the history of world commodity trade and the structure of the world economy in perpetrating environmental degradation and unbalanced economic growth is overlooked. Environmental conservation must take place within the ideology of trade liberalization and the free market, in collaboration with transnational corporations, and without threatening the interests of dominant powers.

The current structure of environmental conservation and development is highly eclectic and contradictory. New environmental concerns have been appended onto older models of modernization without qualitative transformation of policy frameworks. In the present structure, agricultural extension services may be responsible for disseminating high-input agriculture alongside 'sustainable agriculture', without a concern about the detrimental effects of some forms of high-input agriculture on the environment. New paradigms are merely assimilated into the old top-down structures and paraded as slogans. Sustainable agriculture is translated as a part of import package agriculture, related to such technologies as alley cropping, rather than seen as the search for more appropriate models of agricultural development.

If 'rural development is concerned with the modernization and monetization of rural society and its transition from traditional isolation to integration with the national economy' (World Bank, 1975: 3, quoted in van der Ploeg, 1990: 274) and environment is about the regulation of society (rather than the regulation of nature, which is impossible), the underlying rationality which enables these anomalies to exist becomes apparent. If the main obstacle to modernization is the incapacity or unwillingness of rural producers to organize production on the basis of current market relations (van der Ploeg, 1990; Rogers, 1970; Williams, 1976; Konings, 1986), the relationships of producers to their localities, to the environment and to regional systems of exchange form the main avenues of circumventing and avoiding incorporation into the rationality of the world market economy. Hence the importance of the ideology of the tragedy of the commons, which essentially seeks to enclose and commoditize the remaining lands which lie outside the regulation of the market and the state. Interventions at the interface between rural producers and the natural environment thus form a mode of undermining the autarky of rural production in regions where producers have rejected modernization and its technological systems. Provisions of aid, credit and infrastructural support form a method of modifying this interface. These levers facilitate the commoditization of the relationship between producers and their localities, creating the conditions which will facilitate their incorporation into the world capitalist economy. Sanctions for failure to adopt these levers of encapsulation are the reinforcement of marginalization. In this model of development, concerns with the environment are not reflected in the advancement of basic and critical research at the national level, but in the expansion of an infrastructure for the dissemination of commodity packages from international centres of research and development.

In Ghana, the independent research of farmers in rural areas and researchers in national centres of research into regenerative technologies has been marginalized by the expansion of high-profile agroforestry packages concocted by the FAO-UNDP-MoA Agroforestry Programme. These programmes are backed up with large doses of financial inducements. This programme is considered by some researchers in natural resource management as the politicization of agroforestry.

Beyond these political considerations, the human–environment relation may constitute a potentially serious crisis. If global systems of environmental management are an illusion, present managerial frameworks may exacerbate degradation by adding layers of unwanted political control, bureaucracy and ideology masquerading as science.

Adaptation, Popular Environmental Perceptions and Social Structure

In place of managerial approaches and the need to calibrate and interpret environmental change and events in themselves, a second possible methodological approach to the interaction between natural and social systems is to focus on human adaptation to changing environments. This approach views environmental stress as a challenge to society, in which a variety of responses are possible. Some of these responses will result in successful adaptations and others will be failures.

The study of human adaptation needs to be carried out in a historical and structural framework rather than within a systems analysis. While systems analysis is concerned with human adaptation, the study of adaptation or human ecology is not usually placed within the context of the historical development of the economy and society and the impact of political and social antagonisms. Adaptation is usually conceptualized within the context of the interaction between environment, technology, population and human values. It is often presupposed that traditional society is adapted to its environment. Disruption occurs through population growth and modernization creating pressures on the utilization of resources, or through the erosion of human values associated with an equilibrium with nature by increasing commercialization. This approach is difficult to accommodate within a historical framework which recognizes that society has continually been transformed by social and environmental contradictions arising out of the utilization and administration of resources. Within a systems framework social change can only be explained by external mechanisms such as population growth or contact with other cultures, rather than by internal dynamics and social contradictions.

This study has shown that popular perceptions of the environment have changed with the evolution of society, and at different moments different constellations of social and ecological factors have led to different perceptions of the interaction between people and the environment. In Krobo, the development of an expansionary land movement was associated with the building of a military organization. Strategies of land management were associated with extensive cultivation and deployment of labour for frontier expansion. This replaced earlier concerns with intensive cultivation in marginal land. Constraints arising from land shortage in the early period were resolved by organizing a military force for winning land from neighbouring peoples. This change was related to considerable social upheaval and transformation within Krobo society, reflected in the movement of secular authority from a priestly class to agricultural military lords. Increasing incorporation into the world economy and the expansion of a colonial economy with its focus on producing raw materials for the industry of the metropolis intensified frontier colonization. This facilitated the commoditization of land values and the emergence of land alienation for export crop production. The subsequent decline of the frontier and marginalization of Krobo has been reflected in an ecological crisis within the area. This has been accompanied by an increasing realization of environmental problems and attempts by farmers to experiment with more sustainable technologies.

The process of adaptation does not lie exclusively at the interface between people and the environment within a locality. It must also take into consideration the impact of political systems of administering people and resources on human–ecosystems relations.

McGovern (1981) has argued that the extinction of Norse settlements in Greenland by the sixteenth century was a result of authoritarian and hierarchical extractive social structures. The elaboration of status differentiation was associated with an economy which depressed the fortunes of smallholders to the benefit of a few great landholding families, church magnates and aristocrats. This was based on a production base focused on stockraising and control over inner-fjord pastures. With climatic stress, reflected in increasingly cold weather from the twelfth to fifteenth centuries, the ecological base for this stockraising economy became severely eroded. The Norse settlements were unable to make adaptive changes to these conditions, and failed to explore the possibilities of the more viable economy based on whaling, fishing and sealing which characterizes modern Greenland, despite a rich fund of neighbouring Inuit technology and expertise. McGovern argues that the Norse settlements adapted none of the viable economic possibilities, but simply intensified their existing stockraising strategies to reinforce the unequal distribution of wealth and pasture. Crisis resulted in the elaboration of religious ritual and mystification of social and economic relationships and the growing impoverishment of the people. The growth of an administrative and political system on an untenable economic base prevented the development of new adaptive responses which would have created economic security.

In Krobo, farmers have responded to growing environmental crisis by engaging in adaptive experiments with new regenerative technologies and diversification of their production base. However, these responses are seriously limited by an unsympathetic socio-economic milieu. Since farmers have chosen to follow their own adaptive strategies rather than the priorities of the state, they have been seriously marginalized. They may have found themselves in a better position – with loans, aid, credit and important functionaries and foreign experts visiting the district – if they had decided to pursue cocoa rehabilitation, monocrop maize production with Global 2000 and agricultural extension, or agroforestry. However, they would have had to suspend the lessons from their own experiences, their own adaptive traditions, and their intellectual autonomy. Ultimately they may have been pursuing strategies which would lead to disaster – since cocoa is too dry for the district, erratic rainfall may lead to the risk of crop failure in planting maize as the sole crop, and many of the promoted agroforestry species could result in weeding problems and increasing problems in managing fallows. But marginalization equally results in difficulty in creating a viable economic base, in problems of access to transport, market outlets, capital and flow of information. The inadequacy of transport outlets promotes market monopolization by traders and poor market prices, particularly for diversification into new crops. The interest of the state in low domestic food prices (to maintain low urban wages or appease urban protest) also encourages poor market prices and marginal access to resources and services. Thus, the economic interests of the state and its position in the global economy may act as a constraint on the autonomous adaptive responses of farmers to ecological stress.

At the local level the system of frontier development has given rise to the commoditization of land values and growing inequity in the distribution of land. There are a large number of farmers without stable access to land. Up to 50 per cent of farmers may have to lease or sharecrop land on an annual or bi-annual basis, and this has serious implications for the ability of cultivators to develop long-term strategies of land management and regenerative technologies. A large number of farmers are excluded from participating in regenerative technologies or in developing folk knowledge since historical circumstances have robbed them of stable access to land.

An emphasis on folk knowledge is not in itself a panacea with which to oppose transfer of technology approaches, nor does it lead to the empowerment of rural communities as is often claimed. It can introduce biases into the process of technology development as much as the Green Revolution, since the social structure in which technical interventions are made is characterized by social differentiation. Folk knowledge is closely associated with the historical evolution of the production base and cannot be separated from its socio-economic context.

Within the present period there are two pressures of commoditization operating on rural communities. Firstly, there is the commoditization of land and labour, which results from the history of integration into the world economy, ultimately originating in colonial modes of export crop production. This involves a whole series of complex mechanisms through which pre-capitalist social formations were integrated into the world economy, giving rise to a number of transitional forms of agrarian economy and rural capitalism. Secondly, there is the rise of agribusiness in the post-war period which commoditizes the process of production by making profits from transactions in farm inputs (which replace labour and the reproduction of the conditions of production) and destroys autonomous farm production.

In recent years a critique of the commoditization of the processes of production and the transfer of technology approach it fosters has gained ground. Support for participatory technology development and indigenous knowledge is essentially a response to the process of commoditization of agricultural science. It points to the importance of preserving elements of farmers' traditions of production, which through continuous interaction with the environment achieve a sensitivity to environmental conditions that eludes international agricultural commodity research. However, this may simply invert the transfer of technology approach and create the illusion that the solution to the problems of the rural areas lies in establishing a correct interface between science and the cultivator. It does not account for the fact that many of the problems peasant farmers face are a result of the history of commoditization of land and labour, which produces hardship and impossible conditions of production, exacerbates land degradation and necessitates change. Under these conditions many farmers may lose an interest in folk knowledge since it cannot solve the problems they face.

Problems arising from the commoditization of land and labour and its ramifications throughout rural production are complex and extremely difficult to address because of the political interests they call into question. Within the most powerful countries ownership of agricultural land, differentiation of producers, the decline of small-scale farm production and farm debt are problems which have not been solved. Appeals to rationality or economic efficiency for land reform may degenerate into mere posturing or contain ulterior motives, resulting in the further oppression of rural people. It is not surprising that many intellectuals choose to shelve these problems like bad dreams and focus on less troubling areas.

Many of the problems of rural areas are linked to the marginalization of the economy and its integration into the world economy through modes which offer little room for expansion, transformation and change. Many rural areas contain knowledge and skills which point to the potential of an economy based on diverse utilization of the environment. These skills rarely inform policy frameworks for the development of the economy. They often exist as a local backdrop to economic activity, constructed by rural folk within a framework of survival skills to cope with insecurity arising from a vulnerable and decaying economy.

Policy measures which seek to transform this informal sector into a vibrant craft and agricultural processing sector may create a multi-sectoral rural structure, which may remove pressures from the farm sector by creating rural options beyond migration. These may alleviate pressures on the land, remove monopoly control over land ownership, and create options for capital and labour which will transform access to land and control and expropriation of labour. This creation of a more diversified economy which informs policy and the development of infrastructural support may significantly transform the relationship of rural people to the environment.

The Frontier and Colonial Development

In recent years there has been growing interest in the protection of the last remaining frontier areas. There is less interest in old frontier areas. There are few studies of the impact of frontier ideology on the environment and on the development of capitalism. Nevertheless present concerns with the environment are influenced by the decline of the frontier. The end of frontier colonization is now in sight and society must take stock of the despoiled environments of the old frontier districts.

Webb (1951) has argued that the development of capitalist society over the last 400 years has been dependent upon the frontier and that the windfalls from the frontier have generated the wealth which enabled the expansion of capitalism. He sees the development of capitalism as abnormal and its institutions as exceptional, adapted to the boom conditions of frontier windfalls. He argues that the windfalls from the colonial frontier provided the accumulation which built European capitalism. The decline of the frontier has resulted in economic dislocation and results in a crisis which calls for new modes of economic and environmental management:

> The fact that we cannot find a new frontier comparable to the one we have need not make us feel that we are now bereft of a challenge and opportunity. It does mean that we have a different challenge and perhaps an even greater opportunity for achievement. For more then four hundred years we bent our effort towards the conquest and exploitation of the Great Frontier, and we have succeeded perhaps beyond our expectations. In making this conquest, we rarely looked back but rather forward eagerly to what was before us. We considered the task Herculean, and we take pride in our ability to perform it. The task was that of taking a new world and making it over into something of an Old World image. That was what we wanted to do, and that is what we did. The question before us is if we can manage what we have so eagerly taken. That is our challenge and out opportunity. We should not be so obtuse as to believe that the means of management are the same as conquest, or that frontier institutions will necessarily serve a metropolitan society (Webb, 1951: 418).

From a totally different perspective Engels explores similar issues concerned with the economic rationale behind frontier colonization and capitalism, and its impact on the world economy and the relationship between human society and the environment:

> Classical political economy, the social science of the bourgeoisie, in the main examines only social effects on human actions in the fields of production and exchange that are actually intended. This fully corresponds to the social organization of which it is the theoretical expression. As individual capitalists are engaged in production and exchange for the sake of immediate profit, only the nearest, most immediate results must

> first be taken into account. As long as the individual manufacturer or merchant sells a manufactured or purchased commodity with the usual coveted profit, he is satisfied and does not concern himself with what afterwards becomes of the commodity and its purchasers. The same thing applies to the natural effects of the same action. What cared the Spanish planters in Cuba, who burned down forests on the slopes of the mountains and obtained from the ashes sufficient fertilizer for one generation of very highly profitable coffee trees – what cared they that the heavy tropical rainfall afterwards washed away the unprotected upper stratum of the soil, leaving behind only bare rock! In relation to nature, as to society, the present mode of production is predominantly concerned only about the immediate, the most tangible result; and then surprise is expressed that the most remote effects of actions directed to this end turn out to be quite different, are mostly quite the opposite in character; that the harmony of supply and demand is transformed into the very reverse.... (Engels, 1976: 182–3).

The present environmental crisis is a historical product of a system of primitive accumulation which appropriated the windfalls of new frontiers for maximum immediate gain. As long as new frontier land existed the development of capitalism and colonialism could proceed by despoiling areas of their natural resources. Degraded frontier districts were left behind as bust towns and the boom continued further up the frontier. On the global scale whole regions were left to stagnate as new areas were found which could produce commodities cheaper. This pattern was also reproduced at the regional level: the richest producers moved into new windfall districts leaving in disregard the old frontier districts, which had become divested of their virgin bounty.

Within the logic of frontier-colonial mentality it was the potential of a commodity or a narrow range of commodities which led to the opening up of new districts. Minimal scientific investigation was made into the economic potentials of districts or the most rational modes of bringing these districts into production. The frontier settlers usually went into these districts with visions of their potential wealth, but limited conceptions based on old world technologies for the exploitation of narrow ranges of commodities. Environments were despoiled of their diversity to make way for coffee, cocoa, rubber, sugar, cattle, etc. It is only in recent years, with the passing away of the frontier and the development of new genetic technologies which need genetic diversity for their building blocks, that human society has begun to realize the potential of the lost diversity in rainforests and other environments.

Global environmentalism is still focusing on the new frontier, and is concerned with regulating the remaining frontiers, often from the interests of the institutions which have grown out of frontier conquest. The decline of the frontier has also produced an angst: that, with the decline of the windfall of the frontier, nature can no longer furnish the wealth that human society (the metropolis) has become dependent upon, and can no longer support the growth of human population which now fills all frontier areas. This angst was captured by Webb as early as 1951:

> and if our techniques speed up the process of utilization and destruction, as they are now doing, they hasten the day when the substance on which they feed and on which a swollen population temporarily subsists will approach scarcity and exhaustion. Then the scholars will look back on the age when the Golden Door opened, and men marched out to the Great Frontier to create the greatest boom the world has known; they will make myths and legends about it, and in poetry and literature express their poignant yearning for the New Frontiers. They will see the frontier as the great factor in the age called modern, see it clearly as the lost factor which they would so love to find (pp. 27–8).

In place of the perception of economics as an inquiry into the wealth of nations, environmental economics is now concerned with scarcity of natural resources and with the limits of economic growth. However, these debates are largely carried out in the abstract, without much attention being paid to the history of the last 400 years of frontier colonialism, and the qualitative framework of institutions and socio-political frameworks which have informed this process of exploitation of resources and human labour.

This history shows a great waste and sacrifice of old frontier districts, of bust towns and labour reserves which lay forgotten on the margins of the world economy. Without any conscious effort to regenerate these areas, how can it be discerned that the human population is too large to allow economic production to be sustained? The reverse is more likely to be the case: the world economy is too small and too narrowly focused to be able to meet the long-term aspirations of people.

The transition to a more balanced utilization of the natural world must involve the complete transformation of institutions which lie at the heart of frontier-colonial exploitation and which focus on the world commodity trade of the metropolis. Even if the concept of the limits of economic growth are accepted, this qualitative transformation of the institutions of world commodity trade would be essential, unless of course the limits of growth is merely an ideological construct to check the motion of the developing world and to protect the banqueting table of the metropolis.

Regenerating Old Frontier Districts

The basis for environmental conservation and sustainable development must include a concern with promoting the economic regeneration of old frontier districts. This requires new modes and criteria for assessing economic needs and designing development plans.

Under colonialism, economic prosperity was measured in terms of the volume of exports and imports between metropolis and colony. In the post-colonial setting economic prosperity is usually measured in terms of the growth of Gross National Product (GNP). In recent years it has been recognized that development has to be assessed in terms of qualitative indices in addition to quantitative growth rates. Some social indicators are now being used by the World Bank. The UNDP has also constructed some 'human development indicators' (UNDP, 1991).

Nevertheless, these indicators fail to examine the qualitative structure of production within particular nations or regions, the contributions of various districts within a country to overall production, and the diversity, stability and vulnerability of the production base. They fail to examine the relationship between social indicators and economic strategy within a single integrated framework.

The dominant economic policy frameworks being presently pursued in developing countries are concerned with export-oriented growth and greater integration with world commodity markets. The consequence of this type of strategy is to generate a command economy, which responds to the demands of international commodity markets rather than the aspirations and creative potentials of the people. There is at present a fundamental contradiction in world economic policy perspectives, between the operation of commodity market integration and concerns with promoting popular democracy, participatory development and sustainable development.

This study has shown how the opening up of the frontier in Krobo was dramatically altered by world commodity markets. The opening up of oil palm production in virgin forest areas of South East Asia resulted in the marginalization of the oil palm-producing districts in Ghana. A comparative advantage in cocoa production was established for the Gold Coast and the new frontier developed in relation to the cultivation of this unknown commodity. In Krobo this resulted in movements into new adjacent land. By the 1930s serious problems had emerged with the production of cocoa in the old frontier districts and the main area of production shifted into Ashanti. Problems have also emerged in Ashanti and the main area of production has now moved into the final forest frontier areas of the Western Region. With no frontier lands remaining, cocoa rehabilitation programmes have now been devised for the older frontier districts of the Eastern Region and Ashanti. These programmes are concerned with the regeneration of cocoa growing rather than with regenerating rural areas and development assistance is provided for this objective alone. The problems and experiences of farmers with cocoa in the recent past and the search for a more viable economic base to satisfy the aspirations of producers lie outside this realm. Despite the inputs of large capital into the cocoa sector in recent years, few cocoa farmers are taking up the recommendations being disseminated by the cocoa sector. A large proportion of farmers are looking for solutions which involve moving out of cocoa. Thus, the cocoa sector has failed to respond to the needs of the farmer and the development initiatives of the state alienate rural producers by pursuing externally generated policies.

Within Ghana the development of domestic food production has also followed a frontier logic. Production focuses on the new frontier while old frontier districts stagnate. In contrast with the Ricardian principle in which the cost of food crops is adjusted to allow the rising demand for food to be met by expansion into new more marginal areas of production, the opening up of the new frontier of food production corresponds to increasing costs of production in old frontier districts. The new frontier brings a windfall which enables cheaper costs of production of food. But this sounds the death toll for older frontiers which become marginalized. This suggests that the windfalls of the frontier may in themselves satisfy the domestic market for food produce. But this may lead to forms of exploitation which hasten the decline of the frontier and its ecological degradation. It also does little to build upon the potential of all the peoples and districts within the state, or to develop an independent and united national economy. It places serious constraints upon the growth of the national economy to meet the aspirations of the people. These mechanisms work not only at the nation state level, but also in relation to the economic and political interests which inform policy at the district levels. Even within small districts such as Manya Krobo, the rise of new frontier areas and markets has eroded older frontier towns.

In contrast with these developments, the opening up of the agricultural frontier in the Americas and production of cheap grain and meat led to Western European states subsidizing and protecting agriculture in the old European farming districts. Within the USA, the movement of the western frontier did not result in the phasing out of the old north-eastern agricultural frontier but the adoption of new modes of intensive agriculture which replenished the soil. The building of an independent national economy with a manufacturing and modern agricultural base involved both an anti-colonial struggle and a civil war against the entrenchment of modes of production responding to the dictates of commodity markets in Europe.

The logic of frontier development still informs national rural development plans. In Ghana, rural development focuses on the opening up of the

Western Region for cocoa and the Afram Plains for food crop farming. The task of devising strategies for the regeneration of old degraded frontier districts and towns has not been addressed. Little research exists on the historical experience of declining frontiers, the future consequences of degraded frontiers and the impact of the new frontier development on old frontiers and policy frameworks. Environmental plans for the rural and agricultural sector are largely devised in the abstract, emanating from global concerns.

A valuable fund of knowledge of the environment exists within old degraded frontier districts. This could usefully inform environmental policies. This includes knowledge and experience of the consequences of frontier development, attempts to adapt to degraded environments, and innovatory techniques and strategies for land management. Knowledge also exists of a wide diversity of uses of natural resources which are presently marginal to mainstream developments within world commodity markets.

The impact of frontier ideology on the world economy needs to be subjected to critical analysis. In place of concerns with maximizing the production of particular commodities within regions or nations, a new logic needs to be implanted based on maximizing the utilization of the diversity of resources within localities in accordance with the aspirations, needs and wants of the producers. This requires a commitment to strengthening the domestic market, which is the focus through which a more diverse resource utilization can emerge to replace a dependence on narrow world commodity markets.

This would require commitment to a more decentralized political system of administration, which would enable districts to define their own development agendas. In Ghana, as in other states, present policy frameworks are concerned with establishing administrative decentralization. But the main objective of decentralization is to remove the burdens of funding rural services from central government. In contrast, a policy of rural regeneration requires a framework which seeks to build up a radically new rural economy with a more diversified system of resource utilization based on a broader infrastructure of rural crafts and a processing industry for local raw materials. This requires infrastructural support to build facilities to enable rural areas to develop more autonomous forms of production and to generate their own development plans in accordance with the creative potentials and aspirations of the people within the locality. This may in the future create the basis for generating a more stable and diverse regional and world economy with a more balanced exploitation of the environment and a vastly expanded store of wealth. This is a viable path to promoting economic systems which preserve, develop and utilize biodiversity. The economic prerequisites of these objectives must be based on increasing economic diversification.

Rural regeneration requires a new scientific research framework. This needs to move beyond an attachment to technological solutions and narrow commodity sector orientation. It would focus on the interactions between people and the environment in specific localities and regions, and ground development policy in historical experience. The historical experience of people in their interactions with the environment can be assimilated into frameworks which inform both scientific enquiry and the development of actions to resolve particular problems. The study of human adaptation to changing environments is important in providing insights into modes of coping with and interacting with the environment. The study of existing production environments can contribute towards relevant policy frameworks and define technical problems which can then be referred to specialized national and international research centres for solution.

In the struggle for a more sustainable economic system the folk knowledge and adaptive traditions of producers in old frontier districts is a valuable resource. Producers in these districts have been forced to find solutions to problems which policy frameworks are only beginning to recognize. Innovatory research which seeks to build an interface with this folk tradition may lay the foundations for new production systems based on a more diverse interaction with natural systems. This will require the provision of support to build and strengthen folk science and enable it to articulate with institutionalized science. The search for new modes of production which meet popular aspirations and which do not antagonize the environment cannot be the provenance of science alone. All relevant human experience should be encouraged to participate in the search for a more stable economic base. This objective will be meaningless, however, unless it is integrated with a critical policy framework and an analysis of the history of the world economy and its implications for tomorrow.

REFERENCES

Abbiw, D.K. *Useful Plants of Ghana*, IT Publications and Kew Gardens, London, 1990.

Addo, S.T. 'Traditional Markets in the Development Process in Manya Krobo in Ghana, 1700-1970', *Singapore Journal of Tropical Agriculture*, 9(1): 1–17, 1988.

Adu-Tutu, M., Afful, Y., Asante-Appiah, K., Lieberman, D., Hall, J.B., Elvin-Lewis, M. 'Chewing Stick Usage in Southern Ghana', *Economic Botany*, 33(3): 320–8, 1979.

Agarwal, B. 'The Gender and Environmental Debate: Lessons from India', paper presented at United Nations Research Institute for Social Development (UNRISD) Conference on Social Dimensions of Environment and Sustainable Development, Valletta, Malta, 22–25 April 1992.

Ahn, P.M. *West African Soils*, Oxford University Press, Oxford, 1970.

Allan, W. *The African Husbandman*, Oliver and Boyd, Edinburgh, 1965.

Altieri, M. (ed.) *Agro-ecology: The Scientific Basis of Alternative Agriculture*, Westview, Boulder and IT, London, 1987.

Altieri, M., Hecht, S. *Agro-ecology and Small Farm Development*, CRC Press, Boston, 1990.

Amanor, K.S. 'Relations of Agricultural Production in the Krobo District of Ghana', PhD thesis, University of London, 1989.

Amanor, K.S. *Analytic Abstracts in Farmer Participatory Research*, Agricultural Administration Unit Occasional Paper 10, ODI, London, 1990.

Amanor, K.S. 'Managing the Fallow: Weeding Technology and Environmental Knowledge in the Krobo District of Ghana', *Agriculture and Human Values*, 8(1-2): 5–13, 1991.

Ametekpor, J.K. 'The Effects of Seasonal Flooding on the Cation Exchange Capacity Base Saturation and pH of Some Soils in the Volta Drawdown Area', *Legon Agricultural Research Bulletin*, 2: 38–44, 1987.

Anquandah, J. *Rediscovering Ghana's Past*, Longman, London, 1982.

Arhin, K. 'The Structure of Greater Ashanti (1700–1824)', *Journal of African History*, 8(1), 1967.

Arhin, K. *The Expansion of Cocoa Production: The Working Conditions of Migrant Cocoa Farmers in the Central and Western Region*, mimeo, Accra, 1985.

Atkinson, R. 'The Origins of Akyem Abuakwa and Kotoku, 1675–1775', pp. 349–69, in B.K. Swartz, R. Dumett (eds), *West African Cultural Dynamics: Archaeological and Historical Perspectives*, John Wiley, New York, 1980.

Aubreville, A. *La Flore Forestière de la Côte d'Ivoire*, Tome 3, Larose, Paris, 1936.

Austin, G. 'The Emergence of Capitalist Relations in South Asante Cocoa-Farming, c. 1916–1933', *Journal of African History*, 28: 259–81, 1987.

Ayensu, E.S. *Medicinal Plants of West Africa*, Reference Publications, Michigan, 1978.

Baker, D., Oguntoyinbo, J. and Richards, P. *The Utility of the Nigerian Peasant Farmer's Knowledge in the Monitoring of Agricultural Resources*, Monitoring and Assessment Research Centre, Chelsea College, University of London, 1975.

Beckett, W.H. *Akokoaso: A survey of a Gold Coast Village*, Lund, Humphries and Co., London, 1944.

Beckman, B. *Organising the Farmer: Cocoa Politics and National Development in Ghana*, Scandinavian Institute of African Studies, Uppsala, 1976.

Beer, J.H. de, McDermont, M.J. *The Economic Value of Non-timber Forest Products in South East Asia with Emphasis on Indonesia, Malaysia and Thailand*, Netherlands Committee for IUCN, Amsterdam, 1989.

Benneh, G. 'The Huza Strip Farming System of the Krobo of Ghana', *Geographia Polonica*, 19: 188–206, 1970.

Benneh, G. 'The Land Tenure and Agrarian System in the New Cocoa Frontier of Ghana: Wassa Akropong Case Study', pp. 225–40 in W. Manshard and W.B. Morgan (eds), *Agricultural Expansion and Pioneer Settlement in the Humid Tropics*, United Nations University, Tokyo, 1988.

Benneh, G., Agyepong G.T. *Land Degradation in Ghana*, Commonwealth Secretariat, London, 1990.

Bennett, J.W. *The Ecological Transition: Cultural Anthropology and Human Adaptation*, Pergamon Press, Oxford, 1976.

Berg, T. 'The Science of Plant Breeding: Support or Alternative to Traditional Practices', in W. de Boef, K. Amanor, K. Wellard, with A. Bebbington (eds), *Cultivating Knowledge: Genetic Diversity, Farmer Experimentation and Crop Research*, IT, London, 1993.

Berg, T., Bjørnstad, Å., Fowler, C., Skrøppa, T. *Technology Options and the Gene Struggle*, Development and Environment No. 8, NORAGRIC Occasional Paper Series C, Norwegian Centre for International Agricultural Development, (NORAGRIC), Agricultural University of Norway, Oslo, 1991.

Bernstein, H. 'Notes on Capital and Peasantry', *Review of African Political Economy*, 10: 60–73, 1977.

Bernstein, H. 'African Peasantries: A Theoretical Framework', *The Journal of Peasant Studies*, 6 (4): 412–43, 1979.

Biggs, S.D. *Resource-Poor Farmer Participation in Research: A Synthesis of Experiences from Nine National Agricultural Research Systems*, OFCOR Comparative Study Paper 3, ISNAR, The Hague, 1989a.

Biggs, S.D. *A Multiple Source of Innovation Model of Agricultural Research and Technology Promotion*, Network Paper No. 6, Agricultural Administration (Research & Extension) Network, ODI, London, 1989b.

Biggs, S., Farrington, J. *Agricultural Research and the Rural Poor: A Review of Social Science Analysis*, IDRC, Ottawa, 1991.

Boef, W. de, Amanor, K., Wellard, K., with Bebbington, A. *Cultivating Knowledge: Genetic Resources, Farmer Experimentation and Crop Research*, IT, London, 1993.

Bosman, W. *A New and Accurate Description of the Gold Coast of Guinea*, Frank Cass, London, 1964. Originally published 1705.

Box, L. 'The Experimenting Farmer: A Missing Link in Agricultural Change?', pp. 87–95 in J. Hinderink and E. Szulc-Dabrowiecka (eds) *Successful Rural Development in Third World Countries*, Netherlands Geographical Studies No. 67, Utrecht, 1986.

Brockway, L. *Science and Colonial Expansion: The Role of the British Botanical Gardens*, Academic Press, New York, 1979.

Burton, R.F. 'Two Trips on the Gold Coast', *Ocean Highways: The Geographical Review*, 1: 448–61, 1874.

Campbell, B. *Human Evolution*, Aldine, Chicago, 1966.

Colchester, M. *Sustaining the Forests: The Community Based Approach in South and South-East Asia*, Discussion Paper 35, United Nations Research Institute for Social Development (UNRISD), Geneva, 1992.

Collingwood, C.A. 'Cocoa in West Africa: The Economics of Pest Control', *Span*, 15: 74–7, 1972.

Conklin, H. C. *Hanunoo Agriculture: A Report on an Integral System of Shifting Cultivation in the Philippines*, Paper No. 12, FAO, Rome, 1957.

Conlin, S. 'Anthropological Advice in a Government Context', in R. Grillo and A. Rews (eds), *Social Anthropology and Development Policy*, London, Tavistock, 1985.

Cooper, D., Vellvé, R., Hobbelink, H. *Growing Diversity: Genetic Resources and Local Food Security*, IT, London, 1992.

Cordeiro, A. 'Rediscovering Local Varieties of Maize: Challenging Seed Policy in Brazil', pp. 165–71 in W. de Boef, K. Amanor, K. Wellard, with A. Bebbington (eds), *Cultivating Knowledge: Genetic Diversity, Farmer Experimentation and Crop Research*, IT, London, 1993.

Crowder, M., Ikeme, O. *West African Chiefs: Their Changing Status under Colonial Rule and Independence*, University of Ife, Ife, 1970.

Dalziel, J.M. *The Useful Plants of West Tropical Africa*, Crown Agents, London, 1937.

Dean, W. 'Ecological and Economic Relationships in Frontier History: São Paulo, Brazil', in G. Wolfskill, S. Palmer (eds) *Essays on Frontiers in World History*, University of Texas Press, Arlington, 1983.

Dixon, J.A., James, D.E., Sherman, P.B. *The Economics of Dryland Management*, Earthscan, London, 1989.

Djeagbo, G., Mate, A. 'Settlement and Farming in the Manya Krobo District', *Bulletin of Ghana*

Geographical Society, 7: 54–8, 1962.

Ellen, R. *Environment, Subsistence and System: The Ecology of Small-scale Social Formations*, Cambridge University Press, Cambridge, 1982.

Engels, F. 'The Part Played by Labour in the Transition from Ape to Man' in F. Engels, *Dialectics of Nature*, Progress Publisher, Moscow, 1976.

Enti, A.A. *Notes on Synsepalum Dulcificum (the Miraculous Berry)*, Accra, 1979.

Evans Pritchard, E. *Witchcraft, Oracles and Magic among the Azande*, Clarendon, Oxford, 1937.

Ewel, J.J. 'Tropical Succession: Manifold Routes to Maturity', *Biotropica*, 12, Supplement: 2–7, 1980.

Falconer, J. *The Major Significance of 'Minor' Forest Products: Local People's Use and Values of Forest in the West African Humid Forest Zone*, Forest, Trees and People Programme, FAO/SIDA, Rome, 1990.

Farrington, J., Martin, A. *Farmer Participation in Agricultural Research: A Review of Concepts and Recent Practices*, Agricultural Administration Unit Occasional Paper 9, ODI, London, 1988.

Fedden, M. *Forest Farm Husbandry*, Technology Consultancy Centre, University of Science And Technology, Kumase, 1988.

Field, M.J. *Auutu Bereku*, unpublished manuscript, Accra, 1941.

Field, M.J. 'The Agricultural System of the Manya Krobo of the Gold Coast', *Africa*, 14: 54–65, 1943.

Flight, C. 'The Kintampo Culture and its Place in Economic Prehistory of West Africa', pp. 211–22 in J. Harlan, J.M.J. de Wet, A. Stemler (eds), *Origins of African Plant Domestication*, Mouton, The Hague, 1976.

Fowler, A., Dumor, E., Booth, W. *Ghana NGO Management Service Unit: Report of a Mid-term Evaluation*, UNDP, Nairobi, 1991.

Francois, J. 'Forward', in J. Falconer, *Non-timber Products in Southern Ghana: A Summary Report*, ODA Forestry Series No. 2, ODA, London, 1992.

Frankel, O. 'Genetic Dangers of the Green Revolution', *World Agriculture* 19: 9–13, 1970.

Gadgil, M., Guha, R. 'Interpreting Indian Environmentalism', paper presented at United Nations Research Institute for Social Development (UNRISD) Conference of the Social Dimensions of Environmental and Sustainable Development, Valetta, Malta, 22–25 April 1992.

García de Santa María, A. *Le parti inedite della 'Crónica de Juan II di Alvar García de Santa María*, ed. Donatello Ferro, Consiglio Nazionale delle Ricerche, Venice, 1972.

Geertz, C. *Agricultural Involution, the Processes of Ecological Change in Indonesia*, University of California Press, Berkeley, 1963.

Ghana Ministry of Agriculture *Report on Rural Indebtedness*, Government Printer, Accra, 1957.

Ghana National Archives. Case No. 41 of 1911, Bye-laws Made by Konor Mate Kole of Odumase, Letter from Konor to Capt. R.S. Poole, District Commissioner of Akuse, 7 February 1911.

Gold Coast, *Route Book: Gold Coast, Ashanti and the Northern Territories*, Government Printer, Accra, 1906.

Gold Coast, *Gold Coast Annual Report 1937/38*, Government Printer, Accra, 1938.

Gold Coast Farmer, 'Dawa Sutch Cocoa Producers Co-operative Society: A Successful Many a Krobo Society', *Gold Coast Farmer*, 6: 97, 1932.

Gold Coast Department of Agriculture *Report on Survey of Krobo Oil Palm Areas*, Department of Agriculture, Accra, 1952.

Gold Coast Ministry of Interior, 'In the Matter of the Stool Lands Boundary Ordinance 1950', *Gold Coast Gazette*, pp. 93–101, 17 January 1956.

Grandstaff, T.B. 'Shifting Agriculture: A Reassessment of Strategies', *Ceres*, pp. 28-34, July–August 1981.

Greenland, D.J. 'Bringing the Green Revolution to the Shifting Cultivator' *Science*, 190: 841–5, 1975.

Guha, R. 'Eco-development Debate: A Critical Review', *South Asian Anthropologist*, 6(1): 15–24, 1985.

Guha, R. *The Unquiet Wood: Ecological Change and Peasant Resistance in the Himalayas*, Oxford University Press, New Delhi & University of California Press, Berkeley, 1989.

Gyasi, E.A. 'The Oil Palm Industry and its Implications for Rural Development in Ghana', *Malaysian Journal of Tropical Geography*, 18: 1–18, 1988.

Gyasi, E.A. 'Communal Land Tenure and the Spread of Agroforestry in Ghana's Mampong Valley', *Ecology and Farming*, 2: 16–17, 1991.

Gyasi, E.A. 'Emergence of a New Oil Palm Belt in Ghana', *Tijdschrift voor Economische en Sociale Geografie*, 83(1): 39–49, 1992.

Hall, J.B., Swaine M.D. *Distribution and Ecology of Vascular Plants in a Tropical Rain Forest*, W. Junk,

The Hague, 1981.

Hansen, E. 'The State and Food Agriculture', pp. 184–221 in E. Hansen and K. Ninsin (eds), *The State, Development and Politics in Ghana*, CODESRA, London, 1989.

Hardin, G. *The Voyage of the Spaceship Beagle: Exploring New Ethics for Survival*, Viking Press, New York, 1972.

Hardon, J.J., de Boef, W. 'Linking Farmers and Plant Breeders in Local Crop Development', pp. 64–71 in W. de Boef, K. Amanor, K. Wellard, with A. Bebbington, *Cultivating Knowledge: Genetic Diversity, Farmer Experimentation and Crop Research*, IT, London, 1993.

Harlan, J.R. 'Our Vanishing Genetic Resources', *Science*, 188: 618–21, 9 May 1975.

Harris, W.V. *Termites: Their Recognition and Control*, Longmans, London, 1961.

Haverkort, B. Kamp, J. van der, and Waters-Bayer, A. (eds) *Joining Farmers' Experiments: Experiences in Participatory Technology Development*, IT, London, 1991.

Hecht, S, Cockburn, A. *The Fate of the Forest: Developers, Destroyers and Defenders of the Amazon*, Penguin, London, 1990.

Hill, P. *Gold Coast Farmer*, Oxford University Press, London, 1956.

Hill, P. *The Migrant Cocoa Farmers of Southern Ghana: A Study in Rural Capitalism*, Cambridge University Press, Cambridge, 1963.

Holling, C.S. 'Resilience and Stability in Ecological Systems', *Annual Review of Ecology and Systematics*, 4: 1–23, 1973.

Holmes, B. 'Economic and Political Organization in the Gold Coast, 1920–1940', PhD thesis, University of Chicago, 1972.

Hopkins B. *Forest and Savanna*, Heinemann, London, 2nd edition, 1974.

Hosier, R., O'Keefe, P., Wisner, B., Wisner, D., Shaakow, D. 'Energy Planning in Developing Countries' *Ambio*, 11(4), 1982.

Howard, R. *Colonialism and Underdevelopment in Ghana*, Croom Helm, London, 1978.

Howse, P.E. *Termites: A Study in Social Behaviour*, Hutchinson, London, 1970.

Huber H. *The Krobo*, The Anthropos Institute, St Augustin near Bonn, 1963.

Hughes, J.D., Thirgood, J.V., 'Deforestation, Erosion and Forest Management in Ancient Greece and Rome', *Journal of Forest History*, 26: 60–75, 1982.

Hunter, J.M. 'Cocoa Migrations and Patterns of Land Ownership in the Densu Valley near Suhum, Ghana', *Transactions and Papers of the Institute of British Geographers*, 33: 161–86, 1963.

Irvine, F.R. *Plants of the Gold Coast*, Oxford University Press, Oxford, 1930.

Irvine, F.R. *Woody Plants of Ghana*, Oxford University Press, Oxford, 1961.

ISNAR *Review of Ghana Agricultural Research Systems, Vol. II: Annexes*, ISNAR, the Hague, 1989.

Jackson, C. 'Environmentalism and Gender Interests in the Third World', *Development and Change*, 24(4): 649–78, 1993.

Janzen, D.H. *Ecology of Plants in the Tropics*, Edward Arnold, London 1980.

Jebuni, C.D. Oduro, A., Asante, Y., Tsikata, G.K., *Diversifying Exports*, ODI, London, 1992.

Johnson, A.W. 'Individuality and Experimentation in Traditional Agriculture', *Human Ecology*, 1(2): 149–60, 1972.

Johnson, M. 'Migrants Progress' Part 1, *Bulletin of the Ghana Geographical Society*, 9(2): 4–27, 1964.

Johnson, M. 'Migrants Progress' Part 2, *Bulletin of the Ghana Geographical Society*, 10(2): 13–40, 1965.

Juma, C. *The Gene Hunters: Biotechnology and the Scramble for Seeds*, Zed Press, London, 1989.

Kea, R.A. 'Administration and Trade in the Akwamu Empire, 1680–1730', pp. 371–90 in B.K. Swartz and R. Dumett (eds), *West African Cultural Dynamics: Archaeological and Historical Perspectives*, John Wiley, New York, 1980.

Kea, R.A. *Settlements, Trade and Polities in the Seventeenth Century Gold Coast*, Johns Hopkins, Baltimore, 1982.

Kea, R.A. ''I am Hear to Plunder on the General Road': Bandits and Banditry in Pre-nineteenth Century Gold Coast', pp. 109–32 in D. Crummey (ed.), *Banditry, Rebellion and Social Protest in Africa*, James Currey, London, 1986.

Kellman, M.C. 'Some Environmental Components of Shifting Cultivation in Upland Minandao', *Journal of Tropical Agriculture*, 40: 40–56, 1969.

Keystone International Dialogue *Madras Plenary Session: Final Consensus Report of the Keystone International Dialogue on Plant Genetic Resources*, Second Plenary Session, Madras, India, 29 January – 2 Febuary 1990.

Kirby, B. Report of a Journey through Acquapim, Eastern and Western Krobo, 30 January 1882, Despatch No. 149 in Enclosures of Despatches from Governor to Secretary of State, March to May 1882, Ghana National Archives (GNA) ADM 1/646.

Kloppenburg, J.R. *First the Seed: The Political Economy of Plant Biotechnology, 1492–2000*, Cambridge University Press, Cambridge, 1988.

Konings, P. *The State and Rural Class Formation in Ghana*, Routledge & Kegan Paul, London, 1986.

La Anyane, S. *Volta Oil Palm Survey: Afram Areas*, Department of Agriculture, Accra, 1954.

La Anyane, S. *Awoweso: A Manya Krobo Huza*, Department of Agriculture, Accra, 1956.

La Anyane, S. 'The Oil Palm Belt of Ghana: Introduction', *Ghanaian Bulletin of Agricultural Economics*, 1: 7–28, 1961.

Lee, K.E., Wood, T.G. *Termites and Soil*, Academic Press, London, 1971.

Levins, R. *Evolution in Changing Environments*, Princeton University Press, Princeton, 1968.

Levins, R., Lewontin, R. *The Dialectical Biologist*, Harvard University Press, Cambridge, MA and London, 1985.

Litzenberger, S.C., Ho Tong Lip, 'Utilizing *Eupatorium odoratum* to Improve Crop Yields in Cambodia', *Agronomic Journal*, 53: 321–4, 1961.

MacKay, A. 'Climate in Late Medieval Castile', pp. 356–76 in T.M.L. Wigley, M.J. Ingram, G. Farmer (eds.), *Climate and History: Studies in Past Climates and their Impact on Man*, Cambridge University Press, Cambridge, 1981.

Macmillan, W.M. 'African Development' Part 2 of C.K. Meek, W.M. Macmillan, Hussey (eds), *Europe and West Africa*, Macmillan, London, 1940.

Martinez, E., Akposore, M.K. Galiba, M., Hong, C.W. 'The Sasakawa-Global 2000 Agricultural Project in Ghana', in C.R. Downswell (ed.), *Proceedings of Workshop Feeding the Future: Agricultural Development Strategies for Africa*, Centre for Applied Studies in International Negotiation, Geneva, 1989.

Martinez-Alier, J. with Schlüpmann, K. *Ecological Economics: Energy, Environment and Society*, Blackwell, Oxford and Cambridge MA, 1990.

May, P.H. 'Building Institutions and Markets for Non-wood Forest Products from the Brazilian Amazon, *Unasylva*, 41(161): 9–16 1990/91.

May, R. *Stability and Complexity in Model Ecosystems*, Princeton University Press, Princeton, 1973.

McGinnies, W.G., Goldman, B.J., Paylore, P., *Food, Fibre and the Arid Lands*, University of Arizona Press, Tucson, 1971.

McGovern, T.H. 'Economics of Extinction in Norse Greenland', pp. 404–33 in T.M.L. Wigley, M.J. Ingram, G. Farmer (eds), *Climate and History: Studies in Past Climates and their Impact on Man*, Cambridge University Press, Cambridge, 1981.

McKorkle, C.M., Brandsletter, R.H., McClure, G. *A Case Study on Farmer Innovation and Communication in Niger*, Communication for Technology Transfer in Africa, Academy of Educational Development, Washington, 1988.

Meadley, J. 'The Commercial Implications of New Crops', pp. 23–8 in G.E. Wickens, N. Haq, P. Day (eds), *New Crops for Food and Industry*, Chapman and Hall, London, 1989.

Meulen, G.F. van der, *A Real Green Revolution: the Solution for the Threatening World Catastrophe by the General and Correct Application of the Ecological Method System*, ACBT, The Hague, 1977.

Miracle, M.P., Seidman, *A. State Farms in Ghana*, Land Tenure Center, Madison, 1968.

Mooney, P.R. *Seeds of the Earth: A Private or Public Resource?*, Inter Pares, Ottawa, 1979.

Mooney, P.R. 'The Law of the Seed', *Development Dialogue*, 1–2: 1–172, 1983.

Mooney, P.R. 'Exploiting Local Knowledge: International Policy Implications', pp. 172–8 in W. de Boef, K. Amanor, K. Wellard, with A. Bebbington (eds), *Cultivating Knowledge: Genetic Diversity, Farmer Experimentation and Crop Research*, IT, London, 1993.

Moor, H.W. 'Deforestation in the Bissa Cacao Area', Papers of the Second Conference of West African Agricultural Officers, Vol. 2, *Gold Coast Department of Agriculture Bulletin*, No. 20: 125–8, 1930.

Moran, E.F. *Developing the Amazon*, Indiana University Press, Bloomington, 1981.

Myint, H. 'The "Classical Theory" of International Trade and the Underdeveloped Countries', *Economics Journal*, pp. 317–37, June 1958.

Nair, P.K.R. (ed.) *Agroforestry Systems in the Tropics*, Kluwer Academic Publishers, Dordrecht, 1989.

Nathan, M. 'Gold Coast Under the Danes and Dutch', *Journal of Africa Society*, 4(13): 1–33, 1904. A translation of excerpts from Tilleman, E., *En liden enfoldig beretning on det landskab Guinea ob deg betskaffenhed langs ved sø-kanten*, 1697.

Nicholson, S.E. 'The Historical Climatology of Africa' pp. 249–70 in M.J. Ingram, D.J. Underhill, G. Farmer (eds), *Climate and History: Studies in Past Climates and their Impact on Man*, Cambridge University Press, Cambridge, 1981.

Norman, M.J.T. 'Energy Inputs and Outputs of Subsistence Cropping Systems in the Tropics', *Agro-*

Ecosystems, 4: 255–66, 1978.

Nowell Report. *Report of the Commission on the Marketing of West African Cocoa*, British Parliamentary papers, Secretary of State of the Colonies, Cmd. 5835, HMSO, London, 1938.

Nye, P.H., Greenland, D.J. *The Soil under Shifting Cultivation*, Commonwealth Bureau of Soils Technical Communications 52, Commonwealth Agricultural Bureau, Farnham Royal, 1960.

Nyerges, A.E. 'Coppice Swidden Fallows in Tropical Forest: Biological, Technological, and Sociocultural Determinants of Secondary Forest Succession', *Human Ecology*, 17(4): 379–400, 1989.

Oakley, P. *Projects with People: The Practice of Participation in Rural Development*, ILO, Geneva, 1991.

Odonkor, T. *The Rise of the Krobo*. Translated from an original Ga text by S.S. Odonkor, Ghana Publishing Corporation, Tema, 1971.

Okafor, J.C. 'Horticulturally Promising Indigenous Wild Tree Species of the Nigeria Forest Zone', *Acta Horticulturae*, 123: 165–76, 1983.

Okigbo, B.N. 'Neglected Plants of Horticultural Importance in Traditional Farming Systems of Tropical Africa', *Acta Horticulturae*, 53, 1977.

Otsinya, R.M. *Consultancy in Agroforestry*, Ministry of Agriculture, Department of Crop Services/ UNDP/FAO, 1989.

Owusu, D.Y. 'Experiences with Agroforestry', ILEIA Newsletter, 6(2): 8–10, 1990.

Pearse, A., Steifel, M. *Enquiry into Participation: A Research Approach*, UNRISD, Geneva, 1979.

Pepper, D. *The Roots of Modern Environmentalism*, Croom Helm, London, 1984.

Ploeg, J.D. van der, *Labor, Markets and Agricultural Production*, Westview, Boulder and London, 1990.

Pogucki, R.J.H. *Report on Land Tenure in Adangme Customary Law*, Government Printer, Accra, 1955.

Posnansky, M., McIntosh, R. 'New Radiocarbon Dates from Northern and Western Africa', *Journal of African History*, 17(2), 1976.

Rappaport, R.A. *Pigs for the Ancestors: Ritual in the Ecology of a New Guinea People*, Yale University Press, New Haven, 1968.

Rappaport, R. 'The Flow of Energy in an Agricultural Society', *Scientific American*, 225: 117–32, 1971.

Ravnborg, H.M. *The CGIAR in Transition: Implications for the Poor, Sustainability and the National Research Systems*, Agricultural Administration (Research and Extension) Network Paper 31, ODI, London, 1992.

Redclift, M. *Sustainable Development: Exploring the Contradictions*, Routledge, London, 1989.

Reindorf, C.C. *History of the Gold Coast and Asante*, Basel Mission, Basel, 1895.

Rhoades R.E., Booth, R.H. 'Farmer-back-to-farmer: A Model for Generating Acceptable Agricultural Technology', *Agricultural Administration*, 11: 127–37, 1982.

Ricardo, D. *Principles of Political Economy and Taxation*, Everyman, London, 1955.

Richards, P. *Indigenous Agricultural Revolution: Ecology and Food Production in West Africa*. Hutchinson, London, and Westview Press, Boulder, 1985.

Richards, P. *Experimenting Farmers and Agricultural Research*, mimeo, Dept. of Anthropology, University College, London, 1987.

Richards, P.W. *The Tropical Rainforests*, Cambridge University Press, London, 1952.

Rocheleau, D., Wachira K., Malaret, L. Wanjohi, B.M. 'Local Knowledge for Agroforestry and Native Plants', pp. 14–23 in R. Chambers, A. Pacey, L.A. Thrupp, *Farmer First: Farmers Innovation and Agricultural Research*, Intermediate Technology, London, 1989.

Rogers, E.M. 'The Peasantry as a Subculture', pp. 111–35 in C. R. Wharton, C.R. (ed.) *Subsistence Agriculture and Economic Development*, Frank Cass, London, 1970.

Röling, N. *Extension Science: Information Systems in Agricultural Development*, Cambridge University Press, Cambridge, 1988.

Röling, N. 'The Agricultural Research-Technology Transfer Interface: A Knowledge Systems Perspective', pp.1–42 in D. Kaimowitz (ed.), *Making the Link: Agricultural Research and Technology Transfer in Developing Countries*, Westview Press, Boulder, 1990.

Rose Innes, R. *A Manual of Ghana Grasses*, Ministry of Overseas Development, Land Resource Division, Surbiton, Surrey, 1977.

Ruthenberg, H. *Farming Systems in the Tropics*, Clarendon, Oxford, 3rd edition, 1980.

Sanchez, P.A. *Properties and Management of Soils in the Tropics*, John Wiley, New York, 1976.

Sattour, O. 'Botanical Entrepreneurship: The Path from Forest to Market Shelf is Strewn with Good Intention', *Ceres*, 23(127): 17–21, January-February 1991.

Scherr, S.J. 'Evaluating Institutional Capacity for Agroforestry Research,' paper presented at ISNAR/ Rutgers Agricultural Technology Management Workshop, held at the Hague, 6–8 July 1988.

Schlippe, P. de. *Shifting Cultivation in Africa: the Zande System of Agriculture*, Routledge and Kegan Paul, 1956.

Shephard, C.Y. *Report on the Economics of Peasant Agriculture in the Gold Coast*, Government Printer, Accra, 1936.

Shiva, V. *Staying Alive: Women, Ecology and Survival*, Zed Books, London, 1988.

Sutton, I.B. 'The Volta River Salt Trade: The Survival of an Indigenous Industry', *Journal of African History*, 22: 43–61, 1981.

Tan, J.G. 'A Participatory Approach in Developing an Appropriate Farming System in Eight Irrigated Lowland Villages', pp. 215–32 in C.B. Flora, M. Tomecek (eds), *Selected Proceedings of Kansas State University's Farming System Research Symposium*, Kansas State University, Kansas, 1986.

Taylor, C.J. *Synecology and Silviculture in Ghana*, Thomas Nelson, Edinburgh, 1960.

The Ecologist. 'Angry Indian Farmers Destroy Cargill's Seeds', *The Ecologist*, 23(2): Campaigns p. 1, 1993.

Thirgood, J.V. 'The Barbary Forests and Forest Lands, Environmental Destruction and the Vicissitudes of History', *Journal of World Forest Resource Management*, 2: 137–84, 1986.

Thrupp, L.A. 'Legitimizing Local Knowledge: "Scientized packages" or Empowerment for Third World People', pp. 138–53 in D.M. Warren, L.J. Slikkerveer, S.O. Titlola, *Indigenous Knowledge Systems: Implications for Agriculture and International Research*, 1989.

Tuffuor, K. 'Role of Forestry in Biological Diversity Conservation in Ghana', paper presented at Biodiversity Workshop at Department of Botany, University of Ghana, Legon, 8 January 1992.

Turnbull, A.L. 'Ecological Role of Pest Populations', *Tall Timbers Conference on Ecological Animal Control by Habitat Management*, No. 1: 219–32, 27–8 February, 1969.

Uhl, C., Clark, K., Murphy, P. 'Early Plant Succession after Cutting and Burning in the Upper Rio Negro Region of the Amazon Basin', *Journal of Ecology*, 69: 631–49, 1981.

Uhl, C., Murphy, P. 'A Comparison of Productivities and Energy Values between Slash and Burn Agriculture and Secondary Succession in the Upper Rio Negro Region of the Amazon' *Agro-Ecosystems*, 7: 63–81, 1981.

UNDP *Human Development Report*. Oxford University Press, Oxford and New York, 1991.

Unruh, J.D. 'Ecological Aspects of Site Recovery Under Swidden-Fallow Management in the Peruvian Amazon', *Agroforestry Systems*, 7: 161–84, 1988.

Viola, E.J. 'The Environmental Movement in Brazil (1971–1992) and the New Challenge of Sustainable Development', paper presented at United Nations Research Institute for Social Development (UNRISD) Conference on Social Dimensions of Environment and Sustainable Development, Valletta, Malta, 22–25 April 1992.

Vivian, J. 'Collective Action for Sustainable Development: Towards a Theoretical Framework for Research', paper presented at United Nations Research Institute for Social Development (UNRISD) Conference on Social Dimensions of Environment and Sustainable Development, Valletta, Malta, 22–25 April 1992.

Webb, W.P. *The Great Frontier*, The Riverside Press, Cambridge MA, 1952.

Westoby, J. *Introduction to World Forestry*, Blackwell, Oxford, 1989.

Wilkes, G. 'Current Status of Crop Germplasm', *Critical Reviews in Plant Science*, 1–2: 133–81, 1983.

Wilks, I.G. *Asante in the Nineteenth Century*, Cambridge University Press, Cambridge, 1975.

Wilks, I.G. 'Land, Labour, Capital and the Forest Kingdom of Asante: A Model of Early Change', pp. 487–534 in J. Freeman and J. Rowlands (eds), *The Evolution of Social Systems*, Duckworth, London, 1977.

Wilks, I.G. 'The State of the Akan and the Akan State', *Cahiers d'Etudes Africaines*, 22: 231–49, 1982.

Williams, G. 'Taking the Part of Peasants: Rural Development in Nigeria and Tanzania' in P.C.W. Gutkind, I. Wallerstein (eds), *The Political Economy of Contemporary Africa*, Sage, Beverly Hills, 1976.

Wilson, L.E. *The Krobo People of Ghana to 1892: A Political and Social History*, Ohio University, Center for International Studies, Altern, Ohio, 1991.

Wolfskill, G., Palmer, S. (eds), *Essays on Frontiers in World History*, University of Texas Press, Arlington, 1983.

Wolfson, F. 'A Price Agreement on the Gold Coast – the Krobo Oil Boycott 1858–1860', *The Economic History Review*, 6: 68–77, 1953.

Worede, M., Mekbib, H. 'Linking Genetic Resource Conservation to Farmers in Ethiopia', pp. 78–84 in W. de Boef, K. Amanor, K. Wellard, with A. Bebbington (eds), *Cultivating Knowledge: Genetic Diversity, Farmer Experimentation and Crop Research*, IT, London, 1993.

World Bank *The Assault on World Poverty*, World Bank, Johns Hopkins, London and Baltimore, 1975.

Young, A. *Tropical Soils and Soil Survey*, Cambridge University Press, Cambridge, 1976.

INDEX